A FLOWER

IN THE MIDST

OF THORNS

A FLOWER

in the

midst of thorns

Autobiographical essays by
JHAMAK GHIMIRE

Translated from Nepali by
Nagendra Sharma

Edited with an introduction by
Govinda Raj Bhattarai, PhD

Promoted by Hasta Gautam "Mridul"

A Flower amidst the Thorns
(An anthology of autobiographical essays)

Writer: Jhamak Ghimire
Translator:Nagendra Sharma
Editor: Govinda Raj Bhattarai

Publisher/Promoter: Hasta Gautam "Mridul"
Nepali Diaspora-USA
13105 Lipton Loop
Del Valle, TX 78617
gautamhasta@gmail.com

Rights: writer
Taiping: Hemant Gautam
Cover Design: Times Creation-Putali Sadak

This book was printed in the United States of America.

To order additional copies of this book, contact:
Xlibris Corporation
1-888-795-4274
www.Xlibris.com
Orders@XLibris.com
112351

A FLOWER
in the midst of thorns
(An anthology of Autobiographical Essays)

जीवनलाई सृष्टिको सुन्दर फूल भन्दर भ्रमझाइदेर आएको मल ।
र खोइ मैले भ्रर्पसको जीवनमित्र स्वयम् आफ्नो जीवन पर्छ
कि पर्दैन क्रास भाष्ट हेन्)

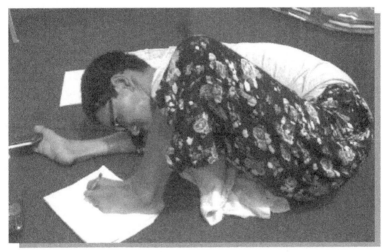

Jhamak writing using his toes.

*For me, life is the best flower of creation. I
don't know whether **my life falls within
the LIFE I myself have defined.***

Editor's Views

A story of untold suffering and struggle for freedom—

 I have recorded in my Journal my meeting with Biswasdip and Jhamak in July 2008 as a great event in my life. They trusted me and requested me to write a **Foreword** to **Jeevan Kaandaa Ki Phool** (literally, *Life: Thorn or Flower*). I spent three years in its processing and development which I have detailed in the **Introduction** to the first (Nepali) edition. (Please refer to the **Appendix** section of the present publication for further details).

The original (Nepali) version of the book first appeared two years later in May 2010. I had made a sincere appeal in my **Foreword**—let every student and teacher, every police and military personnel, human rights activist, social worker, doctor, politician and people from every walk of life read this book—a precious gem, an unprecedented record of suffering and struggle and achievement in a hundred years' history of Nepali literature. I also made an appeal: this book needs to be translated into English first of all, and gradually into French, German, Spanish, Chinese, Japanese and many more languages of the world. After only six months of its publication, it broke all records of sales, and within one year, this won all the prestigious awards and prizes in Nepali literature at home and abroad.

After only three months of its publication an octogenarian scholar gave me a phone call and a surprise: We have translated Jhamak's **Jeevan Kaandaa Ki Phool**, said he.

Who is we *dai1* ?
Me and Safal.
"That's great *dai*. It's wonderful and unbelievable." I spoke.
But they had done it—Nagendra Sharma and Safal. Within three months of its publication, they had completed translating, typing and editing. Then *dai* invited me to his place. He was fighting many diseases, grieving the sad demise of his wife two years ago. All alone, but his heart was filled with grief, fi re and zeal. Out of love and out of generosity he had accomplished this task unbelievably. Safal was there too, however. Without being asked for, without being paid for, all voluntarily, magnanimously. Should we evaluate the task, it is worth two thousand dollars now. In the capacity of the Kathmandu Valley co-ordinator for **Jhamak Ghimire Literaure and Art Foundation**, I was taking care of Jhamak's publication from here (Kathmandu).

She lives in Dhankuta, some 500 kms away in the eastern hills of Nepal. So they considered me rightly a contact person. I was very happy to see a reputed scholar's contribution for Jhamak.

By this time, readers had begun to acclaim Jhamak's masterpiece. She had started receiving great prizes, awards and felicitations. Gradually it reached all those corners of the world where Nepali diaspora are distributed.

1. Elderly, senior brother

One day I received an e-mail from Hasta Gautam (now in Texas). I didn't know him personally, though I was familiar with his creative zeal. By going through Jhamak's work, he was moved to tears. He wrote a long letter, was surprised and wonderstruck to estimate Jhamak's tremendous efforts, courage and contribution to humanity. Human beings owe her much for what she has revealed. Having seen my appeal, Hasta was very much inspired and he proposed that this book be translated immediately into English and he would manage the finances for it.

I already had a surprise in the store and revealed to him that this has already been translated by a famed scholar, writer, and translator, who has command over "Victorian English" as he puts it, because he was educated in Darjeeling and Calcutta during British India days. And his son. He led the project; his son assisted.

"Who is he?"

"He is Nagendra Sharma in his early 80's and his son Safal Dhungana".

"Great".

"Then sir, let us try to publish the work ASAP. We would like to introduce Jhamak, the glory of Nepal, to the wider world."

"We are looking for resources, brother," I said.

"How much will it cost?"

"Almost two thousand dollars."

"I will bear its publication cost then."

Hasta sent me fifty thousand Rupees immediately. I had undertaken the responsibility of editing the manuscript. Nagendra *dai* had suggested **An Ode to the Toes** as the title for the book. He wanted to give importance to Jhamak's struggle, the way she wrote with her toes. Later on, with my conscience and his consent, we made it **A FLOWER in the midst of thorns**, more figuratively. Unfortunately, he lost the electronic version of the type script so I had to get it retyped from the hard copy he had ready, checked, and proofread. This took me another two months. When I started revising the text, I found that *dai* had left along many paragraphs that are much culture-bound and posed translation difficulty and might be quite difficult to understand for the target readers although contained great importance in imparting special meaning of the contents for them. That was one reason he had subtitled the book—*Anabridged version of the Jeevan Kaandaa Ki Phool*.

I, however, talked to *dai* and said—we must reproduce the full text, all texts and words and concepts, the writer wished so, too.

In cases of difficulty, we can create a new concept, or paraphrase or add a glossary to it. Theory provides us with innumerable techniques. He agreed to my proposal and I began to do the job since January last (2011). I had to compare every word and expression; sentence and paragraph before judging its meaning in the target text. It was a 'double bind' responsibility—of releasing the meaning judiciously from the source text, and of arresting the same into the target text. I came across innumerable obstacles; sometimes my knowledge of translation theory and practice failing me. But I didn't yield. It required me some six months of attention; I did it meticulously. Got it retyped, proofread and ready for printing.

• • •

Now I wanted the Translators' Note to appear in the book, but could not request *dai* simply because he was visiting different doctors and hospitals for months then—from Kathmandu he flew to Delhi and then to Bombay and again to Calcutta. Suff ering from cancer, at the age of 81, all alone, only his courage moved him to places. For months he was like that. The edited version from my part was ready by January 2012. But *dai* was still in hospital bed undergoing treatment in Calcutta. I too was bed-ridden, though not in hospital, for the longest period (about four months) so far.

Despite our immovability, Hari Gautam of Oriental Publication contacted *dai* in Calcutta and communicated everything. But *dai* was not satisfied with the editing we had done last year so he wanted to check the typescript thoroughly, once more before it was given to press. Then I sent him the edited typescript to Calcutta through his nephew Narottam Sharma. After three months, the typescript reached Kathmandu,by the last week of April 2012.

The translator had checked every sentence, even every word, every bit of mechanics and interplay of sense and expression.

He had compared his abridged version with my full form—and suggested, marked, showed his doubt and disapproval, struck off, and added page after page in blue ink.

(He wrote—I wish I could use red ink, but it is not handy now.) One can see how his fingers must have trembled, and the old style cursive writing sometimes has twisted illegibly. All the margins are full of his corrections, additions, comments and editing, etc. One can estimate his vigor and courage and dedication despite his severe illness. At one point he has expressed his sincere desire—"I could not write now from the hospital bed, let us Translators be mentioned in passing in your Introduction". The corrected copy, along with his letter in an envelope with a logo of The Mission Hospital Durgapur, Calcutta reached me in Kathmandu. I became quite desperate to read his letter.*

Dear bhai2 Dr. Govinda,

I received your affectionate letter. Thank you so much. Long back, I had written a letter to Hari bhai as well. It could not reach him, I heard, though it will. I am not going to remind you of the contents of that letter, he will convey to you. I know the publication of the book is delaying, I am worried too. You too have worked hard despite your illness, there is no doubt. However it is a question of prestige let it not be 'hataarko kaam lataar', we should not hurry and spoil the thing.

When I proofread, I found some instances that need to be made clear. I hope you will correct them meticulously. Especially in cases where new portions were translated later. I checked it as much as I could, sit on the hospital bed, stealing those moments when the doctors were not around.

Though I could not do it perfectly, I rely on you, my brother. You have shown deep concern on whether I need financial support in order to undergo treatment, at this moment. Thank you so much, your affectionate words are

enough for me and please don't take any trouble of visiting
me at this time. Who else has ever shown such? Affection
other than a brother like you! This is enough for me. 'A
brother in need is a brother indeed'—it's truly said.

2. **A junior or younger brother, a term of address**

My treatment process is lengthening—it is in the
fourth stage, they say, fifth may be beyond repair. Th e
Doctors are trying their best. This requires another two
months. But please don't worry, I am in safe hands. Try
to accomplish the task as quickly as possible, as perfectly
as possible.

I wish you all the best.

Regards
Dai Nagendra
25th March 2012

This is what we did. Nagendra *dai*'s worries are touching.
We all wish him the quickest recovery. Now he is convalescing in
Darjeeling. We feel a great silence in Kathmandu. In the absence
of an energetic guardian and scholar; we feel so. We are waiting
for his return to Kathmandu. Hasta *bhai* is so enthusiastic about
Jhamak's works.

He offered to publish this edition. He has sent us money. And
Oriental has coordinated everything on behalf of the publisher.
Nagendra *dai* checked and edited the text more than three times.
Likewise, Tek Narayan Dhakal, a meticulous person, proofread
it thoroughly. I did three times, and finally Bal Ram Adhikari's
perfect hands gave a final touch to this. Bal Ram, himself a perfect
translator, is a budding scholar. I made some final changes based
on their suggestions.

• • •

It is extremely difficult to strike a balanced point of equivalence avoiding over translation, under translation and Introduction mistranslation. Beyond such surface level, criteria, quality of translation, the use of language as such and the readability of the target text is of highest importance. It is not simply a mechanical task; it is rather a quite serious and delicate thing to handle with. We have tried our best. My experience is that transcription is hundred times more challenging, absorbing and riskier job than creation. But how can we come to each other in this world save for translation? Despite our sincere efforts, we can't guarantee everything. We are doing it with our knowledge and experience of translation theory and practice in mind. I don't know what the target readers will feel. Sense transfer is of utmost importance. *Dai* has focused on sense primarily. I humbly request the readers to trust our sincere efforts that are all.

At this moment I am thankful to Jhamak Ghimire for her kind permission to bring out this version, to Nagendra *dai*, Safal for their hard work and devotion, to Gopal Guragain for co-ordinating these activities on behalf on Jhamak Ghimire Literature and Art Foundation, to Hasta Gautam for sponsoring the publication of this edition, to Bal Ram Adhikari and Tek Narayan Dhakal, for assisting me in editing, to Sewa Bhattarai for translating all of the texts in Appendix section, to Kaushal Khaki for layout design, Sundar Basnet of Times Creation for a beautiful cover design and to Hari Gautam for coordinating its printing/ publication on behalf of Oriental Publication.

There is no final point in perfection.

3rd May 2012 **Govinda Raj Bhattarai**
Kathmandu, Nepal
*Dai's letter from Calcutta

Publisher Views

Experience and Determination

Hasta Gautam "Mridul"

A roof of grass, a house painted with mud, a small stable in the yard, and chickens wandering in the yard. She was sitting outside on a mat upon the porch. Her body doesn't move, and nor does she speak, but she holds a pen and paper in her feet. Her hands and feet are disabled since birth, so she cannot stand, but can stare intently, can crawl around, and can collect many experiences in her short journey. Though she may look disabled or slow from the outside, she is actually very fast and energetic from within. Yet society has been making fun of her on the basis of her looks. Even though the society regards her to be a useless thorn, she is able to conclude that life is a flower, not a thorn. She has the courage to draw the lines of her own destiny by holding the wonderful feelings of her heart in her delicate feet. She has presented the powerful message that talent is never disabled, but may be frustrated within an insensitive society. I got the opportunity to read her book *Jeevan Kaandaa Ki Phool.* I turned its pages along the long route from Texas to Guatemala City. The more I read, the more I became engrossed in her feelings and expression. I too had experienced such realities of life in my childhood at Nathigaar of Rukum. I did not cry easily, but when I did, people pitied me, saying, "Such a handicapped person like me *(him)* is better off dead than alive." But though I was small, my determination was great. I promised myself, "If I live, I will one day walk over the whole earth with these weak legs." And truly, my father Gangaram Khatri brought me to Kathmandu from Nathnagar, with great difficulty by carrying me on his back for three months. I hoped to ride a government helicopter, but no one listens to people like us. My father brought me from Musikot to Chaurjahari, carrying me on his back all the way. He carried me even in the sweltering heat of Chaitra. Though we walked to Chaurjahari many times, we did not get the ticket. Then my father carried me all the way to Tulsipur through Falabag of Satyan *(Salyaan),* where we finally got the ticket. I reached Kathmandu in 2036 BS. My sister Bhim Kumari Shrestha registered me at Nepal Apanga Sangha, Khagendra Nava Jeewan, and from Baishakh five, I began living at Jorpati. After I saw other girls and boys with disabilities, I no longer thought I was the only disabled person in the world. Hence, from Nava Jeewan Kendra, I set a new course for my life, and began struggling constantly to achieve those heights. I fought my disability, my weakness, and I won, which became the success story of my life. In 2050, with the help of UNICEF, I established "National Federation of the Disabled-Nepal 1993," a fortress from where to fight for the rights of disabled people. I became founder secretary, while my friend Nirmal Devkota became its president.

However, the politics of Nepal gradually entered the association, and I stepped out to develop other organizations. My pen was active from those early days. In 2044, I had written and published the novel *Anamika Campus* and *Agnikunda Bhitrako Bhie (Bihe),* and in 2945, I had written *Garud Nag,* a musical story. Due to my determination of standing on my own feet, I had to face a lot of struggles and hardships, but I never gave up on my life.

You lose if the heart loses, and you win if the heart wins!

I just sang this song all through the ups and downs of my life.

I have been residing permanently in America since 2005. The only book that I found that reminds me of that priceless time is *Jeevan Kaandaa Ki Phool*. It has rejuvenated my feelings, and given me more energy in life. I can at least speak, can express myself, and can walk, though with difficulty, but Jhamak cannot even do that. She got neither the opportunity to study, nor any environment for it. The disabled community never got to know who or what governs the country. Instead, Jhamak collected the words that were read and discarded by others, made them her own, and created her own life's philosophy from them. In this respect, though Jhamak is my junior in age, she is much more senior in her creativity.

Only a few people have the ability to light up their lives by expressing such beautiful feelings in creation even after going through such hardships. I pity our inefficient government and politicians—there can never be anyone more disabled than them. By mugging up irrelevant theories, wasting the people's money, and maiming many, they have proved themselves to be the most disabled of all. I pity them a lot. We who are disabled are not sad at our own disability, but at the leaders who have disabled our country. They have gradually made the country more and more dependent on others and frustrated. The country has suffered a lot from greedy leaders who could never think beyond their own advantage. These leaders try to cook on a neighbor's fire, and expecting any progress from them is like cooking Birbal's stew. They promised to bring dry earth from the middle of the pond, but they could not even reach the pond's bank, let alone bring back any earth. These leaders without any political philosophy of their own are scrambling to loot Mother Nepal. What can a disabled person like me expect from decrepit leaders like these?

Hence, the capacities of those like Jhamak are little, and they are silent on our topics.

If my friend Biswasdip Tigela and Dr. Govinda Raj Bhattarai had not made such efforts to publish this book, Jhamak might have been silent *un rhubarb* till now. *The leaders have devastated the entire country, and individuals like us are just drops in the ocean.*

I would like to thank the publisher Lingden and editor Dr. Govinda Raj Bhattarai on behalf of all the disabled people of Nepal. There are many talented people in this society, and it is really hard to imagine a society where they all have a place, but with the help of people like Tigela and Bhattarai, who want to give something back to society, more and more people find opportunities.

I am myself a writer, but the fragrance of Jhamak's writing is very enticing to the heart. Hence, I requested Dr. Bhattarai to publish her book instead of mine, and he agreed. He accepted my request graciously, and I started preparing for publication.

In Jhamak, I see the potential of a journey even longer than Parijat's in Nepali literature. Parijat moved forward progressively, while Jhamak moves forward in favor of life. Those who are in favor of life always flourish. Jhamak has gone beyond literature and has portrayed the essence of living as a disabled person. This is something that the whole world wants to know, understand, and experience.

I am here to assist the realization of her potential in any way. My dearest wish is that she may rise above her hard life and live the life of a creator. I see in Jhamak the capacities of the late Khagendra Bahadur Basnet, who opened the doors for thousands of disabled people, though he could not get up for thirty years. Work is accomplished through intellect, while the body is just a medium. Disability is a beauty of life, not a disfigurement. The one sees disability as ugly is himself ugly from within.

No one can call her life a burden anymore; in fact, she is one of the nation's treasured talents, and can answer anyone who says she cannot do anything.

"Whatever I am or however I may be, I have got life, and there is no need for anyone to pity me. When I have not given up on my life, why should anyone say anything about it? I know how to move on and progress in my life." She can write these words in beautiful handwriting and express herself. Gradually, she will be known as the light of the East, just as Ilam will be known as the pearl of the East. She is not a disabled person; she is a shining light with which she pierces the gloom of a dark society and lives on.

The story of her intelligence, wisdom, and courage will slowly light up the entire world. The world will understand the power that lies in the pen she grasps in her delicate feet. She has proved that the impossible is possible, and shines like a candle in a dark night. She has asked us to think of her life as a gift, not a burden, even though she is born in a society that evaluates lives based solely on the body. She has opened the door to wisdom.

"My sister Mina is the one who has taught me to read and write. I have never been to a school, and yet I have courage to walk the roads of literature. I have golden dreams, and one day I will surely lead others in this society. I have not been able to know any government in this country. I have found *love and support from every member of my family*, at one point or another. Hence, I do not think of my life as a curse. I thrive in my life, I have found energy, and I am learning to make it warmer and better." By saying this, she has already moved a step forward.

Though she has lived in her village all her life and received a limited education, her vision found unlimited possibilities even in her limited surroundings, her small corner, and that frustrated space. By pouring out her soul through her feet in golden letters, she has sent sparks into the society. She had no wish to express any chauvinistic, cynical, foolish, materialized, or blank feelings. Her words were neither plagiarized nor sycophantic. Instead, those were words that had encountered the truth of the soul in the depth of imagination, which had flourished in the fertile land of time. They are flowers, and not the artificial kind without a scent. These are the fragrant jasmines, the *bukis* of the Himalayas, and the *lalupate* of the hills.

Due to her weak hands and legs, she spent many hungry days. She silently swallowed her tears when people called her a walking corpse. When people blessed her at Dashain to die soon instead of *having to endure* such a crippled life, she spoke not a word. She never even knew what school was. When she indicated that she wanted to study, people discouraged because "what use did she have for studies?" But Jhamak did not give up, and learned to write the alphabet with her feet. She has gone through every kind of abuse that society is capable of flinging at a person. How hard it must have been for her to wash her face and use the toilet in her childhood! She gained knowledge just by listening to others reading.

"I did not get the support to live from anyone. My feelings were bottled up until I learned to write with my toes. I had neither paper nor pen to write, I learned to write with bits of coal," she says. She was very hurt when people would say "You don't know anything, why do you want to see a book? What use would letters be to you anyway?" She knew hunger, but had no voice to ask for food. She was thirsty, but had no words for water. Neither did she have a language. She knew neither the wonders of nature nor human feelings. She could feel the sun shining over the hilltop, but could only wonder what it was. She did not know when night fell. She wanted to roam freely like other children, but never got the chance. There was never anyone to carry her around. She began getting around the house by crawling. When she saw a new world at the back of her house, she was quite glad. She got very wet when it rained. Only then did she understand the meaning of rain. When she touched fire, it burned her, and that is how she knew what fire is. Thus, she collected meanings from all around and began storing them in the vaults of her heart. She increased her knowledge and wisdom solely through her own efforts. Through several such hardships, she understood the meaning of each word, and the feelings and expression behind each word. By stringing those words together in a necklace, she made sentences and entered the world of education. She began writing with dew drops on the ground. She tried to write with her toes on the plate she ate from. There is no telling of the efforts that she put in. By collecting words won through so much hard work, she gradually began shining like a star in the society. She was short, but still she carved a niche for herself that was higher than any fully able person. She is a source of power for any person with a weak heart. She is the hope for the hopeless. She is the full moon for those who only see the darkness in life. She is the very life for those who wallow in misery and listlessly wait for death. She has worked very hard to turn the impossible into the possible.

The image of god carved in her soul is her life. She is worthy of worship. She is the only able person who, though being weak physically, is actually ahead of those more able. She is a source of inspiration to the society. Every skill, symbol, and metaphor that she has used has become inspiration for everyone. She does not have the hollow bookish knowledge, yet she can serve the most thoughtful philosophy. Her determination has become much greater than theories of political sycophancy. She is very curious, and is eager to know about other people and society as well. Though people have dismissed her, she has begun a life much more precious than theirs. She is the *Parijat* flower that can see into the heart and soul of every Nepali. By challenging her handicapped body, she has become an inspiration to live with dignity. Time bows down to her, and the society is grateful to her.

Though people may think of her as a walking corpse, she has actually challenged society. *To me, it is the leaders and intellectuals of this country that are handicapped*, not her. I am overwhelmed with feelings at her handicap, because it is surely among the severest in the world. Gradually, Jhamak will be famous not just in Nepal but in the entire world. She will become a pride of Nepal. One day, Mother Nepal too will be proud of having Jhamak, and will declare that she is proud to have given birth to such a one.

At this point, I lay down my pen. In the end, I would like to say that Jhamak is an inspiration to all the handicapped people of Nepal. No one wants to live as a burden to others; everyone wants to live as an able, capable, and progressive member of the nation.

I have one of the dreams to start publication business to promoting Nepali Diaspora literature around the world. So, I determine to publishing first book of Jhamak K. Ghimire, then I get potential co-operation with Professor Govinda Raj Bhattarai, then we create our project to translate in Nepali to English and publishing in Nepal and USA. In this matter I am so grateful with him and also here some special persons to mention in this book. Then I also grateful with Nepali novelist and Poet Homnath Subedi, who was founder of "International Nepali Literature society-USA 1992 and he is board of Trusty of INLS HQ. Who give me his valuable article about Miss.Jhamak K. Ghimire, and I am also so grateful with scholar Professor and Poet Mohan Situal, and my intimate friend Journalist Mr.Lekhnath Bhandari, who was helping sis Jhamak from the beginning of this book preparation. Another courageous brother Mr. Sudarsan Gautam, (his both hand imputed and resident in Canada, who climbed different highest mountains around the world including Mt. Everest). I also thankful with Mr.Abhi Bastakoti for technical support.

Finally, I give thanks to my beloved wife Saru Gautam, who has always giving me her numerous love and support in my life to fulfill my golden dreams.

And I am really appreciated with Xlibris Corporation's, who give me their impressive helping hands to make success dream project.

Thank you in advance from my bottom of heart that respecting all readers to declare her life is beautiful flowers not thorn as a being with disabilities.

The Flower that Failed to Bloom in Spring
Hasta Gautam "Mridul"
Promoter/Author
nepalidiaspora2usa@gmail.com
Nepali Diaspora-USA
13105 Lipton Loop
Del Valle, TX 78617
United States of America
May 8, 2012

Nepali Diaspora: view

Jhamak: Nepali Helen Keller

I had never seen or read literary work of a writer who doesn't use a hand to write before but recently was happy and proud to have an opportunity to read creative work of award winning writer, Jhamak Ghimire who hails from Nepal and writes using her feet or toes. I haven't seen or met her personally but when I read "Jeewan Kaanda ki Phool" and this translation, I felt like I was talking to Nepali Helen Keller of literary world and able to draw live mental picture of her. It is an evidence of her powerful writing. This book is the most powerful autobiographical creation in Nepali literature.

Despite her physical difficulties as you will find reading introduction of the book by scholars who are much closer to her, she learned to read and write using her feet then went on to express and share her feelings and thoughts using it and is able to produce number of award winning Nepali literary books such as Jeewan Kaanda ki Phool. This particular book was recently awarded "International Nepali Literary Society (INLS) Chetnath Ghimire Koshi Zonal Best Book Award 2011" by the INLS Headquarters in Washington DC. As Chairman of INLS Board of Trustees, I would like to congratulate her for this achievement.

She has already become popular with many of her feet-written work in Nepal nationally. As mentioned by Global Press Institute recently, she even has inspired people of her birth place, Dhankuta, a district in Koshi Zone of Nepal, to be self-sufficient [1]. With wining INLS Award, her work has started to be recognized by the Nepali speaking community in the Diaspora and by publishing this English translation of "Jeewan Kaanda ki Phool" or "A Flower amidst the Thorns", she is stepping into the world literature to reach readers internationally including Nepalese in the Diaspora, Friends of Nepal and any literature lovers in general. This will sure continue to inspire people around the world as readership for her writing increases and help spread her message of self-dependent and self-sufficient.

In addition, I am proud that one of the US Diaspora members and life members of INLS, Hasta Gautam "Mridul" sponsored publication of this book. It is my hope that this translating, editing, publishing, promoting activity in the USA will be able to take Jhamak Ghimire and her writings to next level in international literary arena. As with Nepali language version of this book, I am sure this translation will win the heart of international English language readers as well.

Thanks to Jhamak for writing "Jeewan Kaanda ki Phool" and creating world of psychological auto-biographic garden inside and outside Nepal. She is about 32 years old now. By the time she reaches 90, she will have created hundreds of flower garden—all without pen, pain and paper in hand. This is the magic of the literature and human brain. I hope the readers will find her very much interesting. My best wishes for her grand success.

Hom Nath Subedi
Founding President of INLS HQ
Washington DC
05/19/2012

The Scholar' views

Jhamak : From an Earthen Clay to an Enlightened Soul

Almost one year ago a packet of books came to me from a friend of mine in the USA for sharing a reading with him. There were books with various forms and figures but all with wonderful expressions and literary experimentations of the modern realities of life along with Nepalese atmosphere. Most of them had or have the elements of *avant—garde* in Nepali creative culture. They had / have life as a light and light as a life—both towards a continuous 'becoming' from a status of 'being'.  There was life presented as it were, as an ongoing flow of bright rainbow stars full of variety of music and songs of life. Among them there was a book called 'Jeevan Kaandaa Ki Phool ? by a writer Jhamak Ghimire who, from the very birth, is massively disabled with her physical formation. I was really deeply impressed by the sufferings, struggles between good and evil in her experiences, the will power and determination, curiosity of learning, the powerful expressions, discovering life within life, the philosophy, revolt, a sense of forgiveness, *piety* and change as well as the literary flashes of art in letters. There is a challenge in the existence god, as a separate *entity* apart from the divine feelings of man in his/ her sense of compassion. And it is in favor of 'character destiny' of any human being. I had occasional talks with a few friends including Hasta Gautam 'Mirdul' about it. As I knew from him that the book is going to be published in the English medium as 'A Flower Amidst the Thorns'. It has been a very great pleasure on my part too. And Hast told me to write a few words on it. I committed, but could not be fast.

I found the translation to be very good but did not find time to read it in detail. So I mostly depended on the Nepali text, for quotations, which I had earlier jotted down, and on my own passing translation of them.

Various best wishers like Tigela ji, Guragain ji and renowned scholars, including Prof Balkrishna Pokhrel and Dr. Govinda Bhattarai, have elaborately poured their melted expressions of tenderness and thoughtful appreciation along with solid finds of lively facts and promising elements in the book and the writer. Among many other things they have also mentioned about its great literary value. I say, this book is an epic in prose.

Jhamak starts her autobiographical tale in an epic way:

> '*I have now come to interpret life as the most beautiful flower of creation*'.

See ! How beautiful universal a message it is. So poetic! So convincing! It is her discovery of life's meaningful reality. It is as though a jewel of wisdom, wrought after a long battle of experience, and workmanship in an anvil of meditation and experiment comparable to any Vaidic *sukta*.

'*This is an epic novel on the founding of*' a new society of dignity, freedom, talent and justice. It tapes out the crude and dogmatically blind but in some ways ignorant traditional attitudes, limited awareness and unsympathetic frame of mind of the age and society that was very strong and triumphant during her childhood and long earlier. As she somehow went on growing and struggling in her invincible mind with a massive limited capacity of body through her continuous victory, she was changing the temperature of the family and the temperament of the social members. That by the time this epic-novel was written and published the atmosphere was created as well to be itself in a new epoch of social / mental change and progress through her struggling life of sufferings and detached (never autobiographical) positive miscellaneous expressions as a columnist. She says that before this novel she had never expressed her personal troubles etc.

This autobiographical epical novel is written in an unbroken thread of reminiscences to express her ways of discoveries through the struggles of fulfilling her curiosities and the thirst for knowledge of every thing: names of things, event, time, feelings and very many more. They are in a 'stream of consciousness technique' all together.

As every chapter, like a standard *sarga* of Nepali or Sanskrit epics or *canto* of western ones, is a continuation of the previous one as it is a new opening out of a new adventure. The 'beginning' has a relation to the 'middle' as well as with the 'end'. The suspension has been maintained all through as it is contextually unreeled with every event as well as with chapter. In the process of the adventure—aayena-(like the word Ramayana) there are various situations, times, occasions of love, hatred, horror and events of rifts and mental fights being described. The story is driven by the characters themselves. And the situations are woven with the fabrics of bitter pain, irony, ignorance and a sense of zeal to change all. So good. At the same time the situations do not end in themselves unless they derive a discovery, a positive message to the world in general and to the disabled communities in particular. It is a tale told by an adventurer like a Ulysses or a space traveler or the legendary ancient and modern discoverers 'of the great new world' where she found everything strange and lacking and therefore wanted to fulfill the gaps or change the evil ones. She has achieved this in this modern master piece of universal appeal from Nepal.

Here are the elements of fairy tales and the imaginary. They come to blend with the grim reality in the mind and matter of a visionary—the writer. The heroine is the writer herself and her younger sister is the second and rest of the others are the secondary ones, but important with roles of sort. Respecting her grand mother very high she has given all others, including her parents, her due treatment of justice with a sense of respect and sympathy to even the wicked ones who were covered by the ignorant layers of screens of dogmatism and may be due to a kind of frustration in poverty-stricken home and society where the state is all indifferent like the so called god. So fate was to rule the destiny where 'indomitable' as well as rebellious character had to come to challenge it to plough her own corridor of life towards a desired destination. This is the epic treatment of a grand narrative of life and society. At the same time those who successfully flashed her up to the light of the day throughout the wide world are duly placed in high esteem with a sense of sincere gratitude. And she is right. Thus the characters from low level of life—and a great in number in the world as a community or class—and a high mission of human-divine—seem to work on their own realities and they are drawn in a natural manner and art of depiction. There are characters with love, hatred, pride, flaws, falls and rise, the heroine herself with new thoughts of conscious humanity.

Any good literary art is full of the use of beautiful and original imagery employed in describing nature and culture, the characters, events, situations and the like. Here in this novel they abound in plenty:

> 'the ears of the satellites are floating like the case of a ball'.
> 'the morning sun emerged 'like a broken egg'.
> 'even though the night used to be seen very near just in front of me but I could not touch and toss it or make any sport with'.

See the originally wonderful creative expressions:

There are many rhythmic, proverbial as well as poetic pieces in the prosaic sentences:

> 'Neither could I do (garna) anything, nor just die(marna).'

On the one hand she very highly values the moral or mental or spiritual beauty rather than body, whereas, she has also a very high appreciation of aesthetic aspects of physical things, on the other. She has an appreciation of platonic love and again accepts the ideal sexual and psychological matters as well as youth as natural ones. But she puts freedom, self dignity and self-dependant-labor on top of all.

She is an artist not only of letters but colors too. The book in point gives descriptions of such a taste and quality. She says:

> 'Yes, of course, it is very much entertaining to play with colors. On top of it, how comfortable it is to express some of the odd situations and thoughts through colors when it is very difficult in letters.' (P. 202—Nepali version).

Jhamak Ghimire, as a contemporary spirit of awareness, is very much touching with the internal political conflict of Nepal. She is very much critical about it too. She says;

> 'Yes, it is the wound of the conflict, and immense pain, which is very much difficult for man to bear . . .
> I wiped the pus and blood of the wound with words. I wiped the flood of tears with the cloak of feelings'.

These are very high quality figurative expressions of feelings capable only from long labored creative writers of continuous dedication and wonderful genius. No wonder that she has tens of literary publications and so prevail the honors and awards.

There are many dreadful situations and events of hardship in the novel as found in great epics. The one when her grand mother breathed her last at that dead of night is mentionable here. Completely ignorant of death on the one hand and the actual state of affairs of her grand mother at the given moment on the other, she slept fast with her grand mother where the latter was laying down dead calm and quite on the bare cold ground. It was dark everywhere. Even the dim fire was dead. The door was open and there was no mother, no father, nor any of her younger dear sister and brother. It was so cold that she could not resist. So with extreme difficulty she climbed up to the cot-bed, turned the clothes flat and slept. It was only in the following morning when people gathered and prepared for the funeral procession of her grand mother that she heard, (not yet known well) about death and the passing away of her grand mother.

Thus in the novel there is such a wide and varied spectrum of life and the world, very minute details have been described and the situations as well as the activities are all full of the sense of deep compassion(*karuna*), fear and horror, pleasure and plays that it can be called an epic. At the same time there are the elements of a play too. That it is a very big canvas where life and the world have been, as it were, painted in a very lively way.

It has the presentation of the flashes of post modernity when she brings past to unite with the present state, the locale to the universal, the personal to the common. The strange isolation of a conscious but neglected living soul is very brilliantly projected as a light of individual and social life. But this topic needs to be studied in as separate topic. It is an artistic canvas where the universal feelings of sufferings, behaviors, attitudes and the physical minds of the social milieu as well the psychological minds within the human beings have been sharply studied.

She has a reformatory zeal of change and a spirit of raising the low level of life of the disables to the dignified level of respect, talent, achievement and happiness. She says:

> 'There are such traditions in our culture that are full of injustice which do not keep any sympathy with the neglected class. The class which is neglected and humiliated for centuries. Within that class there is a subdued voice which has not been able enough to come out. There is suffocation, tears, anguish and grief, even then there is life, and there is human breath. Hence I have to live by becoming a voice for the voiceless, and

*word for the wordless . . . With this inspiration too, have
I been traveling through life . . . It was a struggle against
a society gripped by the darkness of blind belief and
dogmatism . . . . in which (struggle) no weapons of any
kind were raised, nor carried any explosives . . . . I came
struggling through opinion'* (page 82).

Let us see and feel the expressions! It has the deep seated and heavy torments suffocated for ages. And how determined, dignified, deep and elevated does she become in her expressions of fathomless pains and a strongly rebellious spirit. It is a new document—a dastavej—a manifesto of social reform and change.

I would like to conclude that this autobiographical novel is a jewel of a genius born in Nepal comparable to any great novel and epic. Great Poet Lazmi Prasad Devkota, the greatest poet of Nepal once said:

> *'When the fountain springs forth from genius will
> not it touch the human hears?'*

So is this book and the writer. Were not Homer and Milton blind when they wrote their immortal epics? Were not those disabled writers mentioned in the book and prefaces struggling very hard with fate to change the course of destiny by character? Jhamak is another brilliant example from Nepal—herself a message not only to the Nepalese native disables or of the diaspora but also to the whole of the human beings at large. That this book is necessary to be translated not only in English but also in many more international languages and be prescribed not only in Nepal but in all the classes throughout the globe. I am not ambitious in it but humbly suggestive.

At the same time an organization to take care of the various types of disables in general, Nepalese in particular is necessary in the Nepalese diaspora specially in the USA. At the end, I highly appreciate the great co-operative hearts of our country mentioned above and including Hasta Gautam 'Mirdul' (who himself is an established creative writer of sort—a gazalist, a poet, a song writer and playwright—and disable) who facilitated for the promotion of such a genius who, otherwise could still remain in the suffering shade.

Though still suffering physically as Jhamak is, I wish her continuous success and her heroic message reach in all the bright souls of struggling hearts as well as the generous ones who want to contribute to such a positive earthly-divine cause ! The message is that every disable has a talent. They do not need any mercy from the capable and the well to-do. But like any marginalized social group they need a dignified and meaningful support as well as encouragement so that they can develop their talent to contribute to the society in any way possible for them and thus live a life of self respect, progress and satisfaction. Jhamak is a noble soul of a holy soil. Thank you.

Prof. Mohan Sitoula (rtd)
May 21, 2012
Round Rock(Gol Dhunga)
Jestha 8, 2069
TX, USA.
940-597-9070

Journalist's views

Jhamak: Source of Hope and Inspiration
By: Lekhanath Bhandari

Jhamak Ghimire is an emerging, yet already famous, female writer. There is no need for Jhamak's specific introduction. Her book "*A flower in the midst of thorns*" itself is a reflection of who she is, and what she is. With enormous potentialities to contributing in Nepali literature in the future, she has already set an example.

Jhamak was awarded the "Madan Puraskar" in year 2067 BS. Madan Puraskar is the most popular and prestigious award in the Nepali literature. It is also called the Nepali Nobel Prize. The Late Parijat was the first ever women writer to win the Madan Puraskar for her novel "Blue Memosa". After 44 years, Jhamak became the second women winner of the Madan Puraskar for her book "*A flower in the midst of thorns*". Parijat was the 18th author to win the Madan Puraskar; Jhamak became the 67th winner.

Life: flowers or thorns. Jhamak has written about a dozen books and contributed other literary creative products. *A flower in the midst of thorns* is her most recent book.

Whether life is a flower or thorn is not the question. No doubt, life can be a flower as it can also be a thorn. Not everybody has the same course in life. Jhamak's life is different from that of many other ordinary people. Her life is a blooming flower surrounded by thorny bushes. Life, in itself, is neither a flower nor a thorn; all depends upon the individual, whether such individual makes of the life a flower or a thorn.

"ढुङ्गाको काप फोरेर पनि, उम्रन्छ पिपल
सृजना शक्ती संसारम, कैलाई हुँदैन बिफल"
कविवर माधव प्रसाद धिमिरे,

Poet Madhab Prasad Ghimire once wrote:
"Pipal tree springs out by breaking the corner of a stone; Creative energy, in the world, never fails"

As expressed in the above stanza, Jhamak has, indeed, emerged out of very difficult conditions and, has for herself, established an identity, created a personality and made an image. Jhamak cites these lines by Poet Madhav Ghimire in her chapter "Disability in the eyes of the society". Jhamak is exemplary. She is the new light of hope and inspiration, and indeed, she has been able to give meaning to the meaning of the above stanza by Poet Madhav Ghimire. Jhamak is a rising star. She is a growing flame of courage, hope and awareness. She has immense capacity and is very passionate, and she simply needs opportunity, encouragement and favourable environment to flourish.

Jhamak started her struggle from Kachide in eastern rural area of Nepal, but her fame, now, has crossed the border of Kathmandu and is becoming international. Her name and fame have been sprouting and broadening the rays of hope. This columnist still has it fresh in memory how and when he was introduced to Jhamak in Kathmandu. Even from abroad, during the past several years, this columnist has been following the several creative activities of Jhamak. The columnist had the opportunity to go through some of her latest writings, books, as well as critiques about her writings. Although Jhamak's latest writings are full of awareness and revelations, there is still some room for improvement, from the perspective of artistic way of literary expression. Such a perception may be because these pieces of contemporary writings, mostly in the newspapers, were on modern issues, and they aimed at awakening, creating awareness, and educating the readers on the issues of concern. It would, therefore, not be fair to Jhamak to limit our assessments about her on the basis of such creations only. Indeed, it is not appropriate to evaluate the creativity of a person on the basis of media writings. However, after reading the book *"A flower in the midst of thorns"*, I understood that it has, in a combined fashion, brought about both her magical skills of writing, and her hard struggle in life.

With the help of Nepali publishers living abroad, now, Jhamak has begun her international journey. In spite of the serious lack of financial resources, her book is being translated into English, Spanish and many other languages, and thus is being really globalized, which, in itself, is good news and an indicator of Jhamak's rising identity and respect in the global arena.

This book could be a good source of inspiration for the children of Nepali origin living abroad, especially for those who have become less than creative, with preference to focus more on the so called high-tech gadgets and mundane needs. This book gives readers energy to survive and struggle even in adverse situations.

It is generally not appropriate to make observation about an author's birth, gender, race, physical strength, or formation of the body. Jhamak is physically disabled but is a rare and extraordinary figure. She represents determination and passion. She is the inspiration for many people.

Jhamak has skillfully weaved the truth of her life in her book, an auto-biographic essay. It is about the rise and fall in life. It is the true image of social discrimination and deep-rooted malfunction of our society. It is the story of sorrow as well as joy of family life. It is the struggle of life aimed at fulfilling the ambitions within the limited access of resources and physical disability. It is about love and affection towards life and commitment to face the hard and extreme situations. It is the response to the society and family that treats physically disabled girls, with discrimination. Every individual in the world gets inspiration from some kind of a source. Some people are exemplary and role models for others. But Jhamak is an inspiration for all and forever.

Jhamak's book is really courageous, inspiring and fact-based souvenir for readers. It is of a unique value and falls in a unique category. It is a self-proclamation of a young lady. It gives the taste for life and provides positive message to survive. It teaches and encourages one to struggle hard with extreme difficulties.

Furthermore, this world is a flower in the eyes of a flower; it is a thorny bush in the eyes of a thorn.

Along with Jhamak Ghimire, Madan Puraskar Guthi also awarded another renowned poet Durga Lal Shrestha with Jagadamba Shree award for his outstanding contribution in literature. What a pleasant consequence! Durga Lal wrote, "The world is flower in the eyes of flower"; and Jhamak proved it to be the truth.

E-mail: LNB999@gmail.com

Global Press View

Global Press Institute Renowned Writer with Cerebral Palsy Continues to Inspire

"All our troubles are resolved if we remain self-dependent and self-sufficient."
- Jhamak Ghimire, writer

Born with cerebral palsy, Jhamak Ghimire can't speak or use her hands. She learned to read and write using her feet and eventually launched an award-winning literary career. Ghimire promotes a message of self-sufficiency and empowerment for women.

Courtesy of Jhamak Ghimire,

Tuesday—May 3, 2011

KACHIDE, NEPAL—Jhamak Ghimire, 30, can't speak or use her hands, and her lower limbs can't hold her body upright. She slowly pulls her plate of food toward her with her feet and mixes the rice with dal, or lentil soup. With great difficultly, she takes the food to her mouth, which emits a constant stream of saliva.

Ghimire was born with cerebral palsy, a group of disorders that affect the functions of the brain and nervous system. Ghimire also wears glasses because she has myopia, or nearsightedness.

Yet despite Ghimire's many physical challenges, her mother says she has achieved unbelievable success.

"I had lost all hope when I gave birth to her," says her mother, Asha Devi Ghimire, whose name means "goddess of hope." "I had never thought that a child born with so many complications could one day achieve such success in her life."

Unable to speak, Ghimire taught herself to read and write using her toes, which is how she communicates. Her several feet-written interviews have been published by various media, one which helped launch her literary career.

In addition to working as a columnist, Ghimire has written about a dozen books in Nepali, including four collections of poems, a collection of essays, a collection of articles, an autobiography and two collections of stories that are currently on sale in the local market. She has won a number of national awards.

Her father says his daughter's success has transformed and inspired their entire village in Dhankuta, a district in eastern Nepal, which, like many Nepali villages, lacks roads and telephone service.

"It is unbelievable that a girl with no voice and malfunctioning limbs, who was often cursed with early death, could one day become the reason that changed the fate of the whole village," says her father, Krishna Bahadur Ghimire.

After Ghimire was diagnosed with cerebral palsy, her family members say they didn't have much hope for her. Today, fellow villagers say she has inspired them and improved the living standards in their community, as Ghimire says her goal is to inspire people to be self-sufficient. She also wants women to take the lead in making Nepali society more equal.

There are approximately 2.5 million people with disabilities in Nepal, about half of which are women, says Birendra Pokhrel, chairman of the National Federation of the Disabled Nepal, an umbrella organization representing disabled people nationwide. But only 2 percent of them are employed—of which the female ratio is low.

Typing on her cell phone with her feet, Ghimire says that her parents first took her to witch doctors, who promised to cure her but instead cheated them.

"Despite the chickens, eggs and money they took from my parents as fees, I am still the same," she types.

Ghimire types that her parents finally took her to a hospital, where American and German doctors diagnosed her with cerebral palsy. They said her condition would never improve.

"Henceforth, I tried to make my day-to-day life more comfortable and easy, instead of seeking treatment," she types.

But she says she eventually became interested in the alphabet.

"I learned how to recognize alphabets by hearing my sister, Mina, read," Ghimire writes with her feet. "I would drag myself close to her while she read aloud to identify the alphabets but was often reprimanded for dirtying my clothes."

After memorizing the alphabet, Ghimire began to try to write them in the mud in their yard. But she writes that she was beaten for this, as a popular superstition says that writing on the floor causes bad debt.

"No one understood my desire to read and write," she writes. "The first time I was able to write the letter 'ka' [the first alphabet in Nepali script] on the yard, I rejoiced by blowing dust all around me with a hope that someone would see the letter and realize that a useless disabled girl like me could write. But no one did. Instead I was beaten again for blowing dust."

Ghimire's parents say they never understood their daughter's different abilities. Only after reading her autobiography did they realize the intentions behind many of her actions.

"I never could understand my daughter," her father says. "People like Jhamak could have innate talent, and parents should understand and encourage them."

Her younger sister, Mina Ghimire, agrees.

"As a child, I could not understand the difficulty my sister faced," she says. "While growing up, she would use dew drops to try and write letters on stones."

But she says that once she understood, she started to help her sister secretly.

"After I learned of her desire, I at times stole money from my parents or used the ones she had to buy her pen and notebook to write on," she says.

With her sister's help, Ghimire practiced her writing, which she says made her happy. She says that one of the most special days of her life was when her mother bought her a notebook.

Around the time she was learning how to read and write, her grandmother, who used to take care of her, died. Ghimire says this meant she had to become more independent immediately, as no one is allowed to touch for 13 days after a family death, according to Hinduism.

"My grandmother used to feed me, and with her gone, and the family members, ritually not allowed to touch me, could not punish me," she says. "Initially when I tried to eat with my foot, people tried to restrict me, and on several occasions I hurled the plate full of food away with my feet in anger."

But once they comprehended that she was trying to eat, they let her. During those traditional 13 days of mourning, Ghimire says she perfected eating with her foot and continues to do so, making her less dependent on others.

Ghimire eventually began to share her writing with others. Publishers discovered her when then-editor Bijay Raj Acharya published an interview with her in a magazine.

"She is living her life to the fullest, and the world can learn a lot from her independence, struggle and contribution to Nepali literature," says Acharya, who now owns a publishing house and has published one of Ghimire's books.

She has won nearly a dozen national and regional literary awards since 1998, including one from the Nepali government.

Despite being decorated with so many awards, Ghimire still considers the day her first book—a poetry collection—was published as the happiest day of her life.

"You cannot imagine how happy I was when a book with my perspectives was published, as I had only dreamed of learning the alphabets and being able to read," Ghimire writes with her feet.

Bishwadeep Tigela, the publisher of her recent anthology of autobiographical essays—"Jeewan Kaanda ki Phool," or "Life, Whether a Thorn or a Flower"—says it's just as inspiring.

"Ghimire's manuscript was so heart-wrenching that I could not help sobbing while reading it," Tigela says.

In her autobiography, Ghimire documents instances such as her parents ignoring her desire to study or how she tried to memorize the alphabets her younger sister was studying and practiced them by scribbling in the garden.

"Ghimire's achievements are a source of inspiration even for abled people," Tigela says.

Three editions of the anthology have been published and most bookstores here carry it. Many prominent Nepalis have also named it as their favorite book in media interviews.

Anil Poudel, the producer and director of a documentary based on Ghimire's life, "Jhamak," says he made the film to publicize Ghimire's achievements and popularize her body of work in order to inspire people.

"Reading Ghimire's books and interactions with her has made me realize that most of us are living a dependent and parasitic life without using our unfathomable energy and potential to the maximum," Poudel says. "We should be able to realize our innate potential from the life of Ghimire."

Ghimire is also a regular columnist for Kantipur, a Nepali news daily, and has a large readership.

"Through her column, her potential has been acknowledged—nationally and internationally—not just because she can write with her feet, but because her writing is effective and efficient compared to the contemporary analytical litterateurs," says Govinda Raj Bhattarai, a professor and writer who helped launch her book of autobiographical essays.

Bhattarai says her creativity is unbelievable.

"She has amazed the whole world by creating literature with the help of her legs," he says.

Gopal Guragai, chairman of the Jhamak Ghimire Literature and Art Foundation, a local organization named after Ghimire, says the foundation now organizes programs such as poetry recitations at Nepal Academy, a national academic institution.

Villagers say Ghimire's fame has made the entire district popular. Ghimire says that people constantly flock to her house to meet her and she tries her best to communicate with them.

"I appreciate people coming to visit me and showing interest in me, but several times I am tired and cannot write down every answer," Ghimire says.

Devi Shrestha, a local teacher who has rented a room from Ghimire's family for more than a decade, says that Ghimire's success has improved the local standard of living.

"Initially, the village did not have telephone service, but after Ghimire came into the limelight, we not only have telephones in our house but Internet service, too," Shrestha says.

Now, Ghimire types her articles on the computer with her feet and can access the Internet for information.

Ghimire says that her earnings from her books have helped to support her family. But she says that because of patriarchal traditions, her family doesn't like to acknowledge the financial contributions of their daughter.

"I want to tell all that this thought should be changed," Ghimire says.

She says that discrimination against women is still a major problem in Nepal and that women must initiate changing this instead of waiting for someone to do it for them. She says the most important message she wants to tell people is that every person should rely on what they have and be self-sufficient instead of seeking what they do not have.

"All our troubles are resolved if we remain self-dependent and self-sufficient," she says.

She and others say her story shows this.

"In the past, I was a nuisance and a troublemaker for all, but the situation has changed today," she says.

Read more:
http://www.globalpressinstitute.org/global-news/asia/nepal/renowned-writer-cerebral-palsy-continues-inspire?page=3#ixzz1vR4XuMUu

The Meeting that Day

_____ **Govinda Raj Bhattarai, PhD**

Three years ago, in 2063, Bishwas Deep Tigela was here. He had gone to his native land Dhankuta after releasing his book *Kathmanduma Desh Boknuko Pida*. There he organized a literary program and distributed some prizes before coming back to Kathmandu; he also went to meet Jhamak there. He told me about the experience and further asked me, "Sir, I met Jhamak in Dhankuta. I have promised to take out one of her books. Would you write a preface for it?"

At first, I wondered what "take out" meant. Later, I realized that he meant to publish. "I can write a preface," I told him. "But what will Jhamak say? I have not met her. I did teach in Dhankuta campus once, but that was decades ago, and Jhamak hadn't begun writing then. Back then, I hadn't even heard of her. But now, she has been writing for a decade. Today, who hasn't heard of her or read about her? But I haven't met her myself. To write about a book, I must have the writer's permission as well as the publisher's."

Bishwas had left Jhamak's book *Jeewan Kaandaa Ki Phool* with me back then. After he reached UK, I got a call from him one day. I spoke to mediator Devi Shrestha, and later heard Jhamak's words from him—"Please write the preface for *Jeevan Kaandaa Ki Phool*. I agree to it." I was very pleased that day.

It was year 2067. I finished reading Jeewan *Kaandaa* Ki Phool. There were about fifty pages of typed text in A4 paper. In Shrawan of that year, I went to Dharan as a guest of the "Bhayawaadi Theories" program organized by Desh Subba. The day after the program, I wanted to visit Dhankuta too. My in-laws live there, and also my old house that I had built in my days of struggle, though someone else lives in it now. There also is the college that I used to teach in, more friends and colleagues, and most important, there lives Jhamak. Dharmendrabikram Nembang was with me too. At sunset, we walked toward Salleri with Apar and Adhar walking ahead of us the day after we reached Dhankuta. The wind from Tammar River sighs in those beautiful forest paths under the pine trees. The hills were pushed to one side when motor roads were dug; it was damp but without any grass growing on it. Once you cross the road, the village of Kachide is right in front. There are trees of oranges, tangerines, buckwheat fields, and bushes of pumpkins, and the empty house of Hemchandra Guru. Still on its wall is written "Ram Ram" in dark letters. From there, we went uphill. After walking for a little bit along a dirt road that dreams of being a motor road, there is a house right near the pine trees, at the top of the village and just above the buckwheat fields. That is Jhamak's house. It's an average house in the hills: the house and cowshed are apart from each other. We left the ruminating cows behind in the shed and climbed the wooden stairs to reach the big room upstairs. Jhamak was sitting there. "Baini, I am a stranger. I have come to meet you. We never met before," I told her as I sat down.

She bent down. An open diary was lying there. She grabbed it with her toes and put it over her ankles. Then she wrote on it "Govinda Sir, I know you!"

I remember it as if it happened today. Her face was bright, smiling, and loving, as if we had known each other for years. Right then, Gopal dai arrived there. We had already informed Gopal Guragai, who was the president of Jhamak Ghimire Sahityakala Pratisthan. We sat and talked, communicating in the same way. I spoke clearly; Jhamak could hear well. She wrote in her diary; I read and answered her. As she spoke without inhibition, I found a personality well forged by struggles, with a lot of determination and motivation. I was very glad that I went to meet Jhamak that day.

Around her were racks of books. In front of her were a diary, fax, and computer, while on the other side were her medals, certificates, and paintings she had made. The room was full. In the corner was a bed with bright windows. We drank the tea her mother made and stayed for a long time. That day, I wanted to open my heart out, because her book *Jeewan Kaandaa Ki Phool* had brought me here. I had already read the manuscript that Bishwas had left with me before I reached Dharan. In it, I had found an excellent example of autobiography. I believed that this book would find a special place in Nepali literature, and it would elevate Jhamak's horizons and introduce her to world literature. However, the book still needed to be improved and polished. I wanted to tell Jhamak about the improvements she needed to make. It was good if she made them, and if she did not, it was still my duty to tell her. These were my feelings before I met her for the first time. "Baini, this is an immortal creation. You seem too young to write an autobiography, since you are still climbing the peaks of success. But since you have experienced unique physical struggles on your journey, yet have reached much higher than everyone else, I am very eager to have your story heard by the world. Your poems speak of your consciousness, creativity, and gradual success. The readers can evaluate them as they *fir* alongside the creations of other poets. But this is an autobiographical creation. It will add luster to your entire creation, and all those who want to know your personality will praise your courage through your struggles. This is a different creation—an introduction to Jhamak. This is an inspiration for her knowledge, achievements, struggles, and hope.

"But it still has many places for improvement, many questions unanswered, and many gaps. There are still ways to add power and attraction to this book. Can I speak of these things to you?" I was being careful not to hurt her feelings; I didn't want to end up giving unwanted advice. Many family members, individuals, and organizations have helped her reach where she is now, while I had just met her. I put my feelings to her carefully.

When Jhamak agreed to my words, I continued, saying, "Many things seem incomplete. The curious reader might want to know how Jhamak learned to read. How she began communicating. You have talked about neglect and deprivation in childhood, but how did your body and mind develop then? How did you enter youth, and how did you feel? How did you acquire the mental and physical balance to achieve your surprisingly high goals?"

She knew that she could add these feelings to the book. But she told me that she knowingly left many of them unsaid. "Don't do that," Dharmendra added. "The more you are open, the more credible, respectable, and readable you will become. Every part of your life is slowly becoming public. You should satisfy all our curiosities. This book will not be written again and again. There should be nothing left behind from the experiences of your childhood, though you may add more as your life goes on."

We talked thus for a long time. I was afraid that she might be bored, so I presented her with a book and left. I regretted that I had not visited this struggling ray of light before, and yet I was glad to have met her finally. From today's journey, I learned how she communicates, how she lives, looks, speaks, and what she is like.

Gopal and Bishwas in Jhamak's Road

After two months, I was in UK. Sitting at a cantonment in Folkston, I told Bishwas all about my experiences in Dhankuta. "This will be Jhamak's masterpiece. But there is still a lot to be done. Please don't hurry to publish this book. This manuscript is like a novel or a long story, without any chapters or titles. It would be advisable to add titles like "My Childhood," "My Struggles with Letters," and "Near my Grandmother." It would be advisable to let the reader enter Jhamak's world slowly and then progress further psychologically. Besides, there are other gaps—places where the readers may have questions. At the end of the book, her personality as a writer seems to be overshadowed. Besides, if she wrote about the year 2063, she could also speak about an important period of history!"

Probably Bishwas had envisioned a smaller book. I presented the framework of a completely new book. "I have promised to publish a book of her anyhow," he told me.

"Do publish it," I told him, though there was no need. Bishwas alone has done as much for Nepali literature as an entire institution. It takes time to evaluate such contributions—and I had to convince him that the book needed work.

I returned from UK at the beginning of Dashain. My entire journey was literary. Jhamak's manuscript was still with me. I had read it another time and had corrected it with a red pen—asking questions and suggesting outlines.

Gopal Guragain came to Kathmandu at that time. He was a generous person, a political worker who cared for Dhankuta, Jhamak's talent, and literature above politics. Under his leadership, we organized a meeting at Sahityakala Pratisthan. Many dignitaries were also present at the meeting at the office of NELTA at Keertipur Kumari Club. Gopal put forth a proposal on that occasion—if Jhamak could be given the opportunity to come out of her limited geography and cultural and political surroundings, she would become a writer of national level. That day, we discussed bringing Jhamak to Kathmandu.

Two months later, we had another meeting organized by Gopal. I was made the coordinator of Jhamak Ghimire Sahityakala Pratishthan's Kathmandu branch. We made plans, and Gopal returned to Dhankuta with the news. On that occasion, I wrote a small letter:

> *Dear Sister,*
> *My fond remembrances. I am very pleased to read your autobiographical creation. This creation will raise you from Nepali literature and introduce you to world literature. This country will be proud to have you. But it would be great if you could make changes to this book according to the conversations I had with you, Bishwas, and Gopal. I have written to you some of the things I feel as a reader and a critic. The book will improve if you*

could do them. Do work on it without hurry. I praise
your creativity and capacity.

Brother Govinda

I sent this letter and manuscript back with Gopal. I was slightly scared. Many writers think of their writings as incontrovertible and ignore the suggestions from their readers and critics. But I had never faced that while I critiqued many manuscripts. Yashodhara, Antarmanko Yatra, Baigyanik Goretoma, Neelima Ra *Gadha Adhyaro*, Bich Batoma Byujhera . . . the list is long. I am with the writer, and Jhamak is rather proud. Or she may not want to work again. Will she say that that was her final version?

Gopal came again after three months. We held another meeting in Jhamak Ghimire Sahityakala Pratisthan. We discussed how to introduce Jhamak as a national talent and to broaden her horizons.

After many months came the improved manuscript of *Jeevan Kaandaa Ki Phool*. Jhamak's handwritten words were all over A4 pages, untyped. I had it typed without looking at it. But it was not complete, and the rest arrived after six months. That too I had typed.

An Autobiography in the Immortal Tradition

After nearly two years of patient effort, the manuscript of *Jeevan Kaandaa Ki Phool* was in the last stage. It had been improved, revised, and corrected. It is completely changed. It had increased almost double in volume. It is a composite whole of forty-seven readable essays of manageable length. It touches upon Jhamak's life from her birth in 2037 to the year 2065.

I spent the entire Dashain holidays with Jhamak. Balkrishna had handed over her typed manuscript to me. Dr. Kumar Koirala had studied it deeply. After he had enhanced it with his editing, it fell into my hands along with Kaushal's page setting. I was involved with *Jeevan Kaandaa Ki Phool* the entire Dashain. At the beginning of Tihar, Gopal arrived in Kathmandu again to arrange

Jhamak's stay in Kathmandu. This time Jhamak sent two more essays—"Patraharuma man pokhida" and "Nam sanga bidroha." We included these and began the final preparations.

This book does not need anything said about it, but at this point, I find it necessary to declare that this book is a masterpiece of Nepali literature. There are many proofs of this, but I would like to speak in brief rather than expand all of them. This book is a precious jewel of Nepali literature. Its literary worth will be established as an excellent piece of autobiographical work. This is actually a great decade for autobiographical works have burst into the literary scene. *Jindagika Tipot Haru* by Krishna Chandra Singh Pradhan, *Kaha Gaye ti Dinharu* by Amber Gurung, *Dasgajama Ubhiera* by Ganesh Rasik, *Aaroha Avaroha* by Dhacha Gotame, *Baigyanik Goretoma* by Dayananda Bajracharya, *Antarmanko Yatra* by Jagadish Ghimire, *Mahabhinishkraman* by Madanmani Dixit, *Fadke Tardatardai* by Dr. Tulasi Bhattarai, and so on, are a few of them. Nepali Sahitya has thus climbed new heights.

Each of these creations is a masterpiece. Other writers like Kamalmani Dixit, Rammani Risal also fall under this category. I don't remember any female writers except *Bulku* Sharma who has written an autobiographical piece.

Many writers have presented their autobiography like a novel. Dhruvachandra Gautam's *Badhi* and its sequel *Ghurmi* are autobiographical novels. Krishna Dharawasi's *Adha Bato* is another such creation. The writer's true character can be seen in autobiographical creations. I have raised this issue while talking about *Ghurmi*—there are many changes taking place in the structure and nature of traditional writing. Today, critics are eager to know where and in what measure the writer's life enters their creation. They are dedicated to finding out where the writer's personality is displayed. A renowned literary theorist Roland Barthes has spoken about this issue in Camera Lucida—"It is my political right to be a subject whom I must protect." This declaration encourages the use of subjectivity in creation. Another contemporary thinker Helen Cixous has spoken along similar lines in Root Prints—"Every story tells an autobiographical story of one instead of another." In other words, a character is required, whether real or imagined. In this way, there are many different opinions regarding the hidden or apparent presence of the writer in his creation and its subjectivity. Recently *Candace* Lang has said—"Actually, autobiography is everywhere, we just have to look for it." In this way, the writer can always be found in his creations, and every creation is autobiographical—it just depends on how the reader interprets it.

But Jhamak's creation is different from these kinds of autobiographies. It has literature inside it—but the literature talks about physiology. From the time she became conscious, Jhamak knew that she couldn't move many of her organs, but had a sharp mind. She couldn't move her hands, but had a vivid memory. She could not move her lips, but could hear everything, without any other movement. She has all the organs but they do not work. How terrifying must the moment be when she realized this! Before she realized these things, the opinions expressed about her by the society had already frustrated Jhamak, had engendered rebellion, and touched her with disgust, depression, envy, and angst. She has expressed all these emotions minutely and deeply. It is difficult for anyone other than Jhamak to experience them. Her environment is full of superstition, narrow-mindedness, poverty, and deprivation, a clear river muddied at its heart, a bubbling volcano. It's terrifying to imagine Jhamak's agitation, dilemma, and darkness in life as she tried to break through that wall without any language to express herself. She pierced that fog after seventeen to eighteen years; she tore down the cave and came out into the light, alone, with the help of only her determination, an inner light. She had been buried in dust, but now is in open air. We have never heard from any other creator the struggles of becoming a lettered human being form a dumb animal.

Letters led Jhamak to light, but what inner light led her to the letters in the first place? The world should know how she learned those letters. She speaks thus about the happiness of learning her first letter: "Now that I remember, I could not share that moment's happiness with anyone. I had written again and again on the dusty ground, and had learned to pronounce them in my mind. I broke twigs again and again to learn these letters. I scraped my soft flesh again and again on the ground. Not just that, but I collected the morning's dew in a bowl, dipped my fingers in it, and wrote on a stone, bleeding freely all the time!"

When I read the lines of the piece, I remember Annie Sullivan and Helen Keller. Hundreds of books have been written about her. Recently, the immortal movie Black was released in our neighboring country India. If we could introduce Jhamak in time, the world would descend on her feet while she is still alive.

Shattering Other Mountains

When an innocent girl entered this world, for no reason she was the most affected by the discriminations in this world. When she realized that the society had already foisted its own definitions on her innocence, she fought it and rebelled against it time and again. This creation is a cry of a rebel and reformer.

This book has raised a voice for the fair treatment of children born in unusual situations. In a society where humanism has not developed fully, thousands of children with biological defects are neglected. Children's rights are being discussed today. Humanists have turned their eyes toward disabled, retarded, blind and other such people. Inclusive education is being talked about. However, this is still within the upper echelons and privileged members of society. Children are still neglected and abused in traditional societies. The ones with biological defects are even more neglected. Essays like *Vibhedko Yuddhama Ma Euta Bojh* and *Samajko Drishtima Apangata* portray that abyss. The position of the girl child or young woman is even more precarious, which is what Jhamak has fought against. She has positioned herself against superstition and social ills. She is trying to explain and describe the reasons for her struggles. Being a woman, she has hit out against gender discrimination in a way that disturbs traditional thinking, and opens the door to a new egalitarian consciousness. Right from the days of *Parijat*, the attempt to improve upon social ills had already begun. The major part of contemporary women's writing revolves around it. Geeta Keshari's *Badlido Kshitij*, Prabha Kaini's *Anavrit* (unpublished), Deepa Rai's *Ardhavritta*, Sharmila Khadka Dahal's *Samayako Canvasma, Matra Hoina* and hundreds of other poems, stories, essays, and opinions are evidence to this fact. Many male writers are correcting their own faults in this respect. But Jhamak's battle is different from all of them—more intense and less compromising. There is a fire inside her—a bubbling volcano. She has lashed out at everyone, including her old grandmother, mother, and father and the social ideas supporting them. She has dug to the roots of the religion that has fostered inequality. I think Prabha Kaini's *Anavritta* will help Jhamak too. Morash's *Salijo* will also help this fight against male dominance. Deepa Rai's *Ardhavritta*, Sharada Subba's *Yashodhara,* and so on, will also help her.

The Final Journey toward Freedom

Jhamak has mentioned freedom many times—the freedom to decide for herself and to use her intelligence, the desire to live independently, the desire to live with dignity, and the desire to take her own decisions by breaking the ties to tradition, and the freedom to work for good in her own way. This consciousness has become irrepressible. There are other creations that describe the power of will.

A Self-Made Garden

At the end, Jhamak mentions the names that others have given her: flower of the cliffs, orchid and so forth. They are all very appropriate when you realize how a deprived girl has stumbled, and lost hope many times, but always regained it, fought against the desperate darkness, and emerged into the light. Her life is not just successful but exemplary. When her creation and her positive outlook on life are properly evaluated, then the world will turn toward Nepal. Jhamak's book will become the identity of

Nepal, because she has accomplished something impossible. She is an inspiration for thousands; millions will be inspired by her to continue their struggle with life. She will introduce life as a smile after tears. She will show that life is a positive journey—she will tell this to the world.

When we finish reading her story that she has reached this level without going to school, without learning from a tutor, but sheerly through the light of her own will, then our heads will bow down in shame. When we hear her spread enlightenment to the whole world, we feel that the lives of those who have working hands, legs, and voices are wasted. There can be no comparison to the indomitable courage and consciousness in this human being.

She has rejected the existence of God many times. God may not have a physical form, but I do not feel that all the minute details of creation, sound, colors, sky, and the stars could have come into being without a creator. But I do not want to argue with Jhamak. This world is created by each of our faiths, but it is not shapeless. Let us not discuss this vast topic today—Westerners warn thus: *Do not enter the topics of God, morality, and truth, for you will not exit.*

At the same time, Jhamak is tolerant of people of many religions—she is on the side of intellectual diversity and multiplicity. She has a deep love for culture; she is just aggressive about the ills within the culture.

The Stamp of Time

When Jhamak reached a maturity in her writing, and her capacity to analyze situations was increased, she started writing columns. Through these columns, she expressed her views in public. The time was tough—full of struggles and crises. Thought was always a target, but Jhamak said what she felt and saw. She displayed her courage and spoke without bias. When time handed out a trial by fire, many had pawned their intelligence away, but Jhamak was always in search of the light. She stood unbending in favor of change, novelty, freedom, and republic. She spoke against tyranny. This is her great achievement. Nearly a third of the essays are regarding this phase of her life. She has depicted the political background, ups and downs, murder, rape, loot, abduction, depravity, and the end of the struggle that took place between 2050 (2052) and 2063 BS. Her work is essential to understanding this phase of human history.

Powerful Creation

This is a powerful creation. This is the height of Jhamak's creation, and the height of her thought and philosophy. This is the analysis born out of all her experiences. This contains the typhoon to sweep away all ills. Occasionally, tears flow from the eyes unasked. The reader is hit strongly by her sorrow. He is unable to turn a page. Then he moves on. It is difficult to believe. But here is such honesty that could be nothing but the bare truth. These truths are the sorrows borne by our society. Jhamak becomes a humanitarian above and beyond a man or woman. Is no one hearing this voice? Today the country hears her and tomorrow the world will recognize and respect this indomitable warrior.

At Last

Jhamak is an extraordinary human being who has no equal. There might be hundreds of other born with such a defective biology; they too must have had the capacity to do something, but no one recognized that. Even today, there must be hundreds who bear such banes; they too might turn into Jhamaks.

I feel that society will turn its eyes toward the problems outlined by Jhamak after reading the book. It tells the reader justice can be done only if every human being is treated with the love, affection, and respect that they deserve. Only then can they live with dignity. These findings do not come from a research laboratory, but from knowledge gained from a hard life by a girl of amazing consciousness and courage. This is priceless. Every word touches the reader—sometimes he is shaken to his core, sometimes cries uncontrollably, sometimes is surprised, and sometimes curses himself for wasting his life. I would like to request all the Nepali community to have this book as a requirement for the curriculum in all levels: from the school levels to university level. There has been such a gift to the Nepali citizens in the history of Nepali literature. This tells us what kind of viewpoint we need to have toward children. We can never grow the feelings of humanity and equality unless and until we realize that every disabled child has a Jhamak within herself.

I humbly request the Nepali readers: let us give every student in Nepal the opportunity to read this book. Here is no meaning to education that does not engender the feelings of sympathy, love, and coexistence. These feelings are even more necessary in the *dry* professions like the military, police, politicians, and administrators. This book can fulfill that need. I request all the health professionals, social workers, researchers, students, and all other citizens—you must read *Jeevan Kaandaa Ki Phool*. I am sure that the life of Nepali students and politicians is incomplete without reading this book. That is why I repeat that this book should be compulsory in all schools.

I humbly request all readers—when you go somewhere and meet your friends and relatives, do take this book along and gift it to your near and dear ones. Let us publicize this book far and wide. Let us make people see what a gem is in Nepal, and what mountains of struggles she has overcome.

I humbly request all the Nepali people—let us work toward translating this book into English and other languages. Let the world wear on its head the flower of Jhamak's creation. Let its fragrance reach the entire world.

I humbly request all the researchers, readers, and prize givers dedicated to encouraging Nepali literature—let us recognize this amazing talent among us. Jhamak is a creator for whom all our prizes and recognitions are not enough.

In the end, I congratulate Jhamak on this wonderful achievement. I wish that everyone would praise Bishwas Tigela for his love of literature and his humanitarian heart. If Gopal dai had not dedicated himself to this project, it might have never seen the light of the day. I would like to give him special thanks before I stop here. Having said this, I feel like I have written a new chapter of my life.

An Amazing Talent in the World Literature
(Second Edition)

Jhamak's extreme physical disability is known by the name of cerebral palsy. Jhamak's name be included among eleven writers with this disease. Great personages like Stephen Hawking, Gerry Trailer, Christie Brown, and Chris Nolan belong to this category, and among them is an Asian writer Jhamak.

April 18, 2010 Professor of English
Tyanglaphat, Kirtipur Tribhuvan University
tu.govinda@gmail.com
Kathmandu, Nepal

The Rise of a New Age
in Nepali Literature

Gopal Guragain

Readers of all levels have expressed their desire to get to know the life story of Jhamak, and to understand and study the story of this talented woman at the height of popularity in contemporary Nepali literature. As a result, Jhamak decided that it was not fair to keep her life story a secret for long, and gave birth to this creation *Jeevan Kaandaa Ki Phool*, an epoch making autobiographical work. Jhamak has revealed the mysteries of her life in this memoir that could play a leading role in a new age of Nepali literature. Jhamak has felt her readers' wishes and feelings to understand her life, and thus created this book.

Naturally, no one can remember their infancy, and these memories are gained from one's mother, father, and the elders of the family. Jhamak has made her childhood and present the subject of her writing, and has described the social, cultural, and political situation of the relevant times. This book is not just an autobiography, but is also a mirror of contemporary society.

This book contains the miraculous story of a child who was cursed to death right from the time of birth and has seen the worst of life since then. This book will be an inspiration to thousands of such children in the future. How did a girl who had the cruel destiny of being handicapped from birth struggle with a thousand challenges? How did a girl deprived of speech, motion, and hands spend her days fighting the terrible blows of death? How did the wish to express her happiness, sorrows, laughter, and tears in words arise in Jhamak? How did she gain victory over words in a few days with a foot caked in dirt? How did a girl who had been deprived of books, pens, and notes and who had never seen a teacher or stepped on the floor of a school gain such miraculous success? In an age rife with activists, she never got to know a single one. Even the nation was indifferent to her protection and education. Yet before her childhood was over, words made friends with Jhamak, even in impossible circumstances. Now the same people who cursed Jhamak to death began to see a godly boon in her. How dramatic is the nature of mankind! Jhamak has described these mysteries of her struggle-filled childhood and strange characteristics of human nature as well.

Having faced struggles, neglect, discrimination, and harsh words in her childhood left a deep scar on Jhamak's psychology. Hence, in her adolescence, Jhamak chose literature through which she could express all her feelings. She began dedicating herself to literature, challenging those supposed to be able, beautiful, and superior. The feelings that were previously expressed only in tears and wails could now be expressed in words. The words gave her a leap in life. Right from the beginning of her literary career, Jhamak found enthusiasm, inspiration, and love from thousands of well-wishers. Then energy flowed in her body and mind, which was thought to be useless and freak of nature. A new life and speed flowed through her limbs. Her self-confidence to live grew every day.

Gaining inspiration and consciousness from her own childhood struggles, Jhamak began powerfully expressing her creativity and feelings about discrimination and perversion in society. She became more and more determined in her life, philosophy, thoughts, and values. Gradually, she began the forerunning among young writers. Society's interest in her grew, as powerful creations, thoughts, and expressions were produced from a handicapped adolescent. People of all levels and areas wanted to know, understand, and study her. The number of her helpers and well-wishers grew exponentially. Gradually, Jhamak became a personality of national interest. Her present creation discusses these events.

On the one hand, the followers of monarchy and some members of the elite class approached her to use her talent and creations in their own interests. They advised her to send a letter to request a royal meeting. They dangled the promise of great benefit to her if she acquiesced. But Jhamak was firm in her values right from her adolescence. Hence, these groups were disappointed. In her creations, we find a deep commitment toward freeing literature and culture from the bonds of feudalism.

From the beginning of her creation, Jhamak was determined to use her intelligence, talent, and creation to the benefit of the people, who are the unending source of creation, culture, and power. She decided to dedicate her entire life to the cause of justice, equality, peace, progress, and nationalism of the people. She was determined about the worldwide principles of human rights and freedom. She wrote while standing firmly in the frontlines of the people's revolution for culture and politics in the nation. Her personality and portfolio both grew rapidly as she faced one cultural and political challenge after another. She smiled as a flower even among thorns. The people's daughter lived on in her hut and in the people's hearts. Those who promised the dreams of palaces and luxuries were rebuffed by her. Thousands of pure hearts continued to inspire her. *Jeevan Kaandaa Ki Phool* is the exciting story of such values and belief. This creation has risen as a source of light for thousands of children, adolescents, and youths.

Kartik 15, 2066
Chairman
Dhankuta Jhamak Ghimire Sahityakala Pratisthan Nepal

The Conclusion that God Doesn't Exist, and If He Does, He Is Not As Fair and Kind As We Think Him To Be

by *Bishwas Deep Tigela*

Jhamak Ghimire is an extraordinary talent among thousands of people. She has easily won the test of fire that nature has foisted on her, and her excellent creations have challenged and shamed all of us who are supposed to be physically able.

To understand *Jeevan Kaandaa Ki Phool*, I think it would be easier if the reader could understand the writer's physical condition, and hence I would like to present a short discussion of the past.

Nearly a decade and a half ago, around 2050-51, a rumor spread around Dhankuta Bahumukhi campus that a child in Kachide who was handicapped from birth had learned to read. Many had rolled their eyes and bitten their tongues in surprise at that time. Kachide is approximately one and a half kilometers away from the campus. After that, I went abroad for economic reasons. I continued to get information about Jhamak despite being in a foreign land. When I went to Dhankuta for my first holidays, I bought a book by Jhamak and read it. In the book, I found no trace of her physical handicap and became confused, because those creations were interesting and powerful. Nothing was mentioned about her in the preface or the publisher's note.

The next time I arrived on a holiday, she was scheduled to be awarded the Dhankuta Pratibha Puraskar. There is a strange relationship of trust between two creators. I requested Ramesh Paudel, a senior writer who knew through words and voices, to visit Dhankuta with me. The two of us reached Dhankuta. For years, I had cherished the wish to meet Jhamak, and as soon as we heard of the program, we decided to meet her. In the Pratibha Puraskar program, we saw Jhamak sitting stooped up on a chair. We said *namaste* to her, but she did not return the greeting. That ended the meeting for that day.

The next day, we informed Gopal dai, president of Jhamak Ghimire Sahityakala Pratishthan, and went to her home. We went to Jhamak's room on the upper floor. Jhamak was lying on the bed. Upon our arrival, she got up with great difficulty. Still on bed, she grabbed a notebook nearby with her left foot and rested it on her right foot. She then turned to an empty page. With a lot of effort, she grabbed a pen with two toes of her left foot and wrote on the notebook: "Namaskar, you are welcome!" Then she turned the notebook toward us. I nodded and expressed my thanks. I was dumbfounded on how to proceed. Soon, her sister Mina arrived, and carried her on her back like a child. She changed Jhamak's clothes and brought her back. Jhamak's father, Gopal Dai, Rajesh Bhai, Ramesh dai and I talked about Jhamak. Sometimes, if something struck her, she would smile. She understood everything we said, but could not speak at all. We wanted to take Jhamak's picture, so her sister Mina carried her from the bed to the seat on the ground. After the photo shoot, Jhamak crawled on her own to the 1.5 feet high bed, though it took her a lot of time.

Near her feet on the bed were a lot of books. Her sister Mina showed us all of Jhamak's creations. Jhamak would raise her legs and ask Mina to take up a particular book, and Mina easily understood. Occasionally, Jhamak drooled and Mina wiped it.

I observed Jhamak's situation for a while and imagined myself in the situation. What if both my hands were broken, were flopping uselessly, both feet were dried up and wasted, mouth had been taped so that I could not speak, I am hungry and I want to pee, and I am lying on the ground with my grandmother's corpse in complete darkness? What would that situation be like? We think we are all equal in God's eyes and God treats us fairly, but after observing this situation, I claim that there is no God in this world. Even if he exists, he is not as fair and kind as we imagine him to be. Everything has a limit, but Jhamak's situation is beyond all limits. I express the deepest objection to nature. For a while, I could not speak at all.

We discussed Jhamak's upcoming creation. Jhamak signaled to Mina to give her collection of poetry and autobiography, and gave both to me. I turned the pages and skimmed through it. As soon as I entered Jhamak's room, I felt like I had entered a sacred spot of worship. Suddenly, I felt the desire to publish one of her creations, and asked Ramesh dai as to which creation I should choose. He suggested the autobiography, and I told Gopal dai that I would publish this book. He was surprised. I said the same to Jhamak too, and she replied that she had many other books to publish. She thanked me in writing.

As soon as I offered to publish the book, Gopal dai and Jhamak wanted to make the terms clear. I told them that the copyright would be with the writer herself. All proceeds from the book would go to the writer. I would cover all the expenses of typing, cover, and press. I will take back none of my investments. I guess they were surprised at this proposal. They heartily agreed after a while. I figured that the publication process would cost me as much as three pairs of bulls, but I decided to undertake it so as to provide a little bit of support and help to Jhamak's struggle-filled journey. But I must say that the publication phase turned out to be exciting and productive.

The publication phase took nearly two years, and the resulting volume was twice the size of what was originally planned. More pairs of bulls were added to the list. I had the previous experience of publishing Hariraj Tigela's drama *Apadasta Jindagi*, senior journalist Rajkumar Dikpal's story collection *Aatankako*

Chhayamuni, mar Tumyahang's *Sodhugen Imansingh Chotlung* (an epic in Limbu language), Sesami se Nalbo's *Sobuhangsa* (a khandakavya in Limbu language). This time I had decided to help Jhamak out of my own free will, and shouldered on in the effort.

I downloaded the nearly complete word file and printed it in London. I was in UK at that time. As I read, I cried many times, in many places. I began to wonder how we could make this even more impactful, and in the end decided to request senior writer and critic Dr. Govinda Raj Bhattarai to write a preface. I called Jhamak in Dhankuta to ask her permission, and her sister Mina picked up the phone. Since Jhamak could not talk on the phone, Mina had to do the talking for her. So I hung up and called her again. This time Mina replied that Jhamak had happily agreed. I then gave her Dr. Bhattarai's number and asked her to call him immediately. Bhattarai Sir was faced with not just the preface, but other responsibilities as well. Dr. Bhattarai, who has expended a lot of time, money, and energy into the development of Nepali literature while renouncing his personal interests, began having sleepless nights once he got Jhamak's phone calls. He put aside the dozens of manuscripts that he was supposed to write a preface for, and himself went to Dhankuta to meet Jhamak. Then I received his email—"Bhai, let's not hurry. The book may be late, but it must be good." I regard his energy and active involvement to be a boon for Jhamak. We must respect such helpful hearts and actions.

I am very optimistic that this book will reach the heights of success. If we all could be with Jhamak like Dr. Bhattarai, we will get to read a lot more excellent creations in the future.

The publication process was gathering speed, and many thoughts flitted across my mind then. I googled to find other talented people like Jhamak, and read, researched, and asked people. There were many talented people with disabilities, but none exactly like Jhamak. Hence, I realized that we should make effort to introduce our country, previously known as the land of Mt. Everest, of Gautama Buddha, of brave Gurkhas, and a progressive country, as also the land where Jhamak was born.

Christopher Nolan was one person whose situation and talent nearly matched Jhamak's. Irish writer Nolan typed with his head using a stick. Among his half a dozen books, *Under the Eye of the Clock* was popular and an award-winner. Similarly, Mary Cocks Wales, scientist Stephen Hawking, and writer Helen Keller are memorable people with disabilities. There are also many who were born whole but lost their limbs in accidents and have become famous later. Tika Bamjan, who lost both hands in an accident, is one such writer heading toward greater fame in Nepal. Many capable nations of the world like South Africa, Australia, and the Netherlands have been providing institutional and organizational support to talented people with disabilities. Nolan met his death at the age of forty-three when he choked on food, and the president of Ireland himself relayed this news to the world, because Nolan was under direct supervision of the state. Our nation should learn from such beneficial practices and take many Jhamaks under its wings.

Anyone who reads this book will decide to do something for the country, society, and people. We "able" people will be ashamed of fostering a culture of violence, destruction, rage, and jealousy instead of progress and development. We will be ashamed of being human beings. There will be a change in the way we view the physically disabled. A writer of such an emotional book full of positive message is the treasure of an entire world, and not just her country and village. Life and the world can gain a lot from such a writer. I thank the Jhamak Ghimire Sahityakala Pratishthan for giving me the space to express myself. I wish that Jhamak's writing prowess as well as her fame increase day by day. I express my best wishes for the future on behalf of www.nepaliliterature. com. Presenting this gift from Jhamak to the readers, I take my leave, promising to appear again in future occasions.

January 27, 2010 Founder
Seriya, Brunai Online Nepali Sahitya Munch
biswasdip@ymail.com

From the Writer's Pen

Jhamak Ghimire

These are things that I have never said to the media. Even if I have said, I have said only a part of it. Many people wanted to know and understand my life intimately, but I always made excuses and put it off. In other words, I did not want to waste the reader's time putting forth my personal life to them. I wanted to give people energy and enthusiasm from my pen, words, and creations, and not pain. Hence, I avoided writing about myself.

Meanwhile, readers, writers, and well-wishers increasingly told me, "We must get the chance to know, touch, understand, and feel your life." I used to smile and tell them that it would be open to them in my life's latter half. But they were not satisfied with the answer. In the background, they protested, saying, "The audience cannot wait so long!" I hid from it, not once or twice, but many times. But finally, I could find no place to hide and was forced to write about myself.

I took up my pen, but I wondered how the people would react to something that came out before its time. I felt that I was doing something that should be left to the autumnal days of life. I was afraid of inviting controversies. But anyways, I started this book in the middle of Magh 2062. The month of Magh is very cold, and it is very hard to work in that month. Writing is even harder work than anything else, so I just wrote a couple of pages and left it at that. If I had the heart, the cold wouldn't stop me, but I had no motivation at that point. Besides, my eyes were giving me trouble.

Those pages were stowed in the cupboard for a few months. I did not care to return to them and write more. I cannot say why I had no motivation to write at that point. Then, one day, I met a friend. He asked to see my handwriting; and to show him my handwriting, I gave him those pages of my diary that had been in the cupboard all these months. He began reading it word by word. After reading it, he told me that I must publish this book anyhow. I did not reply to him. At my silence, he repeated that I must publish it.

This voice came directly from his heart. And it was joined by the voices of others who loved me. Should I listen to them or not? Should I respect them or not? My heart was attracted to writing again. After a few pages, my life imploded into me, and I stopped suddenly. I reeled with the pain of a scarred life. I cried alone and lightened my heart. Then I wiped my tears and took up my pen again. I was trying to fulfill a responsibility handed out to me before time, and as a result, many times I stumbled in pain. I paused my pen and concluded that I couldn't explore myself anymore. But then, I heard the voices in the background: "That life . . ." I then consoled myself and moved ahead. In this way, the first draft was written in about a year.

In the meantime, I met the writer Modnath Prashrit at my own residence. In the course of conversation, he proposed to help me publish one book. I could have given him this book, but didn't, and instead gave him something else, because Jhamak Ghimire Sahityakala Pratishthan was considering publishing this book. Sometime later, Dhankuta Pratibha Kosh organized a program where I was invited.

At the program, I met Bishwas Tigela dai who carried a gun in one hand and a pen in the other. He writes about his art, culture, language, and love with the same pen. He is a powerful writer of Nepali literature. The next day, he came to me. There was also Ramesh Poudel, who not only writes well but also paints well. At that time, Bishwas Deep dai requested me specially to publish this book. Jhamak Ghimire Sahityakala Pratishthan accepted this request on my behalf.

Then the manuscript was handed over to him. After a few days of handing it over, Bishwas dai called me and asked, "Do you agree to asking Dr. Govinda Raj Bhattarai to write a preface for this book?" When I gave my assent, he asked me to call and convey it to Dr. Bhattarai immediately. Devibahadur Shrestha Bhai was with me then.

"Convey my assent to Dr. Bhattarai," I requested him, which he did.

I felt happy in a sense, because I felt that having a writer who had read for a long time write a preface for my book was something positive. Days went by and turned into weeks and then months. After some time, I got the chance to meet Dr. Bhattarai himself, and with him was the poet Dharmendra Bikram Nembang. At the meeting, Dr. Bhattarai advised me lovingly, saying, "Jhamak, you seem hidden, you must show yourself."

"I know," I told him. "But it's so difficult to write about personal . . ."

Dharmendra dai looked at me and laughed "Ha-ha, once you write, you reveal it to the world, and it's done! This book will not be written again and again, so you must complete it!"

Why shouldn't I give my time to make it better and more beautiful? I thought to myself. *Why not work a little bit harder?* I gave them a positive answer. In other words, where there was a hidden face before, I would have to render the entire body and its activities. I began to arrange timings for rewriting, and I also had other practical responsibilities. I tried to complete them all together. Meanwhile, I also had to find time to write my columns. I first had to live, and then only write. In this respect, I would like to thank Kantipur Publications because they helped a mother in labor produce her child. In other words, though I did not work hard over my columns then, Kantipur continued to publish them. But maybe they were good despite being written in haste.

Though I had requested for a year's time from my editors and publishers, I actually planned to finish it in six months. It would be unfair to say I was the only one who spent time and effort on this book. Dr. Govinda Bhattarai not only guided me lovingly until the book was complete, but also pointed out its inadequacies and helped improve it, so much so that many times I would stop while writing, the pain rendering me unable to continue, and I would think *So much pain—what good would it do to the world?*

If there were someone near me, I would tell them these things. But I did not tell many people—Devibahadur bhai was one of the few I did. Every time he scolded me lovingly, saying, "Why do you say such things? You must fulfill a writer's role, you cannot hide too much . . ."

His words rang true, and right then Dr. Bhattarai would call me, saying, "Jhamak, there's not enough polish, work on it!"

"I will try, but I am not sure if I can polish it to perfection," I would reply to him in the voice of a mediator.

He would smile in my ears and tell me, "May your attempts bear fruits." After this conversation, I would resume my writing. The creation does contain pain, but they are not unnecessary. They are intimately joined to my life and I have honestly put them forth for the reader. I have presented the naked truth of our society in which I am the lead character and my parents, my sister Mina, and others are secondary characters. Here, I have gone beyond my relationships and observed their nature, behavior, and personality from a writer's eyes. I request my readers to view them with the same eyes, because this book is not just about *my* life, but the life of *all* the people represented in it.

This book is not about depression and frustration. They are a part of it, but this book is also full of struggles, and the meaning of life that has hope and enthusiasm. If, after reading this book, you try to live a little bit more humanely, then this book will fulfill its purpose. If the people have equal rights over hills, forests, wind, sky, air, and light, then only can they be equal, because all these things have life and are important for life. If this book can break a little bit of the wall that divides one man from another, then this book will be meaningful, and human life and humanity can smile.

I always remember my mother and father who gave birth to me, raised me, and introduced me to the colors of life. There is also Mina, who is the junior heroine of this book, without whom this book would be incomplete. I will always remember her. When I reeled with pain at the time of writing, Devibahadur bhai gave me emotional motivation to go on, and with these words I salute him.

I would like to thank Dr. Kumar Koirala who edited this book but kept my original language intact. I would also like to heartily thank Balkrishna Bhattarai who typed it, and Kaushal Khaki who did the page setup.

I also remember Gopal Guragain, the chair of Jhamak Ghimire Sahityakala Pratishthan, and its other members with fondness. The rods of my journey are strong because of their efforts. Gopal Sir has always tried to make my journey easier and better, and has gone through a lot of troubles for my sake. With these words, I would like to thank him as well.

In the end, I will always be indebted toward the intellectual and critic Dr. Bhattarai, who read my book, not once or twice but many times, helped to compile it, and wrote a critical preface for it. If he hadn't spent so much time and effort on it, the book would not have been what it is now. I would also like to thank the publisher Bishwas Deep Tigela, who not only had a humanitarian bent of mind, but also proved that he loves Nepali art and literature with all his heart. Bishwas Dai, I thank you with all my heart. I would like to thank Ramesh Paudel daju for the beautiful cover picture, and Sundar Basnet of Times Creation who designed the cover. And now, I open my life to you that were closed until now.

Kartik 23, 2066
Dhankuta—3, Kachide

CONTENTS

My Life's Beginnings

$\mathcal{I}$ have now come to interpret life as the most beautiful flower of creation. But I'm not sure whether my own life also comes within the purview of this interpretation. As for me, I laughed while my mind was in tears, and every moment of my life tossed was with pain and suffering. Few people may believe now if I say that I have somehow survived under the weight of a heavy burden. Truth is extremely bitter, and reality is most tasteless. At times, when I turn those pages of life and look over, I myself cannot help shedding tears again and again. And it's but natural, because it appears that I was dropped out of my mother's womb along with many unlucky fate lines written all over (my forehead).

On the sixth day of my birth, my mother must have bathed me clean and laid me down with a new exercise book and a pen placed under my pillow. People believed that fate scribbles one's course of life on that night. At that time, you wished that lucky fate lines would be scribbled all over my forehead. But, Mom, that was a mere wishful thinking on your part, because fate never drew a good fate line or a strong luck line for me at all.

Time had only showered misfortunes on my lap—a girl cheated all the time by destiny; I had neither any sweetness in life nor any jest for it. Life is not what one expects it to be. I only survived because I was destined to live. I couldn't tell whether it was an animal's life or a human being's that I was pursuing. The only difference, perhaps, was that even as an animal, I was lucky to get cooked rice to eat—that's all! I lived a life void of sensitivity—a life that feels no pain, no colour, and there is no love for the world. I am sure, hardly would human beings experience such a life. Some poets may be interested to write poems about such a plight; some sensitive hearts may love such a story. At the time, I was so much laden with pain that it was almost beyond tolerance.

I was a person accursed by the gods, as I had been at the receiving end of consequences resulting from the sins committed during my previous birth—so they believed. I was born in a society that believed in infinite number of death and birth cycles. That's why I was regarded as a piercing thorn in the flesh of all around me. Those eyes were never filled with compassion toward me, and the hearts never melted out of love. On the other hand, they were quite abusive toward me and *angered* against me. Was it right and proper that such a thing should have happened to me—a tender, delicate, and innocent little girl? But I had no alternative except to suffer without a murmur of protest. In the innermost depths of my mind, a question used to emerge constantly, "Was I at all responsible for what had transpired to me, after all?" But the tragedy was that I had no medium, no voice, and no means of expression whatsoever, whereby I could have uttered my grievances. I was merely a living organism. How suffocating was my life! Nowhere was there any *outlet for my* pains and suffering. Had there been any, the river of life would have run vibrantly.

Nature be blessed! You gave birth to me merely to be at the receiving end of human cruelty—thereby to awaken me to the meaning of my being, my existence. When I was writing in pain, you stood before me as a mother and showed all motherly love to me. My mother also seems to have given birth to me merely to undergo sufferings. She bore me in her womb for a period of ten months. It was neither her fault nor mine. Only destiny was to be blamed. But can *crippleness* be defined as a mere state of bodily *infirmity* and *incapableness*? If that was so, how is it that the world did not treat people like Homer, Nikolai Astrovesky, and Helen Keller as incomplete? They were also bodily *incapacitated* as I am now. But they also created history, left their marks, and established the meaning of human being.

But what about me? I was born in a world widely different from theirs, in a different geographical location. That was why I had been constrained to live a life of inequity and lowliness that only animals may have deserved. As I started gathering my *sensibilities*, some iota of intellect and consciousness may have begun sprouting. But this developing consciousness is also akin to a curse, because I had no voice to articulate my thoughts; neither were my legs capable of taking a step or two nor were my hands capable of picking up even a flower—basketful of the *makhamalee, godabaree (Chrysanthemum),* and *orchids.* I was dumb, helpless, and a crippled girl who had all these capabilities snatched away from her. I was deprived of all these; I was denied everything. I was a helpless child deprived of all these, though my heart wished I could run along the slopes and walk around the lap of nature; but my feet failed me—they were powerless. How I wished I could talk to people around me, but was deprived of voice! All these desires will never be fulfilled now, and they just fell heavily like a burden in my life.

In fact, I had so much been cheated by destiny that I couldn't even raise myself from the bed. It was perhaps my grandmother, a grey-haired old lady almost like a moon disappearing beyond a mountain, who would lift me from the bed and take me in her laps. She might have wished me, the firstborn child of her son, to address her as 'Grandma!' in its *tote boli* (babbling), and caress her wrinkling skin on her cheeks. But, my dear grandma, I could not fulfill your sincere desires! Other grandchildren did this later. I only troubled you just by holding onto your back; I know how dearly you loved me!

What's more, our family's financial position at the time wasn't all that sound either, so much so that it was difficult even to make the two ends meet. It was said that our parents would often go hungry for days on end, trying at best only to somehow feed us children. Oh my grandma! That would not satisfy you, and you would feed me till I would be full, ignoring your own hunger. Moreover, you put me to sleep with you and feed me time and again throughout the night. Ah, I remember how tasty were the foods that you fed me, my grandma!

Oh my granny, hadn't it been for you, who used to place me in a bamboo-basket woven by the skilled hands of Khok and wrapped me with old rags to keep me warm. I don't know whether, by this time, I would have been wetting the bed or I would also have followed your footsteps. It was simply because of you that I became aware of different hues of life, understood life from a variety of angles and also learned to experience the beauty of life myself. You're *(not)* with us any more, Granny, and that has been your misfortune. But you are nevertheless very much alive, and kicking before my mind's eye.

Grandmother and
Gender Discrimination

My grandmother, who loved me so much, I have only one *fuss* over all the irreplaceable love you have showered on me. How could you forget my own sister? What was her fault to have been born as a girl child? But you blamed an innocent baby girl that had just come to the earth, that had just begun to spread the hues and colors of life here, saw her guilt, and you took it for true. That's probably why if she had been a son, you would have readily showered motherly love and affection for her. But unfortunately, since her birth had been of a female, you could never shower motherly love for her. She would have wanted the same kind of love which I got, but you were never kind for her. Why did you scare her away with sticks in order for her to get shunned from your eyesight? You had, in fact, wanted a son who would open the path of heaven for you. She was born with the gender of a female. That was the reason why you just could not stand her. Even if she had been a girl child, she was, after all, your own children's blood or was meant to be just their seed. You did not do the right thing, for you yourself had been born in the culture; so how could you escape from it?

It is not only you, most of the Nepalese women are born with the very same culture; they get brought up and eventually die. That might have been my mother's wish too; she must have nurtured desires for giving birth to a son who could maintain their lineage, who could have a main share of their property, or be its legal *interior*. She was the very same female who had been brought up in the same culture. The world has, after all, placed the females in the second category. Moreover, how can the backward women think of their own existence? My mother was the very same woman who had not had the time to think about her own rights. If the women from the developed countries were to know that the fetus was a female, they could have aborted it. There was no legal freedom for women for getting their fetus aborted in those days; the use of medicine was considered illegal too. It is said those who could afford to, get this done secretly outside Nepal. Most women consider this (aborting) as sin because tradition has taught them such a lesson. And every year, they conceive with the hope of giving birth to a lovely son; and if they fail to produce one, they add to the number of girl children every year. How ignorant are the Nepalese women, and how utterly vulnerable! But how could the Nepalese women belonging to an undeveloped country, and, on top of it, from a poverty-ridden society resort to such a practice! But those few who could afford it used to go outside the country and undergo an abortion. Moreover, Nepalese women below the poverty line are like exploited under the tradition that regards abortion as a sin and, with the dream of giving birth to a lovely male-child, become pregnant almost every year. In case a son is not born, they only go to multiply the number of female children. How utterly vulnerable are the Nepalese women!

My mother also had to suffer from a similar fate, because despite her intention not to give birth to a female child, two of us girl children had already been born. I don't know whether she considered her own womb or us faulty in this case. It was, however, neither her fault nor ours. The blame lies squarely on the shoulders of the man who could not fertilize appropriate semen as he would have liked it. A mother is simply the earth—she only conceives, that's all. But how is it that in our society people have understood the matter in a totally reverse manner? The culture that is based on such blind faith always lays the blame on the womankind. My poor mother had also been tightly entangled by the chains of a similar tradition that she couldn't snap the chain.

Instead of snapping it out, she began to make it even stronger; it looks like she had an innate desire to give birth to a male-child.

How can one survive without giving birth to a healthy boy baby, a support to one's old age? Who would, otherwise, perform the last rites when they would pass away? As such, she must have been gripped with a feeling that, somehow or the other, giving birth to a son was a must. As if in answer to her prayers, the third time she was pregnant, a son, indeed, was born to her. My sister and I became his elder sisters, and my parents begot a son. They no more had to be blamed as a 'sonless' parents. That in a way also helped open my grandma's pathways to heaven—no longer would she be impelled to hover around, directionless, in the mid-air after her death. The messengers of Death God will not obstruct her path, because she now got a grandson who would remove every obstacle to heaven. Expectedly as it were, although on other occasions she never saw eye to eye with her daughter-in-law, that day she had taken it upon herself to prepare meat curry and rice in order to feed the latter. She was beyond herself with joy.

Thanks to the life of a woman, it will be considered meaningful only when she gives birth to an heir (son), otherwise it is meaningless. A woman will be regarded auspicious, ominous, and great only when she produces an heir who will give continuity to her (husband's) lineage. It goes without saying that my mother was also very much pleased with herself—she had apparently been self-contented too. Even otherwise, Hindu tradition regards a male child as a hidden treasure; which Hindu woman wouldn't be happy and contented when she *could lay hands* on such a treasure?

The birth of our younger brother had truly given rise to an expected pleasure in our minds and lent an exceptionally joyful brilliance to our household. How delighted was our granny, with her silvery hair, to fondle the grandson in her laps! I could not have measured the depth and her happiness though I used to sit close by her. But then I was aware of the situation by now. On my part, I was burning inside myself with jealousy to see Granny carry our brother around. As it is, it is perhaps natural for a child to be jealous on such occasions. I was the eldest sister of two. How could I remain unaffected by a similar feeling of jealousy, because following my younger brother's birth, my grandmother had ceased loving me as much as she used to? Her behavior was verily an indirect outcome of the filth that had deposited itself in the feudal culture and the culture inherent amongst the Nepalese people.

But despite all these, she somehow had a greater soft corner toward me than my younger sister. Wherever she went, she used to carry me aloft on her back. "I'm afraid this kid would also die when I'm no more," she used to tell persons close to her, adding, "She will get nothing to eat after I'm gone." But Grandma, I have somehow been surviving even in your absence—in the company of my parents and siblings. I must keep on surviving even if all of them are gone; they must likewise survive even if I'm gone. This is the philosophy of life.

Drilling After a Demise

It appears as if my grandma had been preserved by death only to allow her the privilege of witnessing a grandson. But she couldn't fondle him on her lap for long. She couldn't even wait to hear *the newly born* baby's babbles. Our younger brother was hardly a year old when she passed away, or, in her own words, left for the heavenly abode. Whether the God of death quietly had the passage to heaven for her or not, I am not aware of; nor whether she could conveniently climb up the stairs leading to heaven.

That night is still fresh in my memory. What a frightful and dark night it was! There was no other human being in that small house of ours except Grandma and myself. Even my mother had gone to our maternal uncle's house along with my younger sibling. Nor had father returned even that late from the town toward which he had headed at daytime itself. Probably he had entered some tavern and started drinking country liquor. Not even the moonlight had fallen on the earth that night, otherwise at least an illuminating moonbeam would have penetrated through the side or back door and smiled. On the other hand, darkness had been so pervading that night as to not make anything visible except the palpable darkness.

Till then, I had not even learned to eat myself—others had to feed me. That night, against the light thrown by the wood burning in the hearth, Grandma had fed me some cooked rice with meat broth and tomato pickle. I don't know from where the meat had been brought in the daytime—I found it fairly tasty that evening. Of course, there was no question of rice with meat not being tasty. But somehow, she herself didn't partake of that meal—I know not why. Possibly she wanted to wait for her son to arrive so that they could dine together. The food had somewhat been covered and placed by the hearth itself.

The fire was still burning in the hearth. On looking outside the door, one could see nothing but lump of jet-black darkness. *Rising within that lump was a black sky with some dim gleam of flickering stars,* which again had been lost behind that all pervading blackness. The vague outlines of Grandma's face could be discerned in the glimmering light of the fireplace. How had her eyes been seemingly burning against that flickering fire? I had not noticed her eyes gleaming thus on other occasions. I had not even noticed that just next to us was a starkly dark human figure squatting. Scared stiff, I moved even closer to Grandma—almost attached myself to her body. Noticing that I was so scared, Grandma was murmuring, "What is this girl so much scared of?" The fire also completely died out. Once the fire died down, the human figure was also no more visible, thus making my mind more at ease. It turned out that the figure was mere reflection, a shadow of a man and the black lump of the smoke. Some kind of quietude prevailed in that infinite *desolate*. There was nothing but the fire gleam in the name of light—and that too had, by now, died down leaving mere black coals.

As I said, man-like figures could vaguely be discerned in the light of the burning coal. Of the two figures, one suddenly slumped on the ground. In other words, Grandma suddenly fell down asleep. I wondered why Grandma had lied down on the chill earth—could be because she felt excess heat of fire. The glow of the coal fire was waning. The stars in the sky looked twinkling. I kept on squatting near the hearth itself—filled with a childish impatience that the moment Grandma got up, I would go to bed with her. But there was not the slightest trace of Grandma ever waking up! Some buzzing sound was heard outside. The dogs seemed to be chewing something. Besides, there was some ruffling noise that made me wonder if father had arrived. I would be elated at one moment—only to be disconcerted at the next when no one entered the house. Now I started suspecting whether Grandma had, in fact, gone to sleep there itself. I dragged myself closer to her and tried to pull her up with my two legs—only to realize that I was not capable of bolstering even her single arm, not to mention of raising her entire body. So heavy was her body, in fact, that I could not even move it slightly—and how could I, a mere child just nearing five years of age? No, I couldn't. Desperate, I started weeping right there—but neither my wailings helped wake her up, nor did they reach anybody else's ears. In the stillness of the dark night, my wailings were merely a cry in the wilderness!

Now I had started to grow goose bumps within myself. The door was also ajar, and what I could see outside was mere darkness and nothing else. Now I got more and more scared of even staring outside the room. Terrorized, I attached myself as closely as possible to Grandma's body and slept even as I had kept crying. Something like a strong wind was still howling outside. After a while, however, the bare earth emitted so much cold that there was no way I could bear it. Father had not arrived yet—God knows in what recreation he had lost himself. It seems man loses all sensitivity toward his family sometimes. My father too had lost all his sensitivity in that recreation. Otherwise, a man who had left home at daytime with only a setting sun like old mother and a small kid like me at home would have returned by the evening; but he did not. Possibly he had lost himself in the sips of the liquor somewhere.

As it is, a tender child that I was, I was getting restless with sleep. There was no trace of Grandma ever waking up either. Nor could I, in the dead darkness, even make out where our bedstead lay. What a great calamity in life! In fact, never in my life have I faced such alarming plight. I had no alternative other than to somehow drag myself about and to grope for bed in that pitch darkness. Thank God, as I started groping around, I somehow reached the cot and clambered myself atop it with great difficulty. But the beddings had been folded up in a heap. In the old-time ground-floor houses, the bedsteads and fireplaces, eating and sleeping, would be located together; our house was no exception.

That was why, possibly, the bedding had been folded up so as to save them from the smoke rising from the fireplace on the ground. It thus called for another uphill task for me to get the beddings unfolded. Ultimately, I somehow unfolded them and laid myself down. Grandma had still been lying on the ground. I thought she had gone to sleep there itself. But it turned out that she had already breathed her last. She is still said to have some undertones of life as father ultimately returned. Alas! Had I even the least indication to that, I would perhaps have poured out some water into her mouth even by toppling the water jar lying nearby. But unfortunately, it never occurred to me that my grandma had passed away right in front of my eyes. It was, nevertheless, possible that I might have been terror-stricken had I realized that she was no more. I could even possibly have passed out myself. Thank God, time probably was on my side; besides, my own innocence might also have played some role in my favor. That's why I could sleep soundly nearby. That was a quiet night and its stillness might also have helped my tender bodily frame go into a deep slumber. I loved that sleep and my innocence.

Even a small noise or sound is enough to create uproar in a silent night. In fact, the commotion created by the abruptly gathered crowd of people had also suddenly disturbed my sleep. Agitatedly, I started arguing within myself as to why so many people were shouting, and from where had those people, along with my father, who were nowhere there earlier, appeared. Having thus awakened from my sleep, I raised my head and looked at the ground where Grandma had been lying earlier, but in the faint light of a small oil lamp, I couldn't see her. She must have got up and walked away from there, I thought . . .

I did not understand what people were talking about. Some spoke—despite being so many members in the family, the old woman had none to give her some water on her death bed; others said—how urgently did death grab her; she could not even speak her wishes before she died; still others said she breathed her last after she fed this girl and put her to sleep. But I did not make out of they spoke. Now I think, it was good, I did not understand anything that hoary night. Had I understood, I could never have enjoyed such a sound sleep. I was free and innocent so I could enjoy such a sound sleep time and again.

By the time darkness was overtaken by light and the day dawned, I observed that Grandma was lying peacefully on the ground by the side of a mound with a holy *tulsi* (basil plant). She was deep in her sleep; a great silence prevailed there. How could she enjoy such a long sleep? My father was sitting in a corner of the courtyard, as if lost in thought. So many people gathered at night; *where are they now?* I wanted to drag myself closer to Grandma, but people said I must not touch her and did not allow me to go near her. I observed their activities. Some of them cut down bamboo trunks, placed Grandma's body on a pair of them, wrapped a white shroud over her prostrate self, and tied the body with bamboo straps. I thought it must have been very painful for her to bear. I was angry at those people. How cruel they are! At last, flowers were collected from somewhere around, and garlands were woven and placed over the body, with red vermilion powder sprinkled over it. It appeared somewhat odd because till that time, she had never even put a red-colored paste on her forehead. What was the sense in covering her body with red *abir* powder now that she was dead? *This is the kind of paradox in the life of Nepalese women*—once they are widowed, they are forbidden to wear anything red—be they bangles, *potay* beads, necklaces, garments, shoes, powder or whatever. They are denied participation in any kind of celebration either. But once dead, they are free to wear red—what a mockery of a tradition! Likewise, they put everything on my grandma's body. Then my father lifted one side of the bamboo to which the corpse lay tied, others joined on three sides, then the conch shell was blown . . .

That spread mournful notes all around. My father's sisters shed copious tears as they wept and the scenario made me weep as well. I feel, however, that I had wept more because I had been deprived of Grandma's company and was unable to accompany her. For it was the first time I had to part with her. On that very day, she had been adorned like a bride and had gone leaving me behind all alone.

My uproarious wailings may have melted some people's hearts, for they tried to console me by saying things such as, "Why are you weeping, dear child? Your grandma has only been moved to a hospital and she will return as soon as she gets well." It is not difficult to console a child; I was comforted too. Then I kept waiting for the time when my grandma would recover and come back to call me. But by evening, all the people who had gone with her returned along with our father who had his head shaved off and had wrapped himself in a thin white sheet. But Grandma had not returned. I felt like asking Father about Grandma's whereabouts. But who was there to understand my voiceless hints? Yes, there was no way, no language, with which I could communicate with other people. What little I could do was to raise my feet if I wanted to eat something and shake them if didn't want. Many days and nights passed away—so did many weeks and months, but my grandma did not return—she had gone the way of no return. My life experienced such tragic events in a tender age before I could understand its meaning. In fact, I was the only person with her; she had breathed her last in my presence.

Hindu culture has its own peculiar traditions of observing mortuary rituals. Accordingly, my father stayed physically away from all of us in an isolation as a *kriyaputri*; my mother followed suit. For twelve long days, they confined to a particular place; they were not supposed to touch any one of us. Even in order to partake of their food, they would remove themselves away to some nearby pond or natural spring every day. All my paternal aunts were also supposed to follow similar rites; so they also isolated themselves from us in order to observe the *jutho* ritual. And, on my part, till then I hadn't learned how to eat—either my grandma or my mother would feed me, and in their absence, Father would do so. Now both of them were secluded and abstained from everything. No one else knew how to feed me except my mother's younger sister. She would feed me when she was around. But it wasn't possible to hold her for such a long period of twelve days because she had her own affairs to attend to.

Both of my hands were non-functional and could not even catch hold of anything. Even if I did so, they would tremble and things would fall. It was also impossible for me to pick up grains of cooked rice off a plate and put them into my mouth. Feeding me, therefore, came up as a challenge for all concerned, although they would try their best. The very taste of rice would be different. Now I began to let my plate of food fall in the floor and began to quarrel with those who fed me. Those who believed in controlling me through beating were in the *kora* ritual. When I showed my discontent to eat by quarrelling, they guessed I was interested to eat on my own. So that came as a blessing in disguise, as it were. For people started letting me do what I pleased with the grains of cooked rice. In the process, I gradually learned to pick up the rice grains, one at a time, with the squat little toes of my feet. That wasn't much of a problem because I had long been habituated to pick up small pebbles off the ground and play with them. What was immensely more difficult was to lift those grains up to my mouth with the help of my toes. When I lifted those grains from the plate, hardly a few were left to drop in my mouth; all the rest fell on the floor. Despite this, I felt happier to play with the rice grains. They left me all alone and allowed me to eat on my own, since the day that I dropped the plate they were feeding and all the rice grains got scattered on the floor. Since then, in whatever quantity I ate, I ate to my taste.

In the beginning, I started eating with a single foot, but since I could lift only a few grains of rice at a time, they wouldn't make a mouthful, thus dissatisfying me. As such, I started learning to make use of both my feet for the purpose. Initially, it appeared to be a futile exercise, but I did not cease putting my heart and soul into the efforts and, ultimately, my hard work did pay off—no matter what an uphill task it had been. I used to dip both my feet into the rice-filled plate, would pick up some grains with the help of the toes of one foot, place them on the upturned sole of the other, bent my head so low as to touch the rice grains with the mouth, and gladly gulped them!

No more was the help of others called for, as I could now feed myself. The one beneficial fallout in my grandma's sad demise was that it ultimately freed me from the compulsory dependence on others just in order to eat. My parents also, as they emerged from their seclusion, must have been pleased to know that their perennial burden of feeding me had now been a thing of the past. This was a successful exercise—a drill, born out of a sorrowful separation. Life traverses that way, along the winding lines and curves; old ones get wiped out, new ones are drawn.

Life within a Void

J endeavored to move my hands around, but failed. My fingers were seemingly devoid of a capacity to stir even a little. My lips were eager to speak, but not a word or sentence came out of them. My legs did not have the capacity to support my body weight either. As it gradually dawned on me that the limbs of my body frame were dysfunctional, I felt extremely helpless and wretched. I had also nurtured, like all children in general, desires to walk around and reach places near and far. But my legs did not support me, thus compelling me to drag and haul myself around. Even when I dragged myself even a few cubits away to some distance, I would feel elated as if I had reached a new place, a new land, and experienced a new perception. It would be a novelty for me to be able to drag myself to some distance and to pluck, and snap a few weeds and leaves for my collection. I had not seen the world beyond. I would consider our house to be much larger and nicer than those of others, simply because I hadn't seen the houses of anyone else!

There was a small hut nearby our house which served as a cow and goatshed. As I saw cows and goats bleating or grunting there, I had a feeling that my life was not much different from theirs. They could neither express a feeling of hunger nor of thirst. They would keep bleating or mowing continuously. Occasionally, when some person gets irritated and beats or belabors them, they cannot even utter a cry of pain nor can they request their tormentor not to torture them. What a despicable life! And how much different was my own life in comparison to them!

I would experience hunger, but had no voice to utter that I was hungry. I would feel thirsty, but had no medium to express it. Life was somehow dragging on even in the midst of such a dumbness and silence. I endured even if it was bitter and harsh. They say all stones are not mere stones—they are *shaligrams* too. So these childhood memories are precious *shaligrams* for me. These keep moving in my mind as if these are unforgettable moments in my life.

At times, I would observe the cows and goats shed copious tears, and would feel that they were weeping for me; and then I would also squat next to them and cry bitterly. Sometimes they would beat me if they happened to see this. If the cows and goats uttered a painful cry, I would feel that they were shouting to be freed, and if I found a sickle nearby I used to cut off their leashes and ropes to which they were tied. My mind would greatly rejoice at such times as they would then move about freely and unhindered. I would feel that I achieved something great. My mother has thrashed me severely many a time as she saw those animals devour the standing crops belonging to somebody else in the neighbourhood. And why would not she beat me when she saw that I had snapped the cords that had tied the animals and set them free!

I remember I was mischievous in my childhood. Sometimes I would fill in the dishes and pots (cleaned) with soil outside and would fill in with weeds and leaves; then my mother would beat me. She slapped my tender cheeks how many times I don't know. Ultimately, I was a child and I could not behave differently. I could not be free from childlike behavior, mischief, and restlessness. Sometimes I would forget after my mother's beatings and would resume doing such things. I thus also savored the taste of life within that dumbness and silence. I cannot tell whether that taste was sweet or bitter; but all said and done, even a life within such dumbness and quiet hard, I felt a peculiar flavor of its own!

A Thin String to
Hang on to

The process of various colors spilling over the pages of life continues without interruption. Yet none, but the colors of agony and tears have so far spilled me. Whether or not any other color will also spill over it is a matter that lies in the wombs of time.

I was just about seven years of age at the time. It appears that the country was going through political upheaval in those days. How could the young and tender brains of an innocent and helpless girl possibly grasp such a development? My brains also could not understand it at all. But whenever a radio was close at hand, I used to hear such sensational news as "There was a public demonstration at such and such place." Or "Police resorted to firing/baton charge at miscreants trying to vandalize the king's statue" and the like. I used to hear such sensational news. Persons of my father's ilk would bite their tongues in surprise, and comment, "What are these people up to?" Those were presumably the times when the popular movement of the year 2046 (the early 1990s) had been raging. And I used to be terrified and trembled within myself. I used to imagine that the demonstrators were possibly a formidable, menacing lot.

On those days, I was an innocent child; how scared I was, how much I dreaded sitting all alone.

Those were the days when our father used to narrate many a tale about demons and giants, thereby filling my mind with a kind of dread. *In those stories, there were different ghosts and demons that used to be more or less alike in nature, with long teeth and tusks, endowed with huge and powerful body frames and so on.* I used to equate the political demonstrators also with such characters. I would be inwardly pleased to hear they had been shot dead. Those days, my younger sister had started attending her school, father would leave for his office, and mother would go out to fetch fuelwood *(firewood)* and fodder, taking along with our younger brother who was too young to be left at home. That would leave me—the only jobless person—alone at home like a kind of a caretaker. At such times, the tales of ghosts and demons narrated to us by the parents would keep on terrifying me.

If the blowing wind budged the doors a little, I thought ghosts had done it; and the falling of tree leaves would also greatly shudder me. At such times, I used to miss the company of my grandma, as I used to feel terribly lonely. Many years had passed since she left. How I had shed tears in her death, but she never returned. Fate had destined that I keep a watch over the house the whole day.

Despite this, life was not so extremely bitter for me anymore. Ultimately, one has to face the orders of one's destiny. I felt I too could go to school with my sister—how enjoyable would have been the school environment! Ah, I could just reach it. But on my part was a heavy burden; such a life *has had nothing* except *quagmire* of grieves and pain.

In those days, I was an innocent girl. How scared I was to be left all alone the whole day! I would keep on weeping with fear and would convulse with the pangs of hunger and thirst. When I could not bear hunger any longer, I would pull down the pots of leftover and stale rice with my feet, and would eat if I could or else would spill the contents all over the floor; the same thing happened with water. On my mother's return after collecting fuel and fodder, she would see all the cooked rice and water spilled around the floor; she would then thrash me thoroughly with a stick, blaming me all the time for having eaten all the food without leaving anything, even for the younger sister and brother. How much would be the quantity of the leftover? I could easily finish, but she would demand the share of my sister and brother, and would thrash me. My body would swell with welts all over. Suffocated with grief and pain, I could not even cry aloud. What a fate I had! Nor was my father any different. He too is the husband of such a wife. I would be beaten even for the fault of spilling a little water. They wanted me not to cross the limits of behavior drawn by them. But a child as I was, how could I shrink myself within those limits?

Those days, I feel, the sprouts of consciousness about the realities of my existence had started germinating in my mind. I realize that the pleasures of infancy that all the other children enjoyed in life were denied to me forever, as my legs didn't have the strength and capacity, which was left in them, to jump or run around. Apparently, my feet were at least capable of slightly moving the fingers about, but my hands didn't have even that much capacity. Nothing was left when I knew. What was more, I had seemingly lost the power of speech too. I could at least crawl myself forcibly and move up to a few 'hands' (*cubits*) distance away, but even that was not liked or appreciated by any of my parents or elders. That's why I had been derisively dubbed a *Saanpey*—a slithering snake! Maybe because I did much mischief though I crippled. As mentioned earlier, my parents would always despise me for being the only useless member in the family. One can give me any name they liked. As they addressed me *Saanpey*, I thought my name must be *Sapey*. Even my younger siblings had picked up the same attitude; when pleased, they would address me as *Thulee*, the eldest one, and at other times, *Saanpey*. Sometimes, when my parents were happy, they would lovingly utter endearing terms like *Baba, Nanee* to address me; I would be very happy at such moments and felt that life was quite pleasant—I thought there were some that loved me too. In fact, everyone does love their young ones. Undoubtedly, my parents too loved me, but I could never experience that, even slightly. As word spread that I was being addressed as *Saanpey* by my own family members, other villagers had also started doing likewise. In our society, people's attitude toward feeble persons is quite different. I was also born in such a society; so how could I expect people of the same society behaving in a different way? On the one hand, superstitious tradition has been deeply entrenched into the society and *more over it being morbid with* ignorance, lack of education, and poverty, how could I expect a different behavior? No, I never got love and respect. The villagers too would address me *Thulee* at the presence of my parents; otherwise, they would call me *Saanpey*. This is the result of the mind-set: you can address a handicapped person as you like.

It appears that I had been a child with a sensitive psychology right from my infancy. I would be deeply hurt at the slightest rebuff. At times, when nobody was around, I would weep to my mind's content, thereby possibly washing all my grief with tears. I thought all my sufferings would be washed away with teardrops. I would feel ill at ease on seeing my younger sister alone going to school; when I saw my father teaching my younger sister with love and affection, I would feel as to how nice it would have been if I were to be taught in the same way. I would also yearn for learning by sitting near him, but that yearning was never fulfilled, because my father, if he saw me getting closer to him at such times, would scold me by shouting, "What's the use of your learning and reading?" How cruel and heartless was that old man? (*chap*)

But whether or not I went and sat beside him, or howsoever harshly he used to scold me, the urge for reading and learning was so deeply ingrained in me that, even as I sat at a distance, I would always be casting a cock-eyed glance at the way he would teach; I would try to copy him by scribbling anything or whatever on the bare floor, without him even noticing. I thus started learning whatever I could with my own efforts and in my own pace. For me, the open and wide earth became an exercise book—the small pebbles, soil, and the little fingers of my feet took shape of pencils, erasers and so on. Even to this day, when I reach closer to the pebbles and the dust, those events and incidents of the bygone days start swirling around my mind's eye without end. I feel like playing with mud and pebbles to my heart's content till this day. But that pleasant and memorable childhood has moved quite far away from me.

Yes, till this day, I have been roaming around the same environs of my childhood, which had been spent in a challenging manner. I feel that willy-nilly and without realizing, I seem to have started smearing my life's pages with newer colors, but the letters are the same that I used to scrawl and inscribe with the help of my feet's tiny fingers on the dust of a bare and open earth. Perhaps, for me, life itself became a canvas, on which the colors of tears were spilled; colors of pains also got spilled. Mine was also a childhood filled with supple and tender desires, dreams and aspiration natural to any child; but how was it that those childlike desires and dreams could not be fulfilled as easily as those of other children in general? Is it that I did not have a soul? If I had, why was that soul so much been slighted and insulted?

When I saw the dewdrops falling from the eaves in the morn, I felt quite happy. My grandma used to beat me many times whenever I wanted to play with it. Now I was no longer worried, and did not care about this; I wanted to play freely. There was none to control me. And I began to play with it and drink it, and don't know what I did with the dewdrops collected on the pot. Nature has a wonderful course of creation—the dewdrops fall at night and are seen in the morning, and it evaporates instantly.

My younger sister used to pronounce vowel alphabets with Father, but I had no voice to utter those letters, although I had powers of hearing. As a result, I would silently and inwardly try to pronounce what I had heard and repeat them twice, thrice, or more. He used to hold my younger sister's hand and teach her how to write those letters, that is क (ka), ख (kha), ग (ga) and so on. On my part, I would collect the dewdrops falling from the eaves of the roof in a crucible, crawl up to a little distance, dip my feet's fingers in that crucible, and with the dew, attempt to scribble some letters at random on a nearby rock stone. When there was no dew collected, I used to break little bamboo twigs, make a 'pencil' out of that and try to scrawl letters, using the flat earth as my 'exercise book.' As I would scrawl with dew-dipped foot-finger on a rock, the force of scrubbing would peel off my soft skin many times without number. But nothing ever deterred me from learning to my tiny fingers as a result of the harsh rubbings. Whether my toes bled, or I mastered writing or not was immaterial to me.

The other exercise—that of learning to write with a bamboo twig on the solid earth—was no fun either! In the first instance, even the effort to catch hold of the twig in-between fingers strongly enough was an ordeal in itself, as the fingers of the feet were not, unlike those of the palm, as long. If grabbing the twig was difficult, writing on the earth with it was even more so. After all, that was also perhaps a trial, a test of my perseverance and doggedness undertaken by destiny. Whatever it was and howsoever difficult, I never gave up scribbling on the earth with a bamboo twig. They had a superstitious belief that scribbling the surface with a twig (or charcoal) leads one to incur debt. My mother would scold me seeing me do this. My father too would show his anger to see me dirtying the mud floor. So I used to do this whenever they could not see it. Sometimes, I even tried to write in an empty space of my mind.

I still recall how much my feet-fingers had trembled and how much they had shaken for lack of balance as I sought to scrawl. It had taken a long time to master the practice of holding twigs with the fingers of the feet like one does to a pencil with hands. Besides, it had taken a much longer time for me to be able to catch hold of the twigs properly with the tiny fingers of the feet than it would have been with the fingers of the hand. Many letters would look twisted, bent, or of unnatural shape as a result of the body's or fingers' tremors and shaking. Even so, in order to successfully write down a letter of the alphabet, I broke many twigs, covered a wide area of the earth with my scrawling, emptied many a bowl filled with dewdrops, caused the soft skin of my young fingers to peel off several times, and also spilled my blood freely. Sometimes I used to sit close to my sister, when father was away, and I used to give a glance at what she had written and would listen to their pronunciations. I would play in my mind the shapes she produced, the movement of her hand, and the pronunciation of the letters or words from her lips. I used to observe every step for every word. Then I contemplated. I kept listening her speak as I had no voice. I had hearing power as of a normal child, and could understand too, but nobody knew about this mystery—not even my father.

He would just scold me, saying, "Why do you disturb your younger sister? She is reading and writing. You get out!" Then I used to stay away, but I never sat idle; I tried to learn something.

But when I wrote alphabets in dewdrops on stones, they would dry out instantly; no trace was left there. And I would weep to witness the loss of my efforts. I was time and again hurt by such experience. I would again collect dewdrops the following day and repeat the action—many times.

They call dewdrops the teardrops of the moon. I happened to smear new colors in my life, happened to draw an outline of new life by writing letters of alphabet with those teardrops.

Every spring season, in association with the earth, lends a new color to life. In me, no color of enthusiasm and ardor had been spilled until then, nor had wings of ecstasy sprung up. But the name of struggle had seemingly been an indelible part of my life's destiny. In fact, the theory of conflict and struggle is applicable to everything; as such, it goes without saying that it was equally applicable in my life as well. The conflict of the conscious with the unconscious, the struggle of colors in the blank canvas appears to be truly strange and peculiar. It is from the battlefield of similar dialectics that the journey of my life is moving ahead—a journey that had in it every element of tears, pains, challenges, and struggle. In a way, all the life's colors were there—except those of laughter and delight. What I lacked was precisely the color of delight and pleasure. The faint traces of smile that occasionally emerged in (*on*) my lips would also be driven away by Father's admonition not to—I knew not where they would disappear, because our society doesn't appreciate the laughter of womankind; on top of it, I was a useless dumb daughter. How, then, would my father approve my smile?

If I failed to obey him, I may *be rebuked* with words like "You fallen girl, a *saanpey!*" My father is quite clever; he was only chosen to laugh. Eventually, what is the difference between dumb and clever? How do you define? If such a question were to be posed before the clever ones, that is, my father, what would be its reply? Why do you keep such questions unanswered? Neither my father nor the clever ones could give an answer to this. How were such people to know that we also had our sensibilities and emotions, wishes and desires, like other human beings? Whoever came to our house those days would wish I were dead rather than living such an extremely horrible life. They did not want my family to suffer my tragic presence and be tormented by it, nor did they wish that I should prolong my miserable existence. The easy way out of both was my demise. But was it proper that they had expressed such a wish? What an insensitive behavior! Why could not the clever ones think it properly—death is not the only solution to everything. All those who visited our home asked him for my death. They did not want my family to suffer more because of me; and they did not want my life to continue with untold suffering like this. The only solution to *everything* was my death. No, death did not snatch me away simply because they wished so. O *Yamaraj,* the god of death, had you snatched away my life at that time, I could never have learned the various hues of life. The meaning of life would have remained limited to that—death followed by life, which is experienced even by animals. By not wiping out my existence just like that of an animal, you did the correct thing, dear *Yamaraj!* You had also perhaps wished that this person should be allowed to scrutinize life's multiple hues and variegated colors. The world of those clever ones, those possessing voice, never ever understood and appreciated that even the dumb and meek ones possess a mind of their own, their own curiosities and inquisitiveness, and long for life. If vocal people assault the meek by demanding their death, who else would be more inhuman and cruel than them? What a traumatic shock would she experience when the clever ones do demand death for her! The clever ones did never think;

they spoke without thinking of a tender mind. These things also kept haunting me time and again.

There was no one but myself to experience the pain in me and the deep injuries inside my mind caused by such asides. But I had no voice and no signs by which to express my protests; I was doomed to merely listen and tolerate them. What a fate! People used to see in my physical appearance a mere life stuck to just a voicelessness, immobility, and inertness. They had not witnessed even a thin ray of hope within me. Nobody had observed anything but hopelessness and a patch of dark cloud. In their view, my future was only tied to the life of my parents, who used to wish by way of prayer to God, saying, "May this girl's breath of life fly away even as her parents are still alive." How was I to describe it? Sympathy toward me or an expression of indifference? If I call it sympathy, they had wished the death of a tender girl by burning human sensibility into ashes; if I feel ignored, they had prayed him only to end my tragic life.

But God never fulfilled their desires because they were unjust. Their god was made of stone. How could a god made of stone award death to me? Their god also probably desired not to impose an unjust death on an innocent girl. I recall now that the wishes of an early death desired for me are burning in the cremation ground. I am standing before that god and asking him to give me death, but only a great death that is acceptable to me. An animal-like one is, however, never acceptable to me. I am standing in such a time which is burning a fire of tradition (custom) on an innocent soul; she is bearing intolerable pain. I am writing these writings. I am telling this to them who wish to read the pages of my recollections; I am opening up these pages. Even if no one ever saw a thin ray of hope in me, I, on my part, was catching a glimpse of some brightness and illumination ahead of me. Possibly, I had started seeing a silver lining even around a dark cloud.

Rays of Hope

Like a sky that looks clear and bright after the patches of cloud go away, I had already started seeing rays of hope even amid hopelessness and disappointment. I felt like becoming the same clear and bright sky myself, but patches of dark cloud were still hovering around my mind. I also desired to accompany my younger sister to the school in order to drive away the darkness around me, to reach up to that light. I aspired to be enlightened.

At times, I would see my younger sister opening the pages of her books, reading or writing. The pages looked so attractive that I felt like touching and handling them. But who was there to comprehend those desires of mine? I used to squat near my sister and, unnoticed by her, would touch the book—even a touch of the page lent me a sense of pleasure and delight. But once my sister knew that I had touched her books, she would pick up a quarrel with me for having tarnished the pages, and even occasionally lodge a complaint to the family-elders. With an apprehension that my tiny dust-filled fingers of the feet would, of course, soil the pages, I was scared to touch them to my heart's content. Sometimes she would angrily tear off and throw away the pages of her exercise book touched by me. Collecting those torn-out pages, I would try to imitate the letters of alphabet a bit further away. How I wished that someone would teach me how to write like my father does to my sister by holding my little fingers slowly! But he speaks even when I looked at her books: "You don't know. What do you look at? What's the use of your learning?"

However, it was my fate to sit at a distance and keep watching how my sister was being taught.

I felt desperate to hear my father say so, and a question occurred in my mind. Is it useless if I know words? So his question did not hurt me that deeply. I think I was growing rebellious slightly. Why should they learn everything and not I? This question haunted me. I loved feeling the soft pages of a book more than knowing its big letters of alphabet. When my father was not around, I used to sit by my sister and feel the soft pages of books. At that moment, I felt I was turning over the five pages of my own life. But that sweet feeling would disappear momentarily. My sister would complain that I was tampering with her book, and she would weep. I was slightly grown up, sturdier too. My parents would express their anger on me.

It was but natural too because I used to trouble her and made her cry; would—her books. Really she was a much? रुन्ची (weakling, tearful) girl in those days. So they were angry at me.

Our society holds a belief that children should be disciplined by scolding and threatening them. This culture is deeply rooted. My parents too were grown under such belief. They naturally imposed the same culture upon their children. The colors of anger and आवेश (agitation) were diluted in the minds of their children in such a way that the whole life would turn into a collage, the more one drinks the intoxication, the more one wants to drink. I was felt with anger and आवेग excessively in my childhood, as a result its impact could be felt subsequently in one's thought, behavior, and activities.

Children are, by nature, curious and fragile. As a child, my own nature wasn't any different from that of the others; the only difference was my being physically handicapped. But my parents would not appreciate my curiosity and agility. On the other hand, they would perhaps think, "When would this girl pass away? It's okay as long as we are around. But what would happen after that?" Or somewhat along those lines.

On the occasion of one Dashain-festival, as my father put the tikaa on my forehead, he murmured by way of his good wishes,

"May you not live longer than us. For, who would look after you after we were gone?" What would I make out of these words—a blessing or a curse? Such words would badly bruise and impair the young mind of a child like me. He blessed my siblings so: "May you live long. May you *possess* a lot. May you be famous." That old man cursed me—*die earlier*. I condemn such a mind as termite-eaten; instead of opening up various facets of life, he wished for the death of a tender bud, and that too on the auspicious occasion of the great Hindu festival Dashain. How unduly am I who got curses, not blessings on the occasion of a great festival! The tender heart was bruised badly. Why shouldn't I live longer? Why don't they *shower* loving blessings upon me? It was a question that the past had to answer, but the past could not find the answer, nor the present tried to do so. The present survives as the remains of the past—the same tradition, practice, and culture. Their lifestyle is similar. They hardly try to change this.

People who are incapable of rebelling against such outdated beliefs and traditions are living like an animal-life even to this date. They also have their desires and ambitions—but who is there to understand and take pity on them? They are alienated from the society, and live a segregated, withdrawn life. How about me? Despite being a member of this very society and the world, I have been a recipient of mere hatred, indifference, and insults. If everybody is entitled to enjoy equal rights, how much of share does fall to this world (of mine)? Or is it only pity? All conscious people should think. But will they, whose mind is moth-eaten, consider this problem? There is still a group that supports backward people. Where are the voices in our favor? Who will raise voices for the emancipation of those whose souls are suppressed? Who is there to raise a voice in favor of people like us whose souls are victimized and suppressed by the society and the world at large? There is nothing but huge walls; when shall we begin living like actual human beings by dismantling the walls? This is a question I pose before this age and the people living this age.

We are also living in this age who, having obtained a human life, could not live this to our heart's content. It is not that we are hankering after pity and compassion. Nor is our world any different from that of the other humans. But why is it that they lure us to live on pity? We are not animals within human frame from a different world. Our world is same as *yours and theirs*. We have a similar frame as theirs—of bone, flesh, and skin. The only difference is we have some defects in it.

But how is it that our world could not be shaped as beautifully as that of the others? Why does the world look down upon us as incomplete and incapable? Simply because we have some physical deformities and disabilities inherent in us? What is the definition of completeness? I ask this question to those who are looking for completeness and who find completeness in themselves. There is an eternal question addressed to them from the world they have labeled as incomplete—where is its reply? There are many such questions, but the so-called civilized world is *shirting*; why don't they answer? How is it that even religion and traditions discriminate against us? Why did that *group* known as God did injustice upon us? An innocent girl would express many such dissatisfactions. Why even the so-called divinities look at us with apathy and indifference? When are these people and their social culture, religion, and traditions to change? This is a question I throw at people who look complete; at those who consider themselves as complete. For even as an innocent girl child, my mind used to be filled with such questions.

At present, as I stand and look back to those dark days, I ponder over the fact that, willy-nilly and unknowingly, I was made to raise a banner of revolt against the society, its religion, culture, and traditions. I feel that the society in which I had been born and brought-up had been inwardly being devoured by the worms of evil customs and conventions. And what positive outlook were we to except from people who had been raised amid such manners and convention? On the part of my parents, their mind-sets weren't also made of a different material. How could they also cross the boundary walls of society and raise themselves above their environs? And I, a person born in the same society, could not remain unaffected by those influences either.

Time was moving ahead at its own speed. Various wishes, desires, and aspirations had begun sprouting up inside me as well. It was because I did not have a heart different from those of other people. Like the hearts and mind of all other children, I also possessed a heart that was young, restless, curious, and at times naughty. However, it was not easy for me to acquire the status of other children.

I had also started seeing new colors in life. I used to feel that rays of hope lay in the letter of alphabet and, as such, their mastery became my life's one and only ambition. I used to collect the pages of exercise books torn and thrown away by my younger sister and go through the letters written therein all through the day—by copying them on the bare earth with the help of a twig, by inwardly repeating and memorizing them over and over again, many times without number. Time was giving me a strange kind of test. Even in my dreams, I started seeing nothing but myself reading and writing. Whatever Father used to teach my younger sister, I had already learned by dint of my own endeavors and practices. I then started learning the composition of words—the exercise of forming words by combining the letters was by no means easy. I used to write all the letters of the alphabet on the ground at a time and then pick up the different ones to combine them into word. For instance, *kalama* (कलम = pen), *kala* (कल = machine), *phala* (फल = fruit), *jala* (जल = water) and so on. Those were the colors of brightness, and light spilled over my life's pages—colors that appear pleasant and delightful even today as I recall them. That is perhaps the meaning of the saying that, without going through the experience of tears and toil one cannot experience the pleasure of laughter and smile. I also experienced laughter inside tears and light inside darkness. I knew life is expressed through experiences. It is sometimes scattered all around. By now my finger no longer trembled; they were habituated to write letters. I knew—one should adapt to different situations in order to survive—my little fingers were quite used to in performing the game of survival.

No more did my tiny fingers of the feet shake and tremble as I wrote—they had been habituated to scrawl the letters. Like others catching hold of a pen with their hands, I used to catch hold of a twig and scrawl letters with the feet. To this day, I write in like manner. Like others using three fingers to hold a pen, I also use three toes of my feet while holding a pen or a pencil, but people have the illusion that I use only tow *(toes)*.

It is truly said that life is also an experiment. It appears that every common and ordinary experiment teaches a person to think in a novel manner and helps him or her to sustain life smoothly. Had I not, when I discovered that my hands could not catch anything, experimented writing with my feet, my body would have been the synonym of a living corpse and I would have been waiting my death in a lonely and dark corner. Thank God, I was spared the fate of a living corpse. But neither society nor family was of any help in all this. What encouraged and guided me was my own conscience, my soul. I have now started seeing a little of the light of consciousness ahead of me. And, seemingly, I am being pulled toward that light in a slow and gradual manner.

Joys that Sprouted with Letters

$\mathcal{I}$ remember now that at the time I first learned to write the letters of the alphabet, I could not share the joy with anyone. I had, nevertheless, mastered the art of scrawling letters even if it was on the bare earth, and had learned to pronounce them although only within my mind. The first day I had been able to scribble the first letter of the consonant क (*Ka*), I had sprayed a cloud of dust in the air out of sheer happiness because I had broken innumerable twigs time and again in order to know this letter. I bruised the tender skin rubbing against the soil. Moreover, my fingers bled when I practiced writing with my fingers by dipping them on the dewdrops collected on the bowl. If ever there lay any reason behind it, it was only to recognize letters and to learn how to write them. When this lesson was learned, I myself raised dust and sprayed it on my body. Besides, with an intention to allow other people also to see that I had mastered the art of writing, I had drawn a large-sized क (*Ka*) on the earth. But there was no question of anyone looking at it; instead, some of them stepped on that letter and erased it. In other words, my first letter क (*Ka*) was wiped out of existence even without anyone seeing it. Alas!

But to a person whose life and existence itself had been as good as erased, tolerating one insult and injury after another seemingly gets ingrained in the mind as a matter of habit; I was also one of such persons. There was none whom I could share my joys with, nor was there anyone to share my sorrows. That day, when the letter that I had joyfully scrawled was stepped over with shoes, my heart was badly torn to pieces. I expressed that feeling of distress by screaming, because the resulting pain was unbearable to me. That scream was perhaps an expression of resentment against those who had stepped over it. But my screams were not taken in that light by other people. They said that I had screamed as a result of hunger or thirst, my goodness! That period of my life is quite adventuresome. I have never revealed this to anyone so far. I am revealing this to you for the first time today.

It's true, there was none with whom I could share my joys of learning the first letter of alphabet. I had shared that joy with this inert earth—I had celebrated the moment by spraying the dust all around and covering my own body with dust.

It was quite difficult for me, unlike others, to write beautifully as on a piece of paper. It's true, I was surrounded by thorns, and I had to write another letter pushing them apart, that too on the bare ground. The second letter I scribbled was ऊ (oo—he, she, that); I was excited this time too. This time, I shed tears in excitement, but I wiped them out so that they could not see them. The third letter I scribbled on the mud was व (wa).

As I could not even maintain the balance of my body properly, scrawling letters of the alphabet was an ordeal in itself. My toes would tremble. I somehow wrote the first letter. After that, it took me a very long time to scribble all the letters. But no matter how long it may have taken, I would be patient. Those days it was an uphill task for me even to communicate my feelings with others. So much that I did not even have either words or signals by which I could tell people I was hungry—I started merely to open my mouth widely to express my hunger and people would comprehend that I was hungry. When I felt thirsty, I used to point to water-vessel and people would understand what I meant. Likewise, at times of nature's call, I would point toward my private parts. These were the few signs or hint—call it a formula or a medium—by means of which I could communicate with my people. Had I been deprived of even such signs or symbols, can you imagine how it would have been possible for me to live?

That's why, *perhaps* people say, "Where there is life, there is also the art of survival." This maxim proved to be true in my case as well. After all, somehow I had to preserve my life and demand the basic necessities of life as I had also, like all others, been born with a mouth to feed and a belly to be filled with from the moment I had been born out of my mother's womb. I had somehow to learn how to satiate my hunger and how to quench my thirst, besides also learning the manner by means of which I could evacuate the system's waste materials. I had to learn all this, and I did. These limited signs and symbols greatly helped me somehow or the other to carry on life. My relatives could not afford to keep a watch over me the whole day. They would help and assist me in passing urine or evacuating feces *(emptying my bowels)* while they were around; but when no one was there, I used to somehow pull down the pajamas with my feet, crawl myself some distance away from house, and would manage to complete the exercise. We had no toilets at the time. Not only was this case with our house, but also for most houses in the village. The elders would move toward some streams or rivulets and hide themselves behind a tree or a bush; on our part, we children would *make do* by squatting on the sides or a slope of the kitchen garden.

My soiled private parts used to be cleaned by the elders of the house; on other occasions, I used to pull out some leaves or grasses with my toes and rub them hard on the affected parts. In that manner, I also learned to wipe out my feces, but my elders would never let me do it myself as, according to them, I soiled all my undergarments in the process—and they used to clean them once again. These are my reminiscences of a time when I was around eight or nine years old.

Times of joy and delight happen to occur but rarely in one's life; likewise, the times of my life's delight and happiness are hard to come by. I have already mentioned joys I had experienced when I managed to write the first letter of the alphabet in life. I never received a word of praise nor a word of encouragement as I accomplished it. But, as I threw dust in the air to express my joy, I have frequently been scolded by my mother. Disobeying her made her thrash me too. But nothing could disrupt those moments of joy—neither scolding nor thrashing. I celebrated that moment by blowing soil powder all around; from that very space, I shed tears of great joy! Oh, I learned that there are times when no one joins you when your life takes a pleasant turn, nor is there anyone to console and fondle you at times of pain and suffering. I would also wish there was someone to share my joys and fondle my hair with love when I was successful; and, when I would be pained and sad, I wished some tapped my shoulders with affectionate hands and encourage me by saying, "Oh, you dumb girl, must you be so dejected and downcast in life?" But who was there to soothe me with such words? I had been a girl discarded and shunned by everybody. Although, on my face, people seemed to display sympathy by uttering words like "Poor thing," "How pitiable" and the like; but inwardly they would want me to die early—a reaction I could gather by their unspoken behavior toward me.

At present I remember them. Having lost the battle of life, they are living a helpless and लाचार (lowly) life. They treated me the way that they had learned. I no more look at them with revenge. I have looked at the world with love; I can see today that their wrong beliefs and thoughts are drifting in the air like any *unusual* waste material from the satellite. New thoughts are *waging* war in their mind. I am quite sympathetic toward them from the very core of my heart. At present, I am filled with a love for that aspect of life that had become a thorn and pierced me, and scratched my young and delicate heart with its claws. And I experienced that had my conscience not been thus pierced by thorns, I would not perhaps have experienced the feeling of a soothing coolness. That's the reason why I love the thorns as much I do love the flowers, and I am equally fond of my life's moments, be they of pleasure or pain. I plucked up the delights that had blossomed with letters of the alphabet and I did also pluck the pains, sufferings, and miseries as well; in other words, I kissed moments of infinite happiness along with the flowers of the letters.

The first word I had scribbled happened to be कलम (*kalam* = pen) because I had been in a dire need of a pen and of which I had been deprived. It had been some kind of ambition with me to avail of one. I had also been immensely happy at having been able to attain the success of composing a word. This time, however, I did not celebrate my success by throwing a cloud of dust around, but by guffawing aloud. But even when I laughed thus, nobody showed any keenness to find out why this girl had behaved in that manner. I went on composing many words one after another. I happened to create a novel path along with that. It appeared that time also flows, drop by drop, along with life. I sought and searched the value of being a human with the help of those drops of time.

Now my father began to teach my sister the lessons of क का कि की, that is, lessons of inserting different vowel syllables to a consonant. She began to repeat (pronounce) the same by pointing at the words with her finger. I too sat close by her, looked at the letters (or words), pronounced mentally, and scribbled them on the *floor/earth*. As she repeated innumerable times, I could easily pitch it up. While practicing writing, she did many times until many pages of her exercise book were exhausted. As mentioned earlier, the pages of the exercise books torn and thrown by my younger sister had always come handy and useful to me. When nobody was in the house at a daytime, I used to pull and drag myself to the spot where the wasted pages lay, collect them together, and go through the letters of the alphabet written on them repeatedly, to my heart's content. Burnt-out cinders and coals would also be thrown at places where it was easy for me to find them. I had now started writing on the rocks with those cinders. Writing letters thus had become my entire daytime routine till my parents and siblings returned home. The moment I would sense that someone was approaching home, I would hurriedly spray mud on what I had written with the toes and would wipe them out by rubbing them with the feet. I would also hide those exercise books in nooks and crannies where it was not easy to locate. And thus, everything lay unsuspectingly usual when they came. Writing with the cinders was usually a taboo, as it was believed that such a practice would invite loans, and children doing so used to be rebuked. My parents were particularly against it. But I used to write or scrawl freely and unhindered behind their backs—for I had attained a kind of mastery over the art of writing. This is how I learned to write letters. Obviously, your might be curious to know about this mystery, so I revealed it to you today.

How desperately a person, who is denied the medium of communicating his or her feelings with others, somehow tries to find a way out—you can imagine yourself. I was the same person deprived of a medium. But I was a human being, not an animal. Even if I had been deprived of many other attributes, I at least had a brain that was capable of thinking and imagining, a pair of ears that was capable of hearing. And, even if a bit blurred, my eyes could see and observe things, while at the same time, at least a little ability to move my toes had been left with me. There were only few things that I could make use of. The rest were all useless, dysfunctional. Yes, with that little I had, I could somehow manage to build a bridge that could help me establish a link with the outside world. I can never forget those precious moments wherefrom I had started filling the pages of my life with golden hues. Of course, there have also been chapters of life which, when turned, rendered me benumbed and delighted at the same time. For instance, how pleasant and exciting were the moments when I had somehow scrawled letters with the help of a twig on a bare earth or with a piece of coal on the rocks? What a pleasant page of life it was! But alas! Nobody tried to open and read it then. On the other hand, when people would see me scrawling on the earth, they would make such disparaging and disheartening comments as "What is the use of her learning?" or something to that effect.

How peculiar are the ways and traditions of the Nepalese! Leave aside the question of bestowing love and affection on the meek and the dumb; our people have a mind-set that regards all the latter as virtually subhuman weaklings. If most of our people possess a diseased outlook such as this, how was I to receive a different kind of treatment from them? But despite the fact that I had received no better treatment at all, I did not deviate even a bit from the path I had determined to pursue.

Those pathways were not smooth. They went uphill and downhill, or were lined up with the turns and twists, filled with intractable boulders and rocks, or were full of thorns. To try to step over them and proceed ahead was by no means easy. These were not graveled roads leveled with the help of excavators, bulldozer, and the laborers and which could be blacktopped easily. It was the thorny, rough road that I had stepped on time and again, and my life has traversed along it time and again. As I walked along that pathway, I *have had* to brave frequent wounds and injuries, and was pricked by many a thorn. Despite all this, however, I still love that pathway and I have still been pursuing the same all along (not that it has now been more smoothened and painless). An ability to read and write the letters of the alphabet had, of course, made things more convenient. That was the joy imparted by the letters—a joy that had filled the heart with pleasure and bliss.

Celebration of Words

Now I would like to tell you how I learned the word formation process—a process by which consonants accept vowel sound-symbols; I will also recount the atmosphere around me.

As mentioned earlier, I had the faculty of hearing intact in my ears and that of smelling intact in my nostrils. My tongue was also capable of picking up and appreciating various tastes. Even if a bit hazy, my eyes were capable of seeing things, while my nerves could feel and recognize various objects as I touched them. With the help of these sense organs, I could experience what was being talked about, what was happening around me, what people were doing and the like. When the sun used to rise and come over the hills, I would be curious to know what it was. As people would say, "Look, the sun has already risen above the hills," I would come to know that it was the sun, and, as I kept looking at it, I would meanwhile catch hold of a twig with my toes and write on the ground, घाम (the sun). When the sun moved from the east to the west, and dark night fell, I pondered in my mind, "Who might be the creator of all this?" They said when the night falls, nothing can be seen, and I surmised it must be night and looked at it wonderstruck. I had no means of expressing what went in heart—no stone, no twig, no soil, or charcoal. There was only the little porch smeared with cow dung and red clay. I wrote रात (night) on that very porch.

But my words would thus be scribbled in a void, and vanished into oblivion. My parents could not see them, and so would not scold me for scrawling on and disfiguring the floor which may invite debts.

As for my eating habits, whatever eatables such as rice, curries, lentils, and so on that mother would give me, I would slowly blend or knead together with my two feet, bend and lower my head down toward the ground, pick up grains one at a time with the help of the left foot, place them on the flat sole of my right foot, raise the latter to meet my mouth, and then put the food into it. Even as I went on eating in this way, I would try to discern and discriminate between the tastes of the various items and then write on the plate from which I ate off—"Rice, *daal* (lentils), curry, pickle" and so on. That would, of course, take time, making my mother shout out, saying, "Why is this girl playing and wasting time instead of eating things quick and fast?" But how would my illiterate mother know that way—even the rice plate would often serve the purpose of a very useful exercise book for her daughter to scribble words on. She never knew that the rice plate, without being noticed by her, became my exercise book.

Various flowers blooming along the edges or slopes of our courtyard would make me extremely delighted, but I was not capable of differentiating their shades and colors. People would say, "Look at this *Taanki* tree. How beautifully it is covered with white flowers!" It was only then that I could realize that the color was white. Likewise, I learned to discern between the blue, red, and other colors; I would look at them intently and with interest, learned about them, and would then compose words like yellow, blue, red, green, purple and so on. I also recognized that the color of the sky was blue. Whenever someone of a darker complexion appeared, they said "black as charcoal." The color of the charcoal with which I used to scribble on the stones and that of the darkness was similar. The only difference was that I could touch and feel the charcoal, whereas the night, though it lay in front of me, could not be touched and played with. I could never do so. One day, a neighboring girl called ए काकी ! (Hey Auntie!). Then I wrote the word काकी immediately. My mother used to say, "I will bring you पापा (sweetmeat, etc.) from the market." I learned that word. My sister would utter words like आउन' (come), जान' (go), दिन' (give), लिन' (take); and I learned such words too.

In like manner, while I heard the various words and expressions uttered by people, I would try to form those words with the help of the letters that I had learned. As they spoke, I would get the opportunity to form one or more new words every day. After some time, I had been successful in forming over a hundred words and adding them to my vocabulary repertoire. When mother used to bathe me, I used to get the feel of water; when I felt thirsty and my younger sister used to give me a glass of water, I could *experience satisfaction* having quenched my thirst. When she fed me a cup of tea, I could experience the taste of sweetness. For, till then, I had not learned to drink liquids. In the cold days of winter, the *balesi* would look white with frost. When touched, it felt cold; I too experienced cold by touching it. With the summer cold would disappear, my hands and feet no longer became numb, and the body would tremble no more. I felt warm those days. And they used to say, "How hot the sun is shining, ooph!" And I used to think, *Ah, that's what they call it hot.* And I would write on the floor नातो (hot). I learned the word आत्था (. . . .) when my mother made fire on the hearth. I knew how to write आत्था but didn't know what it meant. I loved the yellow flames of fire; I imagined what it would be like if I could catch hold of it. While unnoticed by Mother, I did that too. And I felt a burning sensation in my toes. Now only did I realise that the word आत्था stood for burning sensation or being burnt. I also gradually picked up the fragrance of flowers, the greasiness of some stuff like oil, the stiffness or hardness of something like a rock and so on. My sense of touch helped me recognize things that were either oily, slippery, rough, hard, tender, soft and the like, whereas my eyesight came in handy in enabling me to know and learn about the shapes and colors of various stuff. My ears were of help in hearing and listening to things.

Those were the days when my younger sister had started reading the sentences of children's short stories by repeating them over and over again, while Father had started helping her pronounce words that she could not herself comprehend, especially the *conjunct* letters. On my part, I would squat on the floor some distance away from her and listen intently to the stories, poems, essays, and so on, while at the same time pondering over the manner in which she would pronounce various words and expressions. My sole objective would be to concentrate on learning the various letters, words, and sentences she would utter. As she would proceed with her reading, I would go on scribbling on the floor the sentences she used to read.

I had already made myself familiar with, and could now read simple sentences like 'I will eat rice, I am hungry' and the like by scrawling them on the floor. At times, I would move closer to my younger sister and glance over the pages of the book that she had been going through, and, that way, had learned to read and write, along with her, the letters, words, and sentences seen on those pages. But who was there to let me also have the pens, exercise books and the like as my younger sister was privileged to get? For me, the only pens, exercise books, and so on, were the bare earth and the pebbles, mud, and twigs found there and my own tiny toes besides. Nobody would be pleased to see me learn letters, words, and sentences—they would perhaps have been if they had been aware! When my lot was to be blamed for disturbing and to be scolded even when I would go and sit near my younger sister, I didn't obviously give them even a hint of what I had learned simply for fear of my being thrashed and beaten. My poor lot was limited to sharing, only with the earth, whatever pleasures or pains I would feel. Likewise, whatever letters or words I could scribble, I scribbled alone. After that, as I learned combining those words into sentences and enjoyed doing so, I celebrated some kind of festival with the same earth, without giving even an inkling of it to anybody else!

In that manner, I laughed all alone when there was some happiness in life. I also wept all alone at times when it was beyond me to tolerate my troubles and tribulations, pains and injuries. At times, I would shed tears when I was suffering from pain, and I would also shed tears when I was happy and delighted. My tears kept on flowing nonstop when I had learned to design and shape sentences out of words. I could not stop them. What should I call it—a celebration of words or of tears?

□

Shamans and Doctor

People want to insult, dominate, and hate the physically weak and disabled persons. Our religious traditions have clogged the brains of our people with a belief that those who have committed sins in their previous births are born either dumb or half-wit, or with a physical infirmity or *as a woman* in their present lives. Likewise, everyone held the belief that I had been a great sinner in my past life, and, as a result, was reborn in this life not only with my physical deformities and nonfunctional limbs, but also as a woman. That was why, superstitious pregnant women in our village filled with the apprehension that they might give birth to a physically disabled child like me if they cast their eyes on me, would either avoid looking at me altogether or walk at a safe distance away from me. Even after childbirth, they wouldn't come near me with fear that my shadow might afflict the baby with a terminating disease. It was said that they wouldn't even allow my mother to touch their babies, nor would they allow her to sit near the portico or doorway of their houses. How backward is the level of consciousness amongst the Nepalese people! At present, when I remember, I feel as if those events occurred in front of my eyes, and I feel a kind of writing discomfiture. I underwent the suffering of being dumb since I came to discern things in the world.

At every breath and at all moments, Nepalese people put their faith in religion, customs, tradition, shamans or witch doctors, charm and spells, incantations, witches, ghosts and goblins and so on. They hold the belief that these trouble us, and that we should not be able to please or pacify them; everyone may have to suffer a fate like mine. Perhaps, that's why, maybe in order to pacify them, to keep them at a safe distance or to restore my limbs and make them normal, shamans or witch doctors would be frequently made to perform their rituals in our house; or alternatively, I would be taken to such a place where those rituals were being performed. On my part, at that age I would be quite scared of such shamans. I would be petrified with fear as I saw them beating their drums and dancing wildly to their beats, chanting, incantations, jerking, and trembling. On such occasions, I would cling as close to my mother as possible, while the shamans would have us believe that my deformity had been the outcome of ghosts, goblins, or witches having taken possession of my body, and once they could be driven away, I could be restored to normalcy.

I may have, dormant within me, some kind of rebellious mind-set even at that early age. It seemed as if the witch doctors' eyes were made up of some supernatural elements. For I would feel like smashing and splitting those dreadful and wild eyes of the shamans that would look angrily at me as if they were about to swallow me right then and there. I did not dare look straight into those eyes and would often hide myself under the wrap cloth that my mother used as a head cover. I wished I could pierce those red tomato-like eyes. How dreadful and red! Under the pretext of driving away the goblins and witches off my body, so many male chickens, pigeons, and uncastrated he-goats were sacrificed and eaten by those shamans that I have lost count of them!

As I analyze those incidents today, I wonder what else the poor simpletons, the Nepalese, with their brains gripped by ignorance, illiteracy, and superstitions, could think of. What I feel today is that the shamans would, with the help of their *jhaarphook* (exorcism) traditions, try to allay psychological fears and anxieties albeit in crude and small way. They would, by feeding goat and chicken meat at a time when a patient's body is emaciated by sickness, help restore the latter's strength and stamina to some extent. It appears they are somewhat familiar with medicinal herbs and their efficacy in the treatment of some diseases. But despite our effort to dismantle the old foundations of faith and belief, one cannot uproot them so easily. How nice it would have been if we could help these shamans and witch doctors nurture the knowledge and awareness about the procedures of scientific indigenous (native) remedies?

On the one hand, we know science is successful in giving a dying person life, while on the other, at the same age, we believe in the spells of witches and in the power of deities if we don't satisfy them. We believe they have control over on health, and so life. We believe the shamans can ward off the evil spirit and help bring the victim to life by just performing *tantramantra* and beating the *dhyangro*. The witchdoctors and shamans tried their best to ward off witches and all evil spirits. I don't know how many spirits were removed from my body. But I could never recover, could never walk, speak, or move my hands. I still remember those activities quite faintly. I feel bitter to know the status of our Nepali society—how backward and how superstitious it is!

I still remember, though hazily, how the mind of a tender child like mine was harrowed by such things. These are reeling now. The question of believing or disbelieving in the shamans and witch doctors may have its own logic, but it is still vivid in my memory—they had filled the tender heart with great fear. It brought me a kind of आतङ्क (terror/horror). They would implant incomparable fears by drawing images of witches in my mind. I used to tremble with fear. I was scared so much so that whenever someone in dark, dirty dress approached, I took it for the spirit. Scared, I would crawl and slip under the cot.

Our Grandma used to tell us about a knowledgeable shaman, Dalman Bhotay, who lived at some distance above our house. Once I was taken to his place so that he would foretell (*jokhanaa dekhaauna?*) my future. In the process of forecasting, he said to my parents, "She would not merely harm you, but even your children and grandchildren." What else he said I cannot now recall. But even that small sentence of his had shaken me quite severely. I had been harrowed many times by such tomato-eyed shamans. Had I been born merely to harm my father as well as his sons and grandsons? This question haunted the little mind again and again. I thought, *Why do these witch doctors say so?* I would feel like telling those shamans and witch doctors to forecast about their own future and decide about their fates and fortunes. How is it that they only foretell the future of others? Such questions would arise in my innocent mind, but the answers they elicited were always a big zero—it wasn't known why.

When I failed to see any such power in their performance, it is natural for me to be doubtful about them; I had begun question the common beliefs and faith on them. My little heart began to show dissatisfaction about this—aren't you also a human frame like us? Why can't we experience the divided power if you do so? Many such questions occurred in my mind. But on the other hand, there was a crowd of people, all superstitious, who never wanted the wall to dismantle; so they crushed my courage and doubt. They would crush and obliterate my questions, yet they would sprout again—with new leaves the tree would grow. The more they cut it, the more it grew out of the stump, with such new leaves and new sprouts every new keeps growing. I know the seedlings of awareness began to grow gradually.

It appears that the walls raised by insensibilities born out of superstition and bad traditions, as well as the pillars of faith and belief drilled in my small childhood brain, had started being demolished and uprooted slowly and gradually during those very days. Because neither the elderly sorcerer had any answer to the questions raised in my childhood brain, nor had I the voice with which I could articulate what my little brain liked to ask them.

Even if one were gifted with the faculty of speech, how could one muster courage to ask them? So dreadful and fearsome, oh my god! Their red eyes, their bodies wrapped in rags and tattered clothes, and a yellow turban on the head looked abominable, yet they trembled in such a way beating the *dhyangro* drum. Moreover, they used to turn those red eyes time and again toward me. Ah! I was scared in such a way.

They believe their witchcraft and shamanism has some *tantrik* power. But for me, I could see no such power in them. They said their conglomeration of charms and spells so possess divine powers, but however seriously did I observe, I could not notice any.

As I have already mentioned, the various things I would hear about the shamans, ghosts and goblins, witches, and so on, had filled my brain with nothing but dreads and fears. Our father would occasionally sit with us at the veranda and narrate ghost stories thus: "It is said that, in the ancient days, a headless person with eyes on each side of his shoulders would come on horseback up to the mounds at the edge of our vegetable garden, and would return from there after his horse had his belly filled with water from nearby pond." As we would hear such stories, both my younger sister and I would tremble with fear and would stick ourselves closer to him. I thought, *What can we do if such a creature appears before us now? How big might he have been! He might swallow us at a time.* We were frightened too much.

Time passed by, but the shamans totally failed to restore me to normality—that is, to make me a whole person. They failed. It was not merely that they had failed, even medical science could not come to my rescue. It simply failed. There are certain diseases which have no cure at all. As such, even the doctor is reported to have sulked away on the excuse that the bones would improve on their own if they were limp, not otherwise. That was probably all he knew, and there is no sense in blaming him either. But of late, a doctor from abroad had me examined, and said, "The brain, which keeps our body in motion, is itself paralyzed and there is no remedy for this ailment in the entire world." His name was Ruis. I forgot to ask which country he belonged. But he was a pleasant type of a man. He used to work with B. P. Koirala Health Science Institute, Dharan, around the year 2004. I had met him there. There were many people who accompanied me.

As the doctor pronounced that my bones were limp and there was no treatment available, my parents gave up of the task of seeking remedies for my ailment. On my part, however, I had been freed from a kind of bondage, because earlier I was not even permitted to play to my heart's content. "This girl keeps on moving her feet about"—they would say, and put them inside the socks. Perhaps they had hoped that, by restricting the movement of my feet, I might be able to move my hands instead, but no change was forthcoming. I would bow down my head, bit holes in the socks with my teeth, bring out my toes through those holes and play contentedly. As long as my grandma was living, she would thrash me severely on seeing me do so. But no matter how much she could beat me, I did not cease bringing out the toes and playing. But that was blessing in disguise, as it were—for none of the limbs would have been able to move if I had not done that. Dr. Ruis would say, "How could her toes move when her brain itself is damaged?" I would simply look at him and keep smiling. At last, he smiled and told me in his broken Nepali, "It's amazing to see so many different types of human beings. Even if her brain is damaged, she is writing so well with her toes. Very good. It seems that everything is possible as long as there is moral strength." But how was he to know that a severe struggle was called for on my part in order to keep the toes mobile?

Yes, when the socks started getting torn and worn-out fast, they were replaced by shoes. Perhaps that was the last and final test—a tough one. With the shoes on, the little strength I had in my feet would be confined inside them and wouldn't get any kind of support. I would fall down so many times that my head would get severely dashed against some hard object more than ten times, resulting in an acute pain; but even then that wouldn't deter them from confining my feet inside the shoes. I would get terribly frustrated at times, and feel *Ugh! What a miserable life I have!*

Whenever I would be alone, I could crawl up to a nearby rock and hit it with the shoes as hard I possibly could. I would express my anger against those who forced shoes on my feet. Such impacts would result in my feet being injured severely at some places, and I would try to remove the shoes, but to no avail. I would then be left with no alternative but to weep and weep, loudly and alone. Those were the toughest moments of my life which also I had suffered. But once the doctor pronounced that my ailment was beyond remedy, my parents lost all hope and let my feet alone—without shoes. As long as my feet had remained confined within the shoes, there was no way I could indicate that I wanted to pee or pass stool, nor to hint that I was hungry or thirsty. As a result, I would pass urine or stool times without number on my garment itself. And the filth would result in my skin being filled with sore and eruptions.

Those were extremely harsh and cruel times for me. And on top of it, I would receive several beating everyday for the offence of soiling and dirtying my clothes. What a destiny that I had to be beaten severely! My childhood days were thus filled with all kinds of tortures and pain all the time. I was angry in my own mind *to resort*: *You have closed my feet into the shoes and how can I unbutton my dress? You demons! You gave birth to me only to punish this way.* My childhood days were filled with torture and were tormenting. Didn't I cherish the desire of passing my childhood days enjoyably and joyfully as the other children would be doing? But alas, that was not in my destiny! I could not enjoy that life.

Thus, the shamans and doctors had been unsuccessful in curing me. But the fact that they were unsuccessful meant that I had been freed of all restrictions. Once the shoes were taken off my feet for good, my mind started experiencing the delight of a true freedom from bondage. During the days that followed, I would feel like touching and catching everything with my toes or playing with them. I would feel fully free!

The Society's Sense of Beauty and I

$\mathcal{I}$ wonder why the meaning of beauty, as I understood it, was poles apart from the meaning imparted by the society to that world. The society would look merely at the outer surface of things and characterize some persons as handsome or good-looking, while at the same time, describing some others as ugly or unattractive. But I never differentiated some persons as attractive and others as the reverse merely on the strength of their facial appearance. I vaguely recollect that there was the house of an old man adjacent to ours; people would address him as *Laato Saarki*, the dumb shoemaker. He had a great liking for me, would address me as *Saani Mukhini*, the little mistress, and would take me in his lap. I would also quietly move to his loving lap and sit there. I considered that old man as good-looking, beautiful. Those who despised never looked beautiful for me though they might have attractive countenance.

Of what use is internal beauty if the outer appearance is not good-looking, people argue. There is another woman who lives near our house, but who is devoid of morals. Normally, one's first impression of her is that of a charming and youthful lady. As I look at her, I ponder internally over the question—after all, what is the meaning of beauty? But of course, everyone is free to think and feel as he or she would like to. So am I—as free as anyone. It is possible that I did not come under the definition of beauty as was felt and understood by other people.

I had been born with a frail body, which meant, to some others, that I had no soul, no desires, and sentiments either; no beauty. As people would see me outwardly for the first time, they would perhaps find me to be extremely ugly. It was but natural, since the society would look only at the body frame—in other words, only at the bones, skin, and flesh. Naturally, it was valuable for them. It is, of course, true that a person should be physically strong and able-bodied. But if one were to look at it from a slightly different perspective, would it be enough if a person was able-bodied merely from the outside? No, a person must be mentally strong—that's all. Can the society disagree with this view?

The society is happy with well-built bones, skin, and flesh. If not, why do they behave with me in this way? "The strong always dominate the weak"—so goes a saying. This same view is applicable to each and every living being, including the birds and animals. If we were to look at things merely from a materialistic viewpoint, the cycle of creation as a whole has been revolving around this basic point. And since we humans also form part and parcel of this creation, the same rule is applicable to us as well. That's why I refuse to understand life from merely a sentimental standpoint; because we cannot drive life's chariot ahead on the basis of sentiments alone. But at the same time, a human cannot be a mere machine, as mankind is a combination of brain and heart as well. Man is a creature of feelings, perceptions, sensitivities—all bundled together.

A writer had once told me, "I am of a materialistic bent of mind—I don't give much importance to a man's sensitivities." I did not make any reply, but thought in my mind, *There are also such people in this world who are completely devoid of human sensitivities. They regard themselves as creatures of an entirely mechanized world.* But I am not a person who lacks human perceptions, who has no heart, no sensitivities, or no feeling. I do not want to live the life of a person whose human sensitivities are dead. I possess the mind of a human being; that's why I have a life. Sometimes the colors of life's perceptions have spilled over me in a bitter manner; at others, in a pleasant manner. The eyes of this society that merely go by appearances and shades saw nothing but ugliness in me.

We talk of religion, culture, customs, manners, and traditions. Irrespective of the society in which a person is born, he or she cannot remain untouched by such influences. But do our religions, cultures, and traditions have only their positive side? It's true that the society in which I was born is also a pack of good and bad practices. Thus, practices are part and parcels of life, and are unnoticed clearly. These are revealed in their practices. Not so. That's the reason why our minds are filled with such influences as seldom useful. According to our religious scriptures, if a person has committed a sin in a previous life, he or she is bound to pay its price by way of suffering punishment in the present life. By laying down such a maxim, our scriptures have imposed several unjust ethics on people born with disabilities or infirmities. Our cultures have laid down such tyrannical traditions that show no mercy or sympathy toward those that have been marginalized and discriminated against.

I was born and brought up amid the same kind of culture and traditions—as a member of the class that is most despised and disgraced, the class that has been despised and ignored for centuries. There is a suppressed voice amongst people like us which has not been able to come out of their throats. Now I have to live a life that lends voice to these voiceless people. I must survive at least for the benefit of the helpless people marginalized by the society. It is this very enthusiasm that has kept me going along life's journey. It could take a long time to complete this journey.

Even if I had been living a painful life in a society seized by superstitious beliefs, I was waging a war against it in my own style. In the course of the struggle launched against conventional beliefs and superstitions, no weapon was raised and no explosives were hurled. My young mind would have mere protests and restlessness inside it. I proceeded ahead with a battle of notions and conscience. In course of time, that struggle transformed itself into an attainment—an attainment that is truly beautiful. That struggle articulated and brought to light before the society the truth that the disabled and the infirm also have their hearts and minds, their desires and expectations, and their own pretty dreams. It appears that by launching a rebellion against the customs and traditions amid which I had been raised, I may have started laying down the foundation of my own kind of culture and refinement. The construction of a culture in itself is a very difficult task. I was moving ahead among these complexities.

From my very childhood, I had more or less been hearing stories about Ashtaavakra, a mythical character, and I had somewhat been influenced by him too. I started appreciating the philosophy that we should not look only at the physical aspects of his life, but also at the inherent beauty that lay within him. There are several such characters presented before us by the eastern philosophy that have kept on inspiring people to survive one way or the other.

As it is, I am a person who loves life dearly. I hold the view that we should live our life by waging a battle against the circumstances that we come across, not by running away from them. I also appreciate western philosophy. That philosophy also, which I hold, presents many aspects of life in a positive manner.

It is said to be that Ashtaavakra as a person was physically repulsive and ugly. But how is it that the then society worshipped him reverently? Of course, there may have been people in that society also, who would have laughed and poked fun at his physical deformity and skin color. Is it that only persons who look outwardly attractive are humans, and not the others? That's the way the world seems to feel. That's why pretty women keep on taking part in the competition of wearing beauty crown year after year. And their beauty seemingly vanishes and wilts every year, ultimately ending up in the dustbin as something without any value. Ashtaavakra, to me, is more attractive than such beauties; he also unfailingly presents a beautiful aspect of life—an aspect that comes in handy to all people. Yes, from the cultural point of view, Ashtaavakra had been a character to impart a lesson to us that a man shouldn't be good-looking merely outwardly, but should also be equally beautiful internally. If we base our outlook on such a philosophy, and go on searching, we will come across many similar male and female characters amongst us, even today.

Lord Byron, the English poet of the Romantic era, was also a physically disabled person, but he had a streak of beauty in him. I then used to feel like posing a query to people of our society: "Aren't I good-looking?" But these mute questions would always go unanswered. It was natural for childhood minds to be a storehouse of questions—and I was no different. But those were questions which were fated not to receive any answer. It was as if childhood was the privilege of the others alone—not mine. That was why I did not have the right to enjoy a restless, agile, and nimble childhood. Agility and nimbleness would seemingly suit only those who were physically well-endowed. We, on our part, were a class of socially disparaged individuals, who were not entitled to sympathy and social courtesy. Those who regard themselves as fully endowed, shower words of hatred, insult, and contempt on us, on the ground that we are receiving, in our present life, the fruits of sins that we had committed in our past lives, and what befalls us are mere spittle of hatred and disparagement. Despite being a recipient of such hateful spittle at all hands, I had been drawing pictures of a beautiful life ahead; I had perhaps drawn the most attractive portraits of life during those very days. Who won't be happy to see a pair of new pajamas! How beautiful might I look in these dress!

Patched Pajamas and Shame

The objects I loved most were pebbles and mud, with which I could play to my heart's content. After all, I had been a worthless child in the eyes of my parents—and looking after me was a waste of time for them. That's why there was no one to stop me playing with pebbles and mud at any time. In the process of collecting pebbles, I would occasionally drag myself a little away from home, and my clothes would be entirely soiled with human excreta. For me, the mud would also serve the purpose of water. I would rub off, time and again, the excreta stuck to my patched clothes with the help of mud. I recall now—what a hellish life that had been! My father would have thick blue pajama made of canvas or jute sacks tailored for me so they would be tough and long lasting. On receiving a new set of nicely fitting pajamas, my mind would go into ecstasies. After all, I was a mere kid!

Those pajamas would look nice for a day or two—as long as they had been new and unsoiled. When they got soiled, Mother would have them washed and cleaned if she had time; but at other times, who was there to have them washed? The pajamas would be extremely dirty, soiled in winter. During winter, those pajamas would never warm up and give me comfort; and during the summer days, they used to scorch me so badly that I would keep on weeping ceaselessly. But however badly the sun would singe my soft baby-skin, I was bound to wear those very pajamas. The first thing was that it was essential for me to wear them even for the sake of covering up my shame. They were extremely dirty and patched up things. I would be internally pleased as the night approached because there was no more need to cover up myself—no one would see my shameful parts in the darkness. Hence, I would strip myself naked and that made me feel so much unburdened and relieved.

It is normal with the other children to start feeling a sense of shame from around the age of three or four. Children feel uncomfortable to piss or clear bowels by this age. But in my case, I had no realization of shame or shyness until I was ten or eleven years old; because, even if I wore torn and tattered pajamas, no one would either notice or comment until these days. As I would keep on dragging or crawling myself on the ground for some days with the same set of pajamas on me, how long would they last? They didn't. I was concerned about a single problem—how I can save my tender skin from being rubbed against rough stones and prevent possible wound. However, I was not much concerned even if my shame was not covered, because I was not healthy and whole like others. So I didn't need to cover shame; I didn't have to be ashamed before them. On the other hand, I would prefer to remain naked and play nude. I would think that playing nude would never result in torn pajamas, and thereby I would also be spared the bitter words of rebuke at the hands of my parents. But at the same time, I would be compelled to wear them—even if in the difference to my parents' sense of shame. I had to show the society that I had dress on my body. However, wearing them constantly also meant that they would also be torn out faster. My father used to bring a piece of cloth after a week or so, and would get the torn pajamas patched with it. *Once again, the pajamas would get patched. Once again, the pyjamas would look somewhat new, and I would wear them with a sense of pleasure and delight. What could my poor parents do! They knew how to put another patch upon the older one; they did not look for any alternative.*

It was during those very days that I witnessed the great division between the haves and the have-nots—the walls that separated the two classes, and many other aspects highlighting inequalities between men. The patches added and stitched onto my pajamas not only made me aware of an economic ditch, but also made me aware of a very long class-divide (division). My parents would use bad words on seeing my clothes torn out so soon; and in their displeasure and emotional outburst also I sensed the same pain of deprivation. The otherwise desirable childhood of mine was immersed inside a pond filled with tears. I was not privileged to enjoyment, laughter, and smile anywhere, anytime—my childhood was always dipped in tears, awe, and alarm.

A friend, Bharat Adhikari, had once narrated the story of Sahana Pradhan to me thus, "During the war in Burma, Sahana Pradhan had suffered the ordeals of having to walk over the corpse of human beings with herself covered with eight frocks and thereby surviving somehow to come over to Nepal; her life story should inspire us all." My mind argued within myself—the story of Sahana's struggles, sacrifice, sufferings, and tears is one thing; it might be an immensely inspiring story as well. But she could escape away from the ravages of war and was able to save herself because she had a good body and was healthy. She also had eight frocks with her to wear. But how about the pains and sufferings of people who are deprived and disabled? Has anyone thought about their plights? My intention here is not to persuade you to think of Sahana and her struggle otherwise; she performed her brave role and accomplished the task honestly—that aspect has become inspiring to one and all. Where does Sahana's life fall compared to theirs? Imagine the life of someone who has never seen eight frocks. Imagine about people who have to die an untimely death despite their great desires of living—they that have never experienced anything, but wants and scarcity. I am a character who falls within that same class and category, who only rarely would have the privilege of wearing unpatched clothes and who would, at times, even have to cover the upper half of the body with father's old and torn vests. Even during winters, we could not wear anything other than the old and worn-out sweaters of our parents—some so long that we were not required to wear even underwear and shorts! I have never had more than a pair or two of clothes to wear. There were even occasions when my father's sweaters would serve the purpose of my pajamas—I would push my legs into their sleeves and make do with it! I was a bit dirty those days. My mother could not wash and clean everything. Even if she did, I used to soil myself by playing in the dirt. My whole body was filled with it. I don't know what I did. My childhood day toys were pebbles, mud, leaves of wild plants like *angeri* and so on. Whatever may it be, my innocence brought me a kind of bliss.

I was growing up with age. My guardians had also mostly started leaving me free and alone. With the new kind of freedom, I had been slowly building up my own kind of thoughts, feelings, faiths, and beliefs. In other words, my young mind had started drawing a different road map for myself. My young mind had begun thinking, *Am I not a human being? If all of us are humans, why is a distinction made between myself and the others?* A young child with her young mind wanted to demolish the walls of this discriminating culture and create a culture of equality in its place. A little man with a little mind. If you allow freedom to a little man, he can think and do different things. Likewise, if my guardians had not allowed me this kind of freedom, I would not have, I could not feel, touch, and experience so many hues of life.

These days I see some guardians who want to keep their wards under their thumb. I feel pity and sympathetic for the helpless children whose guardians, in the name of love, are in fact keeping them tied to a leash. They say that freedom will spoil their children. I feel pity on such parents, and I want to penetrate their weak mentality so as to sow the seeds of new awareness. And I feel like crying out in the midst of that very crowd, "I am also one of them who enjoyed utmost freedom while I was a child." That I had been incapacitated by a physical infirmity is a different thing. But otherwise, I had all the freedom in the sense that I had been disregarded and discarded by the society as a worthless being. Nobody would bother as to what I did. I was uncared of, however, in the sense that I was provided only two bane requirements—two meals a day and clothes of whatever quality they are. Nothing beyond this was cared of. Being discarded as an ignored figure was not any ill luck for me; instead, it became a means of transforming the ill luck into good fate. Ultimately, the life was mine, no one else's; and I myself had to take decision regarding how it should be lived. But I did not consider society's indifference toward me as a misfortune. To the contrary, such a social attitude of indifference turned to be a medium that helped me convert a misfortune in a fortune. After all, my life was my own—not that of others. How I would live that life was also my own decision and choice. That's why, I feel, whatever my guardians had done was the right thing; even if they had regarded me as worthless and had left me to go my own ways, I was neither as useless as they had thought, nor was I a worthless member of the society. And that freedom proved a fortune to me. Time was passing at its own pace. Together, I was growing with age too.

By then, I suppose I had been about nine or ten years old. A new house was being built for us, and we all were extremely delighted that we would also have the opportunity to live in a new house. Some of the carpenters and masons who came to work there were a naughty, nasty lot. Of course, if it is not those bubbling with youth and kind of romantically intoxicated to be cheeky and frolicsome, who else will be thus inclined? There is a saying वैंसमा स्याल घोर्ले। . Moreover, men are more beautiful than jackals. That's why, even as they appear sober while our elders are around, at other times they would resort to frolicsome banters. Our old house was demolished. We lived in a shed. We used it as kitchen, dining, and bed. I used to spend my whole time around that shed. My parents would go to their respective jobs, and sister to school, leaving me behind all alone.

The masons and carpenters would look at me and comment, "How will this girl look when she reaches the pinnacle of her youth? How will her face and features shape up like?" Till then, till those days, I hardly had even a bit of an idea as to what youth meant. But inwardly, I would think, *What business is it of theirs as to how I would look?*

The blue pajamas of canvas or jute sack that my father got tailored for me had been all torn and tattered, thereby even exposing my private parts. At times, those laborers would make it a fun to particularly aim at my genitals and throw small pebbles or mud balls at them. As my skin had not been tough as theirs, once the missiles found their target, the resultant pain would be fairly severe. But I would not lag behind them either and would pick up with my legs whatever lay around and throw them as missiles at those mischief makers. When they found out that I would also retaliate as badly, they never ventured to tease me again! The elderly people, maybe knowing my behavior, warned the others, saying, "So long as you don't tease this girl, she is harmless and gentle. When you tease her, she will throw anything at you. Do not disturb or abuse her." But the naughty youths won't obey; they, in fact, ignored the advice. I too had grown wild and had developed rebellious nature by then. I thought, *If I am harassed for no reason, the assaulter too needs to be retaliated. He should be hurt instead.* And I aimed at those who teased and harassed me, with whatever I could pick up—whether it hit or missed. That was the result of the freedom my parents gave me.

I feel that, whether or not anyone liked it, that was a sign of a tendency growing inside me that would retaliate against any kind of injustice. I had already crossed the limits of tolerating torture and torments. Naturally, as normal people have, my sex organs were developed. It was weakness on the part of my parents or my owns to be unable to cover them; or maybe it was a compulsion.

What harm had my organs done to them? What kind of pleasure do they gain by targeting at them time and again? My little mind never knew this secret. But I felt pain. I knew the wickedness of men in different ways. I have expressed before that I did not experience shame until the age of ten or eleven. Now too I don't feel much ashamed of, like others. It's because it's through other's help that I get washed, cleaned, and wear dresses. It is an embarrassing thing for my mother, sister, or whoever does this. None of my limbs is under my control, and I cannot move them as I wish. It is quite difficult for them to do all these things by holding my limbs which were not in control. Sometimes they become angry. They might perhaps want to make their job easier. But what shall I do? I know their trouble, but cannot control my own limbs and maintain a balance of the body.

In Nepali society, if the girls do not cover their private *parts* on the basis that they are quite small, they will charge of being <<<IMAGE>>> and nasty. But I did not have to bear this because it made no difference to me whether I was covered or open. I don't know how far I could read my sex organs. But when I crawled naked, pebbles, stones, and thorns would prick, and I would bleed. I used to apply saps by squeezing kind of blades of herbal plants. How hot it was! Unbearable! The black plant and *titepati* would grow around our house. We small children used to play with the leaves of the black plant and would make small toy houses and cattle out of the *titepati* plant. What a pleasant life it was! But that life was not free from pain and trouble. Many a time, the pajamas would tear open and thorns would prick my organs. I have wept many times when wounds bled. As a child, or because of childlike nature, I have enjoyed many times despite all odds.

I was expressing similar incidents. Since then I know what shame is. And my parents too tried their best to cover my genital at all costs. Now onwards, my genitals could never become an object of recreation by targeting at it with pebbles and *mud clumps*. I could not find any difference in the attitude of the society toward me, yet I could notice some changes in the people. You feel happy to find people's behavior slightly better. With my age, I grew more aware of the environment and life.

The Moment I Received
My First Paper and Pen

By then, our new house had been completed, and we had already moved into it. That house was much bigger than our earlier one—fitted with large-sized doors and windows, somewhat giving me the impression of a palace. We were very much delighted to have moved into such a nice house. As we were still mere kids, just two rooms would serve our purpose—one being used as a kitchen and other as a sleeping room. Rest of the rooms were mostly unoccupied, although some tenants had also started moving into it.

During the interval in-between, a phase of my own life was also over—I had virtually mastered the art of reading and writing. But the sad part of it was that I had still been denied access to an exercise book and a pen. I used to feel how nice it would have been if I also had been fortunate to handle books, pens, and exercise books of my own. How nice it would have been if I were given opportunity to write down the letters that I had known! As my urge for them exceeded limits, one day I scribbled on the mud floor requesting my father to provide me with a pen and some paper. But my father apparently felt that those demands of mine were irrelevant. Instead of becoming pleased and encouraging me, he started beating me cruelly with a stick in hand.

That thrashing made a more painful impact on me mentally than physically. My young mind was so much hurt that day, in fact, that the pain turned into tears and rolled down my face somewhat like a rainfall. Throughout that day and night, the flow of my tears was virtually nonstop, incessant. That old man had a heart of hard rock. I requested this old man earlier too, but he paid no heed to it; he scolded me instead. That very day too, I kept on weeping and wailing; he felt further irritated as it were and ordered his wife—"This Saanpey is crying too much, better hurl a stick at her." I had my fill of such cruel behaviors and hypocrisies that would almost always be my lot. Even in the eyes of those whom I called my own, I became like a beggar—one who would gulp the grains of rice both in the mornings and in the evening without giving any return, and even wore a set of clothing, even if they were a cheap variety. I lived a suffocating life—between life and death. It was true that even if I had been born as a human being, I could neither sustain my own life, nor die an early death that would come as a relief to all concerned. My relatives would also curse me in a similar vein all the time. But howsoever harsh the rebukes would be, I took them as a matter of course and somehow gulped them down. It is said that one can get over the injury inflicted by a few blows of a stick more easily; but the wound or bruise inflicted by harsh words lasts a lifetime. I feel that it has been truly said.

Even today, as I recall the occasions when I had begged my father to provide me with a pen and an exercise book, I feel a deep sense of pain somewhere in my heart; resentment raises its head against that cruel behavior of my father because I had asked him with great hope for a *pen and some paper. But my father had silenced that hope brutally. In other words, he beat me with a stick, and must have thought that he achieved a big thing; but in fact, he had done nothing important. It was like adding fact to a burning fire.* But neither that cruel and senseless showering of sticks on an innocent girl could dampen or smother the awareness that was germinating inside me, nor did it stop growing despite the hindrances posed by the other people. I do not know what kindness and affection prompted my mother that day to fetch a pen and an exercise book to be given to me. For the first time ever in my life, I had received a pen that day. But even that sense of attainment somehow failed to evoke delight in me. On the contrary, my tears kept on falling drop by drop, drop by drop.

"Don't weep, Baba darling, don't weep," said Mina, my younger sister, as she stroked me fondly with the tiny fingers of her hand and kept on wiping my tears. (My younger sisters address me fondly as "Baba" while displaying their love.) My tears may have smeared all over her hands, as she rubbed them on her frock to have them dried. Even earlier, at times, Mina would tear the blank, unused pages of her exercise books and would give them to me. She would also spare her pens for me to write and lend her books for me to read. This time she did not complain to parents against me as before; she did not make me beat. Maybe she had grown wiser by now. Whenever I would weep for this reason or the other, she would come and sit near me with a pensive, downcast face. She would also fetch children's books from her school library just for me. They would be on various subjects, and I would read them all with great enjoyment. I used to prefer poems and short stories. I would copy poems and stories of my choice on my exercise books. I used to copy points of general knowledge from other books.

As I have mentioned, I could not rejoice on the day I had received the first pen and exercise book brought for me. But the next day, I forgot everything that had transpired the day before. It was as well that I managed to forget, because merely by recalling bitter things and grieving over them would not have helped me forge ahead in life's journey. Like the warm sun that nurtured my body, the spirits and hopes my father had tried to crush grew fresh with new roots (shoots) today. Yes, the next morning, I saw the white sheets of my exercise book spread before me and the pen lying nearby. It seemed as if the open sheets were asking me to pick them up and fill them with letters of the alphabet. Enthused, I also lifted the pen (with my toes) and ran it on the blank white sheets. How am I expressing (can I express) the pleasure and delight I felt while I scrawled letters, words, and sentences for the first time without any qualm or fear? How happy must I have felt when I got what I wanted for so long, and for which I suffered so much of pain and anguish! Since I had already learned how to form words and sentences, it wasn't strange for me to learn to read from the book and also to write them down.

I have said earlier that my younger sister Mina loved me so dearly as only few other sisters would. Hardly would a day go by when there were not a pile of new books brought by her from the library on her way back from school. Whenever I was lonesome, it was those very books that kept my company and helped me while away my time. I read all the books one by one—meaning that now I had also learned to go through books. I would then occasionally *lay my hands* on other books too. Among them, I liked literature, science, and social sciences. It is in those days I learned how one should express kindness, love, compassion, and forgiveness to people; how one should behave with them; and how one should help others. I learned their humane behaviors; I learned some lessons through books about human beings. While reading the characters in the stories, I would feel pity, love, and compassion for some, while for others I felt hatred and would be angry with them. While reading the good characters, I also wished to imitate their behavior and quality. When alone, I wished to put myself in their place. Sometimes I imagined myself to be a prince, or a fairy from the heaven—the Prince Dikpal or Fairy Sunkeshra and so forth. The world of my dream (imaginary world) was really beautiful, and I enjoyed being in a world of imagination (colorful) than in the real world. I also started reading the magazines and periodicals that were in the house, and would read them behind the back of my father.

At times, I would hear father recite the verses of the Ramayana rhythmically and in a singsong voice. I would move closer to him to listen to those verses and yearn for going through them myself. But he would not even let me touch the book, and would hide it—I didn't know where! I started searching everywhere and ultimately located it under his beddings. That was the first time I had the privilege of *laying hands* upon the holy Ramayana and read some of it. I found that the large *tome* also had in it some attractive portraits of the story's character often regarded as divine.

I had an impression that the epic book might have been written in different alphabets; but once I saw it, my misconception was automatically *allayed*. I felt I grew bigger. Then I remembered those days of struggle; my heart was overwhelmed with joy. I had an opportunity to touch the Ramayana, the first book by *Aadi Kavi*, the first Nepali poet, and even I myself could read it. I was elated and exhilarated on going through it, and could understand, from a close range, about the main characters portrayed therein—one was Rama, a so-called god and the other Ravana, a so-called demon. At that time, my young mind regarded Rama as a noble character and Ravana as a villainous one. What made me form such an impression I do not remember now, but when I read later, toward the end of the book, about the episode where Rama had cast *aspersions* on his wife's fidelity and, as a consequence, Sita was made to vanish into the earth, I was deeply touched and dismayed. In other words, I no longer considered Rama as a noble character either.

In the earlier days, my father had not been much favorably *disposed* toward me—he used to be rather aggressive. I could never make out why. But of late, he had started looking at me from a more positive angle. Even if he would never bring new pen or exercise book for me, he had at least started sparing the blank pages of exercise books that he had left unused and the old pens he had used. It is said that even a stone gets melted with time; my father was after all a human being, and his heart had not been made of stone. As such, he started softening as time went on. Occasionally, he had also started bringing home the unused office pads and handing them over to me. Even those would come in handy to me for practices and exercises. I would be on cloud nine.

My Belief in Ghost, Spirits, and Gods

Despite my matured age, I still felt I had the innocence of a child. I was more conscious about the world but many more years were required to grow fully matured. In those days, there was no source for water near our home; there was a well quite far. Women (including my mother) would fetch water from that well. I, on the other hand, used to play with the used water at home. Sometimes mother would give me some fresh water lovingly. Elated, I would build a small kitchen and a hut out of thrown-away plastic and bamboo sticks. And moving to the walls of the field, I would make small holes (niches) with the help of a sickle point. I would knead the clay and make pots out of it, and keep them on the niches so that no rainfall could damage them.

The following day, I could find the fireplace, utensils, and the *collage* all intact. I started playing joyfully. I used to make small holes with the help of the same sickle point where I could play the game of *dandi-biyo*. I had also made the *dandi* and *biyo* out of small twigs. The game required two to play—one bawler and the other controller, but I managed to play all alone. Likewise, I used to play marbles and the coin-throwing game of *khoppi*. I did this with my legs. You may ask—""Is it possible?"

Yes, it is. My feet are as active or agile as your hands are. Just imagine. *Some people climb the uphill with loads of dog grass* on their back, and I heard them comment, saying, 'See, this girl is playing the game of males.' Yes, it seems so, but I had unknowingly taken a bold step of doing many activities like these, usually thought to be done by males.

I did not play the games of dolls and kitchen. But if children are given much freedom in childhood, they explore the world on their own, and obliterate the distinction between rules of game played by males and females. I learned from my experience. Some of the laborers would stop for some time and watch me play, whereas some others expressed, "How poor! She is all alone without a friend. Even then she keeps playing!" I don't know who those firewood collectors or grass cutters were, but it was me, an object of spectacle for them. Having observed for long, some would express that it was the result of the Karma of the previous birth. I kept wondering what this 'fruit of previous life' might be.

My father had once narrated the story of a king. It was said in that story, that of the king's three queens, the middle one had been ceremonially sacrificed near an irrigation canal, as a result of which the country had witnessed the advent of good or prosperous times. The queen who had been sacrificed had flown away in the shape of a green bird. The story that a female character, who had been a human being in her previous birth, and had turned into a green bird and flew away in her later incarnation, had left a deep influence in my young mind.

Our folklores and mythical stories replete with characters who take several incarnations and thus live externally, leave an illusion and a superstition in our minds. Traditional beliefs are rampant amongst us that God punishes us in later life for the sins and misdeeds we may have committed in our previous life. I was a person born with similar beliefs, and it was impossible for me to demolish the walls of such superstitions in one go. But the notion of a god would often make me furious, because howsoever frequently I used to pray during times of hardship or calamity, never would it appear in front of me and bless me. That is why I have often thrown or hurled away the objects (stones or images) which I myself had earlier worshipped with flowers and other objects; likewise, I have often demolished the shrines that I had myself carved on the mounds of earth forming the barriers of our sloping terrace.

When my younger siblings were near me, I would play some games with them; but at other times, I would be left alone. They would leave for their school with dreams of becoming successful in later life; I would also have liked to go to school with them, but my legs didn't have the strength in them to reach me there. Crawling or dragging myself up to the school was impossible; as such, I could never make it to the school.

All people who observed me used to comment that God himself had shaped me thus. My mind wanted to find out as to what kind of a creature called God looked like. I had heard from elderly people the stories of deities such as Rama, Krishna, Shiva, Parvati, and Durga, as also of demons such as Ravana, Hiranyakashipu, Kansha, Shumbha, Nishumbha and so forth. The characters featured in the stories I heard had evoked in my mind some kind of a belief in God. I also wanted to undergo a religious penance, with the hope that God would appear before me and bestow an alluring boon on me. Yes, I had a keen desire to be a devotee of God such as Prahlad had been, or God's favorite such as the child Dhruva had been. That's why, whenever I was left alone in the house, I would meticulously hew rough shapes out of stone (resembling some kind of a god), would make garlands out of the sacred *dubo* grass for them, would draw portraits resembling a human face with the help of black embers, and place such 'statues' in a hollow niche carved on the sides of the earthen mound; thus would my virtual temple be built and my virtual god be placed in it.

As I said, I used to worship the same gods in the same shrines improvised by me, make offerings of garlands made of grasses, leaves, and flowers, bow down to pray, and weep. Every day, I would implore and plead with God that I also be made like all others. But despite the unfathomable faith I reposed in him, the lifeless god neither listened to my pleadings and prayers, nor could I ever become like either Dhruva or Prahlad. I have started realizing now that he was incapable of granting my prayers; how could he, for *he himself had no existence*. However, these so-called divine characters *left such a lasting impression in my mind that they left a deep impact on my life and thought process*. The characters like *Hiranykashipu, Shumbha, and Nishumbha left a deep, terrifying impression in my mind*. Really, I got scared to enter my home; the home then was no different from a small, dark cave. It was a small structure made up of stone and mud, with mud floor, a single entrance door in the front, and a small, narrow portico. There was a small window on the other side. There was a single window on the first floor.

Our mother, at times of heavy rain, would take us upstairs to the attic for the reasons of safety. But that attic of ours was not much different from the hole of a porcupine. The child that I was, I would never like staying there for long. What would we do, my God, if a ghost emerged from there? My mind would be filled with such an apprehension all the time. So even if I entered it, I would come out immediately and close the door behind me.

Our traditional beliefs are so much laden with superstition that we believe in dead people coming back to life, that their eyes are located on their shoulders, that they have long tusks and teeth protruding out of their tummies, that the backs of their bodies are hollow, that they are headless, and that their feet are turned toward the rear. The elders in our family had instilled such terrifying ideas in my mind. When I would be left alone in the house, I would be constantly terrified at the idea that my grandma might return to the house in the shape of a ghost. Harrowed by this fear sometimes, I used to leave home and play a bit further away as I imagined that I would have to face the ghost that would come out of my house. I could not differentiate between a ghost and a demon—as both were, I thought, capable of gobbling up at once if they caught me!

The children seemingly also love their life dearly. Otherwise, I would not drag myself as far away as possible from the house (that I felt could be infested with ghosts), nor would I cover myself up from top to bottom with the help of old and torn shawls of my mother and hide myself under the cot. Terrified that a demon may gobble me up, I have hidden myself under the cot many times. During those terrifying times, I have repeatedly wept and prayed God from the depths of my mind.

In fact, if there was anything besides silence that kept me company during those lonely days of childhood, it was the god of stone that I had myself set up. But when such gods that I would shape failed to react to my prayers, I would express my resentment and get enraged. Why doesn't this god shower affection on me as he did in the case of child like Dhruva and Prahlad? Why does this god discriminate between man and man? My mind would be filled with such questions addressed to God. At the same time, despite the fact that I had thrown and hurled away god again and again, the belief and faith in him I had reposed in my mind, slowly and gradually started turning into disbelief, as also a lack of faith and reverence. After sometime, I *would pick the stone, unwrap its* rags, and sleep the baby on the bed. I made such babies out of bottles and stones—even I made babies of rags.

I wanted those babies to eat like we do. But those inert things were lifeless unlike we people. It was natural for me to have that desire, because a child compares everything with herself. I wanted my babies to address me 'Aama' (mother), as I had seen small children do so. But my babies never did so. Had I been born in a developed country, I could have enjoyed an opportunity to play with toy machines that can weep and cry and laugh. But unfortunately, I was born in an underdeveloped country, and moreover, people associated my physical infirmity with different things; but then, I played with those toys or babies of glass and bottle, rags and stones freely, carelessly. Seeing me with those objects, people used to say, "See, this dumb girl is like this. See how she sleeps her baby." If other normal babies would play, that would be considered natural, but they did have a different attitude toward me. Whatever it may be, my childhood days were quite pleasant, which I enjoyed fully.

A Burden in the War of Apartheid

A human being apparently feels a kind of pain as the sprouts of consciousness start germinating a little in the mind. Life is more delightful when one is innocent. When everything about me had started being observed from the viewpoint of infirmity and disability, I had imperceptibly begun to experience a kind of pain in life, so much so that when I would myself take out the stale rice out of sheer hunger, I used to be scolded for displaying the characteristics of dumbness. It is their nature or characteristic, and they will show it. They are mannerless.

"How wretched, you see!" my parents would complain. How लाचार would I have, I would just keep grinning, or else sit there just shedding drops of tears. Like the clever ones, this dumb girl never knew how to deceive and do a कपट (malicious). The world of dumb does not know how to cook up stories. When I had been beside myself with hunger, I had taken some stale rice, not anything of great value. But then, what would I be scolded and rebuked for while no one would say anything, as other family members did the same thing? Of course, I was bodily different from the others—the others would take out rice from the utensils with their hands, whereas I would use my feet for the purpose. However careful I would be in cleaning my feet, they would always look dirty in the eyes of others. Even if I also belonged to the same category of humans, I would be placed in a separate caste or category. Perhaps the most (उपहेलित हर्ने) marginalized even amongst those marginalized. (p. 103)

From this, I came to know why the strong dominate the weaker ones. I had a question to ask: Aren't I a human being? Aren't the dumb and deaf human beings? Then why such a discrimination? Yes, as I too belonged to the group of the feeble ones, I had to face such discrimination. We were the dumb group among the clever ones. I belonged to that 'species,' so I had to be scolded time and again just for eating some stale rice. I have to put a question to the group of the cleverer, 'sound' ones: *What has gone wrong with your kind or group?*

It is then that I realized how the castes were separated. That also taught me why the strong ones in our society suppress the weaker section. My questions would be: Are the dumb and mute people not humans? If they are humans, why were they discriminated against like that? Yes, I also had to face similar discriminations simply because I belonged to the category of the weaklings.

Here people do not treat the dumb and mute humanely because they are simply not human beings. This is the true picture of a backward society—it has to be changed for the better. Some humans haven't been receiving the status of humans simply because of the structure of our society—I didn't receive such behavior either. My young mind would feel bruised and pained, as I couldn't receive a humanlike treatment at the hands of people. I have already mentioned that I had belonged to a different caste, a separate category—a category of humans that the others did not even like to look at. Even as it is, I was dumb and mute; and on the top of it I was woman, a female. I would be identified as a dumb and mute woman.

The first term to identify me was a *laatee*, a dumb one; then came the term female. By then, I hadn't developed into a complete woman, although all the characteristics of a woman were naturally present in me. I would thus be slighted at the hands of those who were known as *vocal, clever, or wise*. When the 'higher' people scold us women, they say, 'This type of women will not follow anything. They will show their own behavior.' Whether we have developed all features of a woman or not is a different thing; they call us as थाइने caste. Ultimately, we are थाइने too because we conceive babies in our wombs, give birth to them, and look after by wrapping them on the rags when they are small. Moreover, I am a dumb woman. I had been oppressed my times by the so-called civilized and clever people. I had been a fine object of entertainment for them, a nice toy and plaything with some traces of human quality. I would never be addressed by my name—only by that of *laatee*, a dumb girl. Even my father would make me an object of ridicule when some guests visited our small hut. I did not like jesting or unnecessary things since I was small. But what would I do? Life, I realized later, is verily a battlefield, where various types of wars are constantly being fought—cultural or religious wars, wars against apartheid and discrimination, and wars for the cause of equality. And human beings are being constantly thrust into such wars with the torch of humanity held aloft. Poor suppressed humans! They keep on fighting with the hope of winning the battle until their last breath. I had also been waging the war of life by mingling and mixing with the same crowd of the pitiable human beings. I had to fight battles against all barriers—religious, cultural, and social.

To suppress and disparage the weak and the meek is a well-ingrained tradition in our society. That very mentality heaped loads of suppression on me also to the extent possible, so much so that even my own parents wouldn't look at me as a member of their family. They took me to be a mere guest in their house for a couple of days. But death refused to take me away as easily as they would have liked. The death as desired by everyone else was running away from me. After all, why was only I considered a guest for just a matter to decay? Are all the other human beings born on this earth immortal and unlikely to decay? Was the desire to perpetuate life and existence merely limited to the others, except me? But no one was there to appreciate my desire to continue living, and therefore it was a lot to be assaulted over and over again. Never was I taught to fight for my survival, but only to run away and escape from life. At times, I would even feel so: since I was such a burden on everyone, why couldn't I be aborted before being born, in the womb itself? How nice would it have been if my mother had smothered me to death the moment I had been born?

Sometimes the so-called kith and kin used to express, saying, "Why was she born as a burden on earth? Better she could have been aborted." Nobody thought about the consequences of such words. How could they know this? I was young, moreover, a woman. Perhaps they regarded me from that perspective. But I too had a tender heart, that could feel all bitter or pleasant results, would cry in pain, and would rejoice when I was happy about something.

It is usual with a child to weep and wail for a while, but be pleased the next moment. But even such young minds are at times seriously hurt by the unceasing rebukes received at the hand of the elderly people. My young mind would also weep very much when it had been hurt by the injuries received in the shape of abusive words. But again, how can small children keep on weeping to their hearts' content when elderly people are around? Even if I was considered a burden on earth by some, as a pricking thorn for others, and still as a perennial burden for all the others, I still kept on surviving. I would even consider my life to be a burden, a heavy load on myself. Yes, I had developed an extreme disinterestedness at one time. The only thing I would pine for was *death*.

Life, however, continued flowing on its course even amid such blows and counterblows. I do not know how I kept on surviving even as I would die every moment. My heart shivers even today as I recall those times. What am I to consider this life—a pleasant one or the reverse of it?

Life went ahead with its ups and downs—struggling against unusual and strange circumstances. In other words, my childhood was heading toward maturity. The wheel of life went on turning uniformly in its own speed. As I grew up, my life started becoming more and more burdensome; the buds of consciousness were raising their heads in my mind. The growth of consciousness was also akin to a process of suffering increasing pain. As it is, life also, in a sense, was nothing but a pain. I would drag my life somehow through pain and suffering. In the process of dragging thus, never did my mind smile with pleasure. But even by way of a faint smile, I would laugh with amusement. The sprouting of consciousness wasn't merely a cure—it was also like opening the curtains of possibilities and build up a pathway for myself to walk along. Till now, I have lived my life amid great agony and distress. Will my life take a turn for the better in times to come?

Casteist Divisions and I

People of many different castes and communities inhabit this land. They have their different languages and cultures. On top of it, they are categorized into the touchable and the untouchable. However educated, civilized, and cultured our people may be, their mind-set and thoughts are under the influence of untouchability as a custom—a person born inside a social structure that does not treat human beings as *humans.* Although born in an upper strata of the caste hierarchy, I never subscribed to the notion of caste, nor of untouchability, because, since my very childhood days, all people I could see were born with the same skin, bones, and flesh. Besides, it was the people who are said to belong to the lower-castes that loved me most. They would invite me to their houses and treat me with the food cooked by them. I would also partake them with relish. But my parents would discriminate between men and men and, until now, do not partake of food either touched or cooked by the latter. They considered the make of their skins, bones, and flesh different, and still now they don't eat food touched by them. However, it is the choice of every individual as to whether to partake of a food or not. But they never could appreciate the idea that no person is entitled to discriminate against any other, because they were only human beings, as it were, and not the others (belonging to the lower-castes).

My parents would talk of higher—and lower-castes. They said when a girl gets all her teeth grown in her mouth and a boy gets his *karmakanda* rites performed, they should not drink water from the hands of the lower-caste people; if they do so, their life span will be curtailed. They taught us that we should not allow them (the lower-caste people) to enter our homes. I, on the other hand, felt as to why they (my parents) don't allow them to enter. What speciality did they have? There were also times during the lifetime of our grandma, when she would even chase away the untouchables if they approached our house, on the grounds that they were uncouth and unchaste. She would drive the children away throwing stones at them. She was puffed up with the idea that she was the daughter of a 'nobility' known as the *Thakuris,* and others were supposed to address her respectfully as a *Maiyaasaaheb*; possibly because she had been raised in a feudal household, her nature was unjust, dominating, and torturous.

Even though I would not tell her anything those days for fear of being beaten, my mind would feel like questioning her, 'Grandma, are you alone a human being? If not, why is your behavior toward the others so unjust and cruel?" But there was no choice but to keep silent. She believed that one should oppress the weaker ones. It was *or* conventional belief.

The blame lies on the unscientific structure of our society that never allowed our brains to think about and appreciate human civilization. The walls and barriers that have been raised in our society have not permitted new ideas and consciousness to sprout in the minds of people. When my grandma used to come home after shopping in the weekly markets or bazaar, she would take a water pot and go to the spring lest some untouchables touched her. She wanted to wash it away. She washed the body that the untouchables had touched it. She only cleaned the dirt of her body; she could not clean the dirt of her mind nor could she wash the unjust and dominating behavior that the customs and tradition had put layers in her mind. Our parents had also sustained the faiths and beliefs inherited from Grandmother, but they couldn't, as strictly, be orthodox as herself. Their thoughts and ideas were also alike, although their behaviors were more relaxed and liberal; as a result, those people, who had not dared to be seen around our house as long as Grandma had been alive, had at least started coming up to our verandas, and their children had started joining us in our games. But they were still barred from entering our house. Many children would gather in our house on the days when the school would be closed, and we would all play together; there would be no distinction among castes and no question of touchables and untouchables. That was our small world.

So long as I was in that world, I had no anxiety or worries any time, nor was I burdened with any responsibility. I used to play the whole day. After the evening meal (white rice), I went to bed. The following morn, as I awoke, it brought me innumerable hopes. The young sun would rise atop the hill and warm my young body. The tender buds of my dream would bloom. I still feel a great joy when I remember those happy childhood days. During school holidays, the children would gather in our home because of me, as I could not go out to play. Perhaps they too had affection and love for me. They wanted to play with me. They would gather other children too, and we played hide-and-seek and doll making games and so on. Parents would not stay at home. I was the eldest child at home. Until they returned, I ruled all. In the game of hide-and-seek, anyone might be a *doom* (the wretched, victim character in children's games). My little sister would whisper in my ears, "Mother will kill us. Don't tell that Kamalas (girls from untouchable caste) entered our house."

I would ensure her, saying, "No, I will never tell this to mother."

I saw that everyone had similar skin, bones, and flesh; I never noticed any difference between them and me. I believed then there is nothing (nobody) that should not be allowed to enter our home. Whenever the little dirty type of people entered it, I just thought, *My parents, I don't see any reason if your house is polluted because Chimri, Kale, and Mini* (derogative names of children from so-called untouchable castes) *entered your house. Aren't they too human beings like me in little frames?*

Once back home, mother used to ask me, "Dear *thuli*, my daughter, did any of them enter our house and do any mischief today?"

"No, mother, nobody entered there," I used to satisfy her. Assured, mother would enter the house and begin her chores. I, on the other hand, would laugh secretly and mentally tell my mother—*Mother dear, you are eating rice in pure house, you believe. What is the difference between one caste of men and the rest?* But I could not tell this openly or else I would get bamboo sticks. So I never made any mistake of revealing that secrecy. I had tested that there was no difference between men. Though I was right, my parents would always be suspicious. They were bound to obey their old culture and belief so I never revealed the truth. Had I done so, no opportunity would have been left for the new sprouts of consciousness to germinate. My parents would never have been positive toward the people of the so-called lower-castes. It's natural *who* will be ready to get disconnected from the beliefs and traditions all of a sudden. I never told my parents that the so-called lower-caste people like *Saarkee* (the shoemaker), *Kaamee* (the blacksmith), and *Damaai* (the tailor) ever entered our house. Despite the fact that I belonged to a higher (touchable) caste, I lived the life of an untouchable in practice because I belonged to the caste of the most untouchables among the untouchable ones, that is, the caste of the dumb.

The caste that had been confined to a narrow room had no right to get mixed up with the society in the broad world, whose sight would spoil the good omens of the big people. However, in this connection, my family showed a slightly liberal attitude—they never confined me to a space; they didn't prevent me from going out. That is how I got a small opportunity to mix with the world.

I wanted to subvert the hierarchy between high and low (castes)—I could not uproot it; however, I did not accept this practice as ideal and did not put it into practice in my life. One day, I saw a so-called low-caste carpenter's fingers bleeding. He had cut it with the sharp blade of his tool. The following day, I saw my mother's finger bleeding; she had cut it with her sickle while harvesting some grass. She came bleeding. I saw all men have same skin, flesh, bones, and blood—there is no difference.

Then why do they draw the lines of difference among them? Some of us may be sharp-nosed, other with flat, some short, and others tall; the only difference is that of caste, language, and culture. All are human beings. The earth (world) is commonly shared, the sky, the earth, the water, the air—why is he not knowing this? Had this world been free from all sorts of differences among men and no jealousy and hatred, how beautiful might the world have been then! I imagine secretly—how nice would it be had the world been like that!

The Awareness about Adolescence and Curiosities

$\mathcal{Of}$ late, my mind had started experiencing a different kind of physical and mental uneasiness. It was but natural that various kinds of curiosities would be born in the minds of children who had outgrown their childhood and were entering the adolescent stage. And I was no different. I had started seeing myself as quite a grown-up person. Occasionally, as I looked at the mirror, I would look fairly pretty too! I would minutely examine my various limbs and be astonished. My consciousness was also getting somewhat matured. My hunger for knowledge had been enhanced by my habit of reading various books and periodicals that were available in the house. I would always endeavor to satiate that hunger in me. As I sought to quench my thirst for knowledge, the plant of my consciousness slowly started growing as if it had found a fertile ground. It was no more a problem for me to communicate with others—I could express any of my feelings and views with the help of letters scribbled on a piece of paper or an exercise book. I had been capable of understanding everything and think over them. I would also feel no more eager to yearn for the company of grown-up people. For, if I sat with them, people would voice various comments at my cost. That's why I would be disinclined to be at places where people would gather together.

An adolescent person also has a tendency to feel shy. People would target me and talk much nonsense. Some would be quite naughty and poke me. I would be the object of ridicule or talk.

I still feel the pain when I remember those moments; I even feel काउकुती (tickling). During the adolescent days, one undergoes strange behavior. One thinks of oneself as strong and brave. One considers oneself as stout and courageous. The clothes I used to wear earlier had started getting either short or tight, and the new ones bought for me would not last long either. If I refused to put on short garments, I would be severely beaten with a stick; how cruel was my father? I would feel furious with the old man and would utter to myself, "Is there another idiot like you in this world? Let there be no one like you anywhere." I would also curse him, saying, "Why should such a person like you beget children at all?" Whatever it may be, I was passing through the adolescent phase of life. Whether sweet or bitter, life was passing in its own pace.

In a sense, life is seemingly fanciful; if your fancies are sugary, you feel life is sweet; the reverse is also equally true. But is it possible to imagine a happy life amid adversity and a sweet life amid bitterness? During the adolescent years, many of my questions and curiosities would be of a biological or anatomical nature, and also connected with sexual psychology, which would not find a favorable environment to express themselves unabashedly and easily. My adolescent period was frustrated—there was no outlet anywhere. There are many social and cultural barriers in our society. To raise questions revolving round health, sex, reproduction and the like are considered obscene and vulgar; I was born in a society that entertained these very beliefs and opinions. What's more, I was a girl with a disabled body—and if I were to raise questions on science and psychology, I would be scolded as an upstart, lacking decorum and the like.

It was for reasons such as these that I could never express my feelings freely and openly in front of anyone. After all, what is the criteria of decorum? Is the mere exercise of suppressing one's feelings and not expressing them in public an indication of a civilized, decent behavior? The lust for life or curiosity had so much been awakened in me that I would be inclined to do the very things that I had been asked not to. There is a traditional belief in our society that a woman is not supposed to indulge in assault and killing; I would wonder why, and had a keenness to know about it. That's why, whenever I was left alone, I would kill small chickens by flinging stones at them. I would enjoy pelting stones at them; but when an injured chicken would convulse with pain, go down to the ground, and die, I would be disturbed by a sense of guilt and would hate myself for it. I would then hurriedly dig a pit for the dead chicken and have it buried into it. Had they known this act, they would have created problems for me; but who tells them?

Meanwhile, I would mentally argue as to what would happen if a woman is indulged in killing or assault and would feel elated with a sense of self-praise. And I would enjoy the sense of pride. But again, when I would see the mother hen start calling her chicken and looking around for it, her motherly affection would burn me with a growing sense of repentance. My sense of guilt would also make me promise that I would never again indulge in such a misdeed. I also used to get frightened as to whether something would go wrong, but the day would pass and the night and no misfortune would befall me. I would get up the following day and analyze that it is all a hypocrisy that a woman should not do this or that. Despite my having thus taken the life of an innocent chicken, I have since then not indulged in any killings knowingly, except perhaps some flies, mosquitoes, or ants.

By that time, I had become fully literate. My younger sister Mina has made a great contribution in making me literate. I would possibly never have been literate had it not been for her unstinting help and assistance; I can never forget that contribution of her all through my life. She did everything she could for me since she was aware of my situation. Had she not helped and supported me, I could not have become literate. I will never forget her contribution. *Oh Mina, you never complained against me even if we quarreled. You kept waiting for me. Whatever times I beat you, you would not return.*

By virtue of my growing age, my consciousness was also slowly ripening. My parents would never even spare a few rupees for me; they would, on the other hand, thrash me. On my part, I would also yearn for some nice pens and exercise books; such an urge I would fulfill with the help of money pilfered from my parents. I would give such money to my younger sister, cajole her, and obtain pens and exercise books through her. She would also fetch such items for me on the stealth, unseen by anyone. I have pilfered money quite often—perhaps that was also a revolt against deprivation. I knew it was a mischief, but I would do it nevertheless. On top of it, I would also occasionally enter the rooms of students staying as tenants in our house and tear off some pages from their exercise books. They doubtlessly knew about it, but would never complain against my tearing off their pages. To that extent, they also displayed a bit of goodwill toward me—I must say. How helpless and desperate a life it was!

I would occasionally feel ashamed and guilty about such misdeeds; but such a feeling would never last long, because I would indulge in such mischief not for nothing, but to learn and know something; such thoughts would help console myself.

One's life is not even—it is full of ups and downs. I too was not an exception. It is not simple and comfortable. My younger siblings would go for tuition with our tenants, while I would merely sit nearby and keep on looking at them. At times, when they come across me these days, they falsely claim that they had tutored me. I am amused at their baseless claims, because they didn't know how I communicated; no two-way communication could be possible unless I displayed in writing on papers. It is true, however, that I used to copy down in my exercise books whatever they would teach my siblings. I still keep recalling those days. How can I ever forget those moments when my life was somehow instilling faint ray of hopes in me? I was trying to follow the track of life. But my own people never tried to understand those sentiments of a young heart. On the contrary, they would always express resentments and anger, which would keep on bitterly scratching my mind. How cruel and heartless was destiny too—it also crushed and suppressed me to the extent possible.

Tolerance also seemingly has its limits. Those days, I was crossing over the footholds of childhood and entering into an adolescent stage. It is natural for an adolescent to be filled with agitation and excitement. If they treated me with anger and emotion, I could not respond to them otherwise. I had acutely felt, at the emotional level, the lack of love and affection at the time. Loneliness had started pestering me. I used to feel that there was no one in this world who loved me, or understood my thoughts or sentiments. I would not find anyone who was benevolent and sympathetic toward me. Nobody tolerates oppression. It was natural for me to be intolerant about their behavior. But I don't know why my response to petty things would arouse retort in my family. I never knew why. I was all alone despite being among my own people. As a growing adolescent, I would crave for greater freedom and desire that there be a place reserved for me in everything. But that craving and desire had no way to be fulfilled because I had been born with a daughter's genitals. Had I been born with a son's genitals, I would perhaps have rightfully received first priority and would have received a share in everything. Such thoughts would keep on constantly pestering my mind. I would condemn myself for my failure to be the first heir. When will the social, political, cultural, economic, and religious structures be more favorable and supportive toward womankind? Howsoever much you paint, color, and decorate old houses, they will continue to remain weak. The cultural structures of ours are of such a nature that without first pulling them down, no new structures can possibly be constructed.

Rebelling against a Name

At my birth, I was named Jhamak, that started with the letter Jha (झ) of the Devnagari script. On the eleventh day, the priest must have pronounced my name Jhamak on the day of the naming ceremony. As I was born a female, the feminine epithet 'Kumari' was added as a middle name later. Thus, I became Jhamak Kumari. But strangely, I was never addressed by that name. I would be called *Thulee*, meaning the eldest, at home. When asked with Father, they wanted *Balika*, not *Thulee*. Subsequently, when I started getting recognized in the people's mind as an adolescent girl writer who uses the toes for composing literature, I realized that my name was Jhamak. I heard this name (Jhamak) since I was ten or eleven from my parents' mouth, as they pronounced this name given to me on the naming ceremony. I thought why were they calling other names (Thulee, Balika) since I do have such a nice name as Jhamak.

Somehow, I would never feel at home with epithets (middle names) that would be used in order to denote the feminine gender—such as Kumari, Devi, Maya and the like. Better use such a single word as does both (indicates name and gender). When I was hardly sixteen years old, I received my Nepali citizenship certificate. At that time also I had urged my father that I would take my citizenship certificate by the name of Jhamak Ghimire, but he would never agree with me. He was adamant that I must add Kumari to my first name. Finally, at the office of the Chief District Officer (CDO) also, I expressed my desire once again. But the CDO also insisted that there must be an epithet to indicate (differentiate) my gender. If that was so, I requested him to prefix my name with a 'Miss.' He refused to oblige me. Ultimately, in the year 2053, I received my citizenship certificate by the name of Jhamak Kumari Ghimire. As I had been of a slightly rebellious bent of mind from my very childhood, I resented the tradition of distinguishing males and females even while naming them. I preferred a short name for myself. I would very much like my name—an unusual and different kind of a name, although the word 'Jhamak' didn't carry any meaning!

I would dream of making my name, Jhamak Ghimire, blossom and shine in the literary firmament. I wanted to be recognized by my favorite name. In my creative writings, I never added the epithet (middle name) Kumari after my first name, Jhamak. People would ask me, "Are you male or female?"

I would reply in an easy and casual manner, "I am a human being."

My readers often ask me, "Why don't you add gender indicating middle name 'Kumari' although you are a female?"

My reply to them is this: My parents' daughter and a Nepali citizen was named Jhamak Kumari Ghimire. She has also been born in the literary world as Jhamak Ghimire. I wonder what name would be agreeable to you.

Whatever it may be, my dear name is Jhamak Ghimire. This very name will shine in the field of creation.

In fact, the word "Jhamak" has no specific meaning. But this meaningless word also aspired for a meaning signifying her identity and existence. Yes, I not only rebelled against my own parents, I could not be satisfied with the name given to me by the priest either.

In me, my parents had given birth to a humble (worthless) child; the priest also gave the girl child a similar name. Time snatched away many things from Jhamak, but it could not snatch away her self-esteem. In the course of her rebellion against her own life and times, she has rebelled against her name as well. Whatever agony her mother had to go through while giving birth to Jhamak, she has had to go through double that agony while giving birth to herself. You have the freedom to address her or to recognize her by whatever name you would prefer. But I would like to make myself known by the simple name of Jhamak Ghimire, if you please, because this is the only name that is endearing to me—a name I could not obtain by begging, or find by searching, but had ultimately to take by snatching! In the same manner as Ratnakar became Valmiki in the ancient days and Bishnu Kumari Waiba became Parijat, I also became Jhamak from Jhamak Kumari.

𝕏𝕏

Menstruation and Youth

$\mathcal{I}$ was also a female, and all the limbs natural to a woman were present in me. The busts (breasts), buttocks, and genitals were gradually growing and taking shape. Youth also was flowering along with them. Menstruation is also natural to a woman. This is a priceless boon of nature, but our society regards menstruation as something impure. At the time of every menstruation, a woman is supposed to withdraw herself into a seclusion for five days. No one else is supposed to partake of the foods cooked or prepared by them, as those stuff are considered impure. But as I started attaining awareness and became a little literate, patches of the dark cloud emanating from nascence and ignorance were being torn apart. The dimmed sky of unawareness was being brightened and cloudless.

Just as the various fruit trees like peach, pear, and guava are covered with blossoms and joyfully smile as they attain youth, and flower plants like लाल'पाते, मखमली, jasmine plants blossom in their season, I could not remain untouched by the wind of youthfulness and maturity. The cheeks started purpling. No bodily organ could remain uninfluenced. Menstruation also meant the full flowering of youth. In the western countries, the first time menstruation occurs in a girl is said to be marked with a kind of festive joviality. But we do not have such a practice. According to our cultural tradition, a girl is supposed to run away from the house on the first sight of menstruation! She is not supposed to see the faces either of her father or her brothers—it is believed. In the event of her seeing their faces, the father and brothers have their life span shortened and could even abruptly die—so goes the popular belief, and many people take it seriously too!

The first time menstruation was sighted in my person, my mother had also shut me in a room with the admonition that I was not to see my younger brother's face or touch him. She did not even allow me to sleep on my usual bed. Father had been away in a distant land to pursue his career. I, along with my younger sister Mina, had to sleep on the floor in a separate room. The change of my usual bedding deprived me of sleep and I kept tossing about until late night. I had also wept bitterly out of fear on seeing me lose my blood for the first time. I had a vague idea that it flows out in the course of menstruation, as I had seen mother's garments occasionally soaked in blood, which she would try to conceal for fear of being seen by the others. But from where would the blood come out, I had not the least idea; that was why, when I saw blood as I urinated, I had been thoroughly scared. On top of that, when mother shut me up inside a room, how must have I felt?

Even if I had advanced slightly in years and was becoming much more aware, the childishness in me had not entirely gone away. As I have said earlier, I wanted to do those very things that I had been warned not to. Even if mother had confined me within a room, it was not possible for her to keep an eye on me all the time. My sister Mina used to visit my room and chat for sometime. My mother too would peep through the door sometimes. My brother was also just a kid at the time and could be easily enticed—he would come close to me the moment I hinted. Mother had kept me in a room she could not guard me all the time. At times, when mother's attention was diverted elsewhere, I would even invite my brother inside the room, would play with him, and even share the food offered to me, which he would gladly partake of. I would do so out of mere curiosity to put our superstitious beliefs to test; if I had a firm belief that he would die, I would never have done it. My lack of belief in superstitions had prompted me to do so, but the day mother saw it, she rebuked me badly and again put me behind closed doors. Even if no one was amused at what I had done, I had been internally pleased. But my mother saw me do that and scolded, threatened, and endured me in that room again. I smiled and secretly said, "I touched your son today. Let's see how his life is curtailed—how he will die." I became happy in my mind. Though nobody was appreciative of my worth, my heart was pleased that day, or I was much delighted and happy.

The next morning, as the mild rays of the sun were providing some warmth to the earth, I suddenly woke up and looked outside. The rays resembled the yellowish color of yolk spilled out of a freshly split egg. How beautiful the rays looked as they fell on the flowers of oranges and tangerine and made them sparkle! *What a beautiful sight you see when the sun's rays fall on the flowering junar trees!* But a girl is not supposed even to see the sun at the time of her first menstruation—what a queer custom! In fact, everybody requires the sun's rays directly; moreover, in such a period, women need more sun, its shining rays, and cleanliness so as not to give chances for different bacteria to attack so that germs would be killed. On the other hand, they prevent the girl from exposing herself to the sun during her menstruation. Mother had advised me not to see the sun, but I did see it and bask on it fully. I looked at it to my heart's content and even went out to bask in its warmth. Mother would shout, "This girl doesn't listen to anything." In fact, I would not listen to anything nor would I obey the other's instructions. I wanted that I should personally experiment with things before I could believe in them; I had to be convinced whether they were right or wrong. In fact, the beautiful atmosphere that I had witnessed outside the room next morning made me celebrate as if I had won a battle. The scenario had ridiculed at the characters who had been living yesterday on outdated beliefs. My mind questioned that day—*How is it that such a natural boon—in the absence of which it is impossible to conceive of this creation—is considered impure by our people?*

Mother had scolded with the belief that if I touched my brother during that period, his life span would be curtailed. Poor Mum, how you know that the life cycle has been running through this blood. She disrespects this unknowingly. She thought that menstruation is an impurity. Poor dear, she had not been able to come out of the beliefs instilled into her mind by social, religious, and traditional cultures. She could not come out of it. Her strong fort of life rested our such beliefs. But me? A girl having a mind that carried nothing but curiosity and inquisitiveness. I had to obtain a reply, based on analysis, to almost everything. I had reached a stage in life when it was no more problematic for me to communicate with others—I could jot down questions on anything that I desired to know or learn. Those days I would also keep on pestering the elderly tenant-students with one question after another. They would say, "We should answer *Thulee's* questions only after a proper thought. If she is not contented with our answers, she keeps on asking again and again. We ourselves do not know answers to many of her questions." Anyway, I could learn quite a few things of enlightenment and science even if my question might have annoyed them all the time.

It appears that the seeds of awareness against wrong traditional views and beliefs had already been sown in my mind. That's why I sought to demolish the walls of my mother's blind faith and superstitions. But how was it possible for a mere adolescent girl to break down those walls of culture and tradition that had been lasting for so many generations? I feel, however, that I could at least make a small dent in those walls of blind traditions.

The companion who befriended me in the mornings, evenings, and nights was my younger sister Mina. I had not learned how to drink water or tea on my own, nor could I myself eat and wash my mouth. She used to help me with those chores. I would, however, be left alone during daytime. Mother would ask me to stay put in one room. The door used to be left half closed. I would sit there and somehow keep myself busy. Although I would not be disappointed, I nevertheless would be astonished to see that those who made me sit thus kept their beliefs in worn-out and outdated things still intact. She did not believe me even to see her daughter alive.

After me, it was my younger sister Mina's turn to undergo a similar ordeal. Mother would also put her under a more strict discipline. Mina would also obey each and every instruction given by mother. How difficult it may have been for her! But she was bound to obey. On my part, however, I would not obey all of mother's instructions as I did not have that much faith in old traditions. I was waging my own kind of battle against time, a battle of my own kind. Even if no one gave me company, my tears, pains, and above all, my life lent me their support. It appears that I had perhaps started my search for a different kind of an existence on the strength of that struggle itself.

It is true that human beings start seeking a space for themselves in everything from the age of adolescence. Man starts questioning that if he is a human being, how is he different from the others of his kind? He starts analyzing things and searching on his own, for the meaning of being a human. Similarly, it was not unusual for me to seek the meaning of being a human being. I would find myself fairly beautiful; even as it is, I had been a well grown girl with a newly developed youth and pink-colored, soft cheeks—like a freshly blossomed, beautiful flower. I never saw myself ugly and unsightly; I wonder if it was because I looked at myself with good-looking eyes.

Whatever it was, I was passing through adolescent age; in other words, the process of my turning from a bud into a blossom was on. In the process of flowering, one had to face and brave hailstorms, clouds, rains—everything. I was also a blossoming flower like that; I had been braving and struggling against natural and unnatural hurdles in my endeavor to flower and bloom. The dream of a beautiful life ahead would make me forget all the pains, troubles, and tribulations. Under whatever circumstances, I did not cease to dream of a beautiful life; that's all. The dreams of boys and girls just on the verge of youth are all the more colorful and lively. Also, the color of my life's dreams was neither black nor white. It was colorful all the way.

Search for Possibilities

Those days we were not allowed to spend even one rupee without the permission of the parents. We were not supposed to use even the money given by them to us. The gift money I received on festive occasions such as Dashain and Tihaar, I would hand over to Mina for purchasing exercise books, pens, pencils, and erasers. She would bring them for me. My parents would consider those things as unnecessary. Both of us sisters would be scolded and beaten with sticks. How foolish were our parents—the administrators and rulers of our lives! To ask them to buy these things meant a waste. In their opinion, the used, old, and inferior stuff were enough to serve my purpose. They would keep on telling me, "What's the use of your reading or learning? After all, you would not be able to go beyond the four walls of the house" and so on. They would constantly keep on scratching my heart with such harsh words, thereby badly hurting my sentiments at times. I would feel that my living was meaningless. Sometimes my youthful mind was hurt. But despite all this, life was an assemblage of experience and I also had my share of experience—sometimes sweet and sometimes bitter. In fact, my struggle with life had a different shape and color of its own.

Others might not see anything unusual about it. But as I belonged to quite a different species of a human being, I not only had to struggle during those days in order to be a person like others, but also in order to be my own self. Later on, however, my parents had started to allocate some small amounts for purchasing some exercise books, pens, pencils, and erasers for me as well, although in a limited quantity. Also, whenever the senior students brought some newer books from the campus library, I would borrow them for a couple of days. They would let me have those books and I would take down items of my choice in my exercise books so as to be able to revise and reread them whenever I liked. By the time I had my fill going through them, those exercise books would also be torn as a matter, of course. I never knew how to keep my exercise books carefully, nor other things. Gradually, my curiosity led me from one answer to another. Those curiosities went on opening a new road for me. The fate was the exploration of the possibilities within me. What shall I do? What is my future like? I began to ponder over such questions. My level of knowledge was expanding gradually. Some spoke, saying, "We should exhibit her on the crossroads, perform some tricks (magic), and earn money." Others suggested that I be put on roadside so that I can survive even on mere begging.

Father would occasionally invite his friends to the house and feast with them in the company of country liquor. His alcoholic companions would be village people of status. Once drunk, they would tell me, with their eye reddened, "Thulee, a person like you in foreign countries take to reading and writing. They have thus attained greatness. We can also make arrangements to help you attain similar greatness. We can also make arrangements to help you attain similar greatness by publicizing your activities."

My parents would also add, saying, "These are very compassionate people. They can do anything for you if they want." Hopes would also rise in my mind that they might do something to help me make my future better; but they could do nothing. Their talks had merely been inspired by the wine.

Some of them, intoxicated by local spirit, would turn their eyes red and would console my father, saying, "O Krishna, how unfortunate you are! See, your daughter will pester not you alone but your son too. Your son too is unlucky, you know." My father showed no reaction to this. How could he, as he was worried his close friend might be angry with him. On the other hand, he must have realized whatever that friend spoke was correct. And he would agree—it's like this, a reality. I, however, wanted to give them a curt reply. This angered me; who were these silly people to say so and comment on me? I wished I could slap them. I was enraged to hear such words. I don't know, such an anger had enveloped me because of my hot-blooded adolescence.

Had my father not been there, I could have given them a proper reply; I could have slapped on their cheeks even if it were with my feet. But my father was there. I was also very infuriated at my father. "Why had he brought such men-animals at home?" I asked myself. There is a limit to tolerance. Beyond that limit, tolerating is impossible. There were also people who would have liked to exploit my physical infirmity by placing me by the roadside and turning me into some kind of a beggar. But I could never see eye to eye with such people and told them in writing, "Beware! You are not supposed to say such things in front of me. I will never beg, nor am I an object to act like a showpiece and collect money as you would like me to do."

They had been quite furious with me and replied, "You will rot and die right inside your house."

I added again, "Even such a fate is acceptable to me. But I am never prepared to sit by the roadside and beg." Since then, no one dared suggest anything like that. Perhaps because I had, by then, developed a capacity of countering verbal attacks and of protesting against such unwanted, slighting remarks. I don't know why, my heart never imagined a day when I would beg for my stomach. Nor did I ever think I could live by begging. I thought, *What shall I do, this life is like this.*

One day, my father's drunkard colleagues sent me a bundle of blank foolscap papers along with some painting materials to help me draw pictures and portraits. Highly pleased, I started painting some pictures of natural objects around me—objects like animals, birds, trees, and plants to the best of my capacity. When they came to our place the next time, I displayed those paintings in front of them. They also highly praised the paintings and assured me that they would send my works to foreign countries. I was delighted that a new career option could open up before me.

But neither did they send my paintings abroad, nor made any other arrangements for my benefit. Those paintings ultimately got tattered and were thrown away along with their false promises. Despite that, however, I was happy that by providing me with papers and painting materials, they had provided me with an opportunity to play with colors a little bit. Since then, I felt that I too possess some potential. I had developed interest in playing with colors. How can I nurture that desire? I didn't have money to buy colors and papers. Despite the presence of possibilities, the lack of opportunity dampens one's gift. The more opportunity and open environment one gets, the more his or her capacity multiplies. Though I had the power and the capacity to play with art, it got shrunk and confined within me. In other words, I tried to expand my space, and my life too tried to bloom and flower.

Entering the World of Books

It appears that the hunger and thirst for knowledge is somewhat strange. It cannot be satiated or quenched howsoever hard one may try. I know the thirst for knowledge is really insatiable; I could not either. By that time, I had managed somewhat to go through books beginning from Laxmi Prasad Devkota's *Munaa Madan*, Lain Singh Bangdel and Lil Bahadur Chhetri's novels, Shyam Prasad Sharma's collection of children's songs, in addition to some essays. Those books, I found, were simple and uncomplicated—easy for me also to read and comprehend. The narrow world of my knowledge started expanding a bit. I have shed tears many a time while going through Devkota's *Munaa Madan*. I was immensely moved by pains of its characters, including the compulsion of having to leave one's homeland amid poverty, hunger, and grief. In fact, the lives of common people, humanity, and nature have been very touchingly portrayed in that folk epic, a book of long narrative poem. I wanted, from my very childhood, to uproot the very base on which the walls between the upper castes and lower castes, between touchables and the untouchables had been raised. Poet Devkota's lines that "a man attains greatness not by virtue of caste, but by virtue of his greatness—kindness of heart," I felt, had expressed his humanitarian thoughts which I liked very much—in fact, that book became my favorite.

I had borrowed the book from someone and I had to return it to its owner, but I coveted the book so much that I wanted to retain it with myself. That's why I had forgotten all the pains and pangs of earlier days and had urged my father to buy a copy of that book for me. I do not know what whim came over to him this time—he bought that book for me. In fact, that was the first book which he had ever bought for myself. I feel kind of proud even to this day as I recall that experience because the first book that my father bought me was *Munaa Madan*, one of the most famous work by a great poet of Nepali literature. I was extremely delighted. I looked at the book turning it side by side, and I read it innumerable times. As times went on, the habit of reading one book after another became so deep-rooted in me that I reached a stage when it became impossible for me to stay without reading something or the other. I would feel highly distressed on the day I would have nothing to read.

It was also time that I had to think my life ahead. Howsoever I tried to make myself at home, I would find my life meaningless when I observed the golden life of the others. I would weep to my heart's content the moment I would be left alone, but I never displayed my weakness in front of others. No matter how burdensome I would find my life, I presented a smiling face in the midst of people. One must not display one's pain in front of all. There are many who ridicule you and laugh at you. That's why I never showed my pains or injuries to anyone. I have presented all pains, sorrows, and wounds secretly to the time, because I no longer have any painful moments of grief of bygone days; when I found it impossible to bear life's blows and counterblows, I nearly committed suicide by stabbing myself with knife while I had been left alone at home. As mother arrived at the very moment, I hid that knife quick and fast. Nobody got an inkling of it.

That was a time when I had been quite discouraged with life—quite disappointed. As I recall that moment today, I say to myself as to what a cowardly step I had nearly taken—. Yes, juvenile stage is apparently quite delinquent. If a person does not receive proper guidance, love, and affection at the time, he or she is capable of taking any false step. I would also find myself lonely and discarded, would become distressed and disappointed, precisely because I couldn't experience any tenderness around.

At the time, I could not recognize and appreciate the beautiful aspects of life. I would see darkness all around.

Life went on moving amid similar hopes and frustrations. Although my parents had started being a bit favorably disposed toward me, their behavior remained as harsh as ever. There was no way of getting even the smallest thing without their order to consent. I never would like my parents' tendency to issue instructions even in unnecessary matters. I would feel that their instructions were like a noose forcibly hung around my neck.

Didn't we have our own desires and ambitions? Don't we have any freedom to do something for ourselves? Why do our parents impose their rule in everything? Why must we conduct ourselves as per their wishes just because we happened to be their offspring? My mind would keep on searching answers to such questions. I would feel that they had not done the right thing in reining in our adolescent desires and sentiments. They issued order and may have thought of themselves as rulers. But they had not done any good by forcing a hook on our tender desires, because younger people too have their feelings; even the little minds do have their own desires, ambitious, and hopes. Why do these grown-ups try to put hooks on our ambitions and desires? Is guardianship a string to stifle us and not allow us to be free, or is it a chauffeur or pilot to teach us how to steer our life's vehicle toward a right and proper direction at times of need? Wherever there are no restrictions, a person gets to enjoy his or her freedom to a fuller extent. If nothing was to be forcibly laden on him or her, how beautiful and attractive this world would be! Colors of anger and resentment would pour down toward the present. I always remained hungry for love and affection that did not sniff of any artificial odor. In fact, I had been so much troubled by the orders of my parents that I was not even allowed to get the books or other stuff I needed, even by making use of the money they themselves had given me.

One day, I asked my younger sister Mina to bring some books out of the money I had received and collected. She went to a bookshop and got me a copy of a Nepali drama *Swaasnimaanchhe* (The Woman Folk), one of the plays written by Balkrishna Sama.

I was highly pleased. Whose heart won't rejoice to read a new book! I saw and read the drama; it was very interesting. I liked that play and enjoyed reading it. But my parents created a great problem by presenting her with questions as to who had ordered her to bring the book for me. They also rebuked me by asking me as to why I had sent for the book without their orders and the like. That incident gives me a feeling of chill even today. They also scolded me, saying, "You cannot cross the boundary of the house." When I remember this event, my heart is filled with a kind of shock. I read many books—literary and others—and naturally expanded the store of my knowledge. I used to get lost with the characters and would cry with their troubles, grief, and hardship. I was long absorbed by the books and their characters—a world of fancy.

My restless and fretful mind would feel delighted and free in a world of imaginations. I would feel that one's adolescent days could be greatly restless. At times, I would feel like weeping all the time; at others, like laughing all the time, like doing one thing at one moment and another thing at the next. I also had natural tendencies such as keeping on constantly looking at myself and, at the same time, feeling highly elated if someone called me pretty or good-looking. Even if people would count me as one belonging to a different and separate category, nature never differentiated me in her bounty of showering on me all the qualities such as features of beauty shades and youthfulness that she would provide to the others of my age. I would consider myself quite pretty and beautiful; I would see myself as attractive as the others. I would even liken myself to the beautiful female characters that I had read about in various books. My wishes and desires had also begun to develop wings of imagination, as it were. My wishes and desires could not be subdued despite the attempts of others to press them down. I would spend the entire day in weaving garlands of sweet and fanciful imagination. I would imagine building a separate imaginary home for myself where I would enjoy an unrestrained freedom, where there would be no trace of characters that despised me. My dream of a separate new house was perhaps born out of the various slights and insults that I had been at the receiving end of. But those dreams never materialized.

By the time I had reached that turning point in life, I had learned many things, both by way of studies and also by way of experience. Anyway, my adolescent and restless mind kept on wandering wildly in the world of books which were only ones that could satiate my hunger or quench my thirst—whatever I may call it—for knowledge.

Buds of Creation

$\mathcal{I}$ was getting myself lost in dreams of golden days ahead and the tears of a painful past were in the process of drying up. But whether or not my tears would be outwardly visible, the pains, pangs, wounds, and injuries in my young and tender heart remained as they had been—without an exit or outlet anywhere. If there was any outlet, it was to let them flow down in the shape of tears. Weeping would also help the mind to be unburdened at times, it appeared. At the time, I had been on the lookout for an outlet from a life of tears.

As I would browse through books, I would feel how nice it would have been if I was also in a position to create characters that were different from the ones read in the stories and poems and write about them. How nice it would be if I also could learn to write similar stories and poems? But what was the use of such desires merely surging up in the mind? I would know nothing despite pouring (pondering) over the books for hours on end, pondering over them and rereading them again and again. If my fretful mind saw a butterfly in front of me, it would keep on thinking about butterflies; if it saw a bird, a sparrow, a craven, or a swallow, I would keep on pondering over them; it was likewise if I saw a human being. I would imagine various aspects of their life. In the process of such imagining, many a story would be woven around them, but never was a single one written.

It appears that my intention to write had truly reached the limits of an ardor, a yearning, an earnestness. To begin with, I wrote about the birds and animals observed around me; but I showed them to no one and merely tore them and cast them away. I would also try scribbling a few lines of poetry on the bare earth, but didn't like them and deleted them. A lot of time was lost in the process. Those days, if I would hear someone singing nicely, I would also like to sing; if someone was even dancing, I would be interested to do likewise; if someone would paint a nice picture or write nicely, I would be eager to do the same—what a restless mind I had!

Amid this very fidgetiness, I had started, knowingly or unknowingly, sowing the seeds of creativity. They had seemingly started sprouting. I had developed a habit of reading literary books and of copying lines from pages that I kept in exercise books. This also helped me sow the seeds of creativity in me. When I would go through the biographies of some struggling or rebellious individuals, I would feel like following their footsteps. It was then that I had stepped into the field of literary writing. Those writings would not be good either, but since they were slightly better than the initial ones, I was encouraged a bit and showed them to a person elder than me, who lived as a tenant in our house. I could not remember his name now. He was fairly fond of me. If he would come home with a new book, he would share it with me and would suggest that I ought to read that one. *Even if you had loved me so much, I neither recall your name now nor know about the place where you were or wherever you hailed from. Do please forgive me—for I could not recognize you.*

Yes, as he read them and said, 'It's good, try to do better,' my pleasure had known no bounds. Such moments of pleasure had come but rarely in my life—so I can never ever forget that day, because one never forgets such golden moments. Whatever be it, the seeds of creativity had begun splitting to sprout and bud. Now, the colors of enthusiasm had started slowly spilling over my life and, along with them, the rays of hopes had also been spreading. The process of reading and writing went ahead nonstop. Many people who visited our house on some errand or the other would return astonished at my activities. They would particularly be fascinated at the words I wrote, and would say, "It is surprising that this girl can write so nicely—and, that too, by holding the pen in-between her toes. God's ways are astounding and inscrutable, beyond our comprehension." For them, I might have been sent to the earth by God to perform some *leela*. And they thought our little mind does not understand the ways of God.

It is likely that those very people may have spread the words around that there existed an unusual girl. Some of our tenants may also have done the same thing. Anyway, I am unaware as to how the world outside came to know about a miraculous girl who writes with her toes. That resulted in more and more curious people occasionally trickling to our house.

Time proceeded ahead along its own lines. Gradually, the seeds of my creativity were germinating. After a spell of time, this news started taking the shape of some kind of sensation and I became a censure in everyone's eyes. Our house, which had hitherto appeared like a mortuary, started to be a centre of human activity. The beeline that people started making to our house had turned it into quite a different place. It was then that the walls of casteist division in our house got pulled down and the traditional belief that low-caste people weren't to be permitted entry into it got shattered. I had been extremely delighted to see that the walls of apartheid that had stood there for untold number of years had gone. After all, I had always carried the credo that all human beings were equal. The same credo had now been won, and our house was gradually taking the shape as the place with a commonality of thoughts and ideas—anyone could come and go. This place was marked by the same behavior toward people of all castes, creeds, genders, and classes. My parents would, however, occasionally express their dissatisfaction and point an accusation toward me. I would tell them that all were human beings.

Meanwhile, the garden of my creativity had started to be filled with well-grown plants, as it were. Ultimately, they grew mature—or, in other words, my writings had started fructifying. The buds and flowers of my creativity looked quite healthy and attractive. In a sense, I started seeing my life as worthy and meaningful.

⚭

Walking along a Wider Path

Of late, scarcity of exercise books, pens, pencils, and erasers had been a thing of the past. People visiting our house would bring them for me, and some of them would also gift a little bit money. As I had no earning of my own yet, the few rupees gifted by others would also appear like a windfall. I was a daughter of the have-nots. I had myself started purchasing clothes for me with the money thus collected. The family had also started getting a little support. The exercise books and pens that would be extra, I had started sparing for my younger siblings. I was thus being established in people's mind as an unusual girl who wrote with her toes. My life had taken a turn for the better—it was a pleasant and delightful moment. I started seeing my life as a beautiful thing.

People hadn't merely started expressing their admiration and displaying goodwill, but were also placing a kind of faith in me and respecting me. As words spread and people started thronging around me, a few media persons had also started visiting our house. Perhaps I was being taken as someone newsworthy. What more would I expect? That was in itself a great thing for a young girl like me.

I was around fourteen or fifteen years of age at the time. I had started making news in the local media as a girl who wrote with her toes. Until then, my name as a literary author had been new to the readers. I had just started coming in the newspapers of the capital, that is, Kathmandu. I do not recall now as to who were the people to give me a place as a news item or those that penned write-ups about me; I must express my gratitude to them.

Yes, my journey had started going along wider paths. On top of it, life was becoming more colorful, and I had started enjoying those colors. As I have said, I would accept some money given to me by visitors, but I never begged from anyone. But somehow, some unwanted and baseless rumors had also started circulating. I felt that poet Bhupi Sherchan had named this country a land of rumors and gossips, for nothing. But if one proceeds along a correct and proper path, gossips can make no difference. In my case also, there were not only negative aspects, but positive one as well—and the positive aspects had been swallowing the negatives ones—a public life, I feel, really a different from the personal. I was also being drawn toward a public life without realizing it. Despite the fact that my personal life had been dogged by various pains and tensions, I started forgetting them as I kept on meeting the various people who would visit me, and getting engaged in chats with them.

It was around those times that I came across local media persons or literary figures such as Geeta Adhikari, Ramesh Chandra Adhikari, Alaka Adhikari, Umesh Chandra Adhikari, Tanuja Pokhrel, Girish Chandra Pokhrel, Pushkar Joshi, Sanjaya Sontoshi Rai, Vujay Subedi and others. Acquaintance with them created, in a way, an easier environment along my life's journey. All of them had their contributions either by way of publishing news and write-ups about me in the papers, or by way of talking to other people about me. They also gradually started getting closer to me, till they ultimately became my intimate companions. I shared with them the moments of joy and grief. I had started enjoying the happy moments of life. Though I was away, I was being recognized as a girl who writes poems. Although I hadn't been far removed from literary world, I hadn't made my mark as a female literary writer until then. But as I would show my creations to friends, they would be astonished, turn the writings this way or that, and say, "It's very nice." Though one of my identities was a girl who knows how to write with her toes, this was establishing a different identity of mine. Time also did not want to limit my experience.

It was a separate kind of journey. There were many a character who gave me company and, by holding their hands, I have steered my life's ship and have moved it ahead. A girl who had figured in some news stories as one with a moderate education, I had gradually been spreading my wings in the literary firmament. By then, I had already attained sixteen years of age. I had also already gone through many books and literary, cultural, political, and social subjects. I cannot remember all those titles now; however, I don't want to underestimate their value. The process of literary creation was going on unabated; I had not stopped analyzing the environment around us, our social customs and manners, our way of life and the like. I had also, by the time, been slowly making myself known as a young female literary writer instead of a girl who scribbled alphabets with her toes.

Along the same journey, I came across Lekhnath Bhandari, Shova Gautam, Ramyata Limbu and Sameep Sharma (*delet*). My journey started becoming easier in their company. They started extending creative support to me; one of them, Lekhnath Bhandari, kept helping me out until much later. By that time, I had finely gone through the works of many, including Parijat, Modnath Prasrit, Khagendra Sangraula, Ramesh Vikal and the like. I had also read some books of Russian, Chinese, and Vietnamese languages translated in Nepali versions and had been influenced by them. Naturally, one is quite sensitive in their youthful age. The philosophy that influenced them in that age would leave a lasting influence. I studied books on Russian Revolution, Chinese Peoples' Revolution, and Vietnamese Revolution very closely. I read novels of revolution. While reading the strugglesome life of the characters of those novels, I used to think *How brave, how strugglesome, and how truly beautiful lives!*

I used to be allured by their lives and feel like living the kind of life they had lived. But alas, I could not live the life of my choice. Even though I had not been able to live a life as desired by myself, I had started hating people who oppressed the common people and those that heaped injustice and tyranny on the weaker sections of populace. Even if my life could not be as beautiful as those of the heroes and heroines of novels and stories, it was also blossoming and opening up on its own. Even if it tumbled down by tripping over something, it would promptly rise itself and recover; even if it suffered from an injury, it would get cured in no time. And it was bound to be—otherwise it could not go ahead in its journey.

A co-traveler that I had then met used to run a periodical called *Navapratibhaa* at the time. He is said to have hailed from Pyuthan. He gave me a nationwide publicity by way of publishing my interview in that children's magazine, although I was slightly over-aged. Likewise, another monthly periodical, *Nawayuvaa*, had an investigative write-up on me published in its issue of the *Bhadau* month in the year 2053. That was penned by Bidur Subedi and Shova Gautam. I must also remember all the members of the publication house known as Mulyankan Prakasahn Griha, nor must I forget that publication which helped make Jhamak blossom by making the soil fertile. I am remembering all hands engaged in that publication and, as I stand on the threshold of the present, I make, by means of these words, an offering of respectful bouquets to all the characters who had, at the time, helped widen the narrow road of my life, and to those who gave me company in some point of life or the other. I salute all those helpful hands.

Life's Colour in Letters of the Alphabet

Be it the various rumors or the talks and discussions, they not only acted as a factor to encourage my adolescent heart, but also created in me a feeling that I must do something. No more was I subjected to negative comments about myself. The visitors to our house would not wish I was dead as it was the case earlier. On the contrary, they would extend their wishes for my long life and progress. I felt life was beautiful. The desire to live, which was once extinct, began budding up afresh. My literary journey was also taking its course. By the time, a few of my poems and verses or lyrics had also got into the print. I no more have those periodicals in my collection, nor do I recall their names. The one periodical I remember is *Nawayuvaa* monthly, which not only had a write-up published about me, but also helped reach my literary creations to many readers, admirers, and well-wishers by having them published. I have always remained obliged to that publication. I express my gratitude to it as I beg it to have me excused because I cannot remember every detail today. Those who wanted to see me alive must have been delighted. The appearance of one's creations published in the media, I found, makes one feel extremely elated. On my part, I had also been so much excited to see my first composition appear in print, which I fail to translate that moment of delight into words.

I wished I could show my published compositions to all. I desired that all should read them and, as such, I would keep them with me. I would show them to the visitors to our house. Some of them might also have been vexed at times, but in those moments of enthusiasm and ecstasy, I was unable to realize their internal feelings. A vanity that I also am something also appeared within me. But I had heard from the elders the adage that one shouldn't give way to nervousness at every little trouble, nor should one be intoxicated even at a little happiness. Where my vanity would also vanish somewhere around, I did not know. I did not consciously display my vanity toward anyone, but if it had leaked out without my overt knowledge, I will say to those minds, which may have been unconsciously hurt, "I am sorry, okay?"

Be that as it may, a little bud was in the process of blooming. Someone could also have plucked it and thrown it the meantime. But there were some others, the so-called educated and enlightened people in the village, who would, on seeing me compose poems, say, "This is an intellectual field, not meant for a girl like you. You would better use your legs in sewing clothes or rolling breads and earn some money."

I felt contempt toward those people; I would get the intellect of such so-called enlightened and civilized people. I would get inwardly furious at the level of thinking of those people, but I would suppress my emotions and scribble down such words to tell them, "It isn't for you to say whether or not I can do it—the future will show. Do not take me for an object to make money by displaying tricks."

On hearing me say so, they would get angry and say, "If it's so, you'll rot and die."

I would add, "If you think I am destined to rot and die, you may as well spare yourself the trouble of shaping my future." That would disperse them away—I don't know where!

Even if they felt offended and walked away, nothing happened to me. Their own faces got darkened. On my part, I had to carve a track of life for myself. I was doing so and also walking along it. In any case, my literary journey was becoming meaningful on its own. Many people would call me a litterateur of the future and also bless me. Their blessings were yet to fructify. A sense of different kind of responsibility was inwardly scorching me, because I would feel whether I could live up to the expectations of such people or not. I also had a doubt about myself. They have such a great faith on me even as I have just appeared in print; *what must have made it so?* I would keep on thinking inwardly that people must have seen some promise in me so as to repose their faith on me. Such thoughts would make me pleased with myself. Youthfulness had just been touching me.

Only one desire had cropped up in me—it was to keep on living by doing something on my own. In fact, I had started feeling awkward in having to survive on the earnings of others. No more was I a child. I could understand everything, perceive, and sense everything. I would feel that I was becoming a burden on my family and relatives. I would despise living like a burden on anyone. But I had no alternative either. What a helpless, disabled life! But no matter how sour the taste of life was, I kept on dragging it.

Talks and comments about me had spread quite far and wide, even on the basis of rumors and gossips. My stray writings had started appearing in print. Weeklies such as the then *Vijayapur* (published from Sunsari) and *Karkamal* (Biratnagar, Morang) particularly used to carry my writings. The then editor of *Karkamal* was a sister (*didi*), Kamal Kasaju by name. I had also met her. Likewise, there was another sister (*didi*), Ganga Baral, working for the *Vijayapur*, through whom my write-ups would appear in that weekly. I had no work of mine published in a book from until that time. I could not find publishers too. But I hadn't stopped writing. I was getting established as a known face amid many contemporary friends such as Tanuja Pokhrel, Alaka Adhikari, Geeta Adhikari and many others. We used to recite our poems or listen to those of the others when we would meet. They were senior to me both in age and in creations, but they would appreciate my writings. I had thus gradually made an impression on my contemporaries. My life was also flowing like a poem. I would like to quote a poem published in my anthology *Sankalpa* (1998):

Determination

Why do you ask me
For the definition of life
Life is decorated in itself
Please experience it.

Every moment, look
In the innocent throbs
The reality of life
Whenever you find the existence of life
Then you will know the definition of life.

How beautiful is the life
How sweet
You will know it
Ah, I wish I could
Ever traverse
Along the path of life
I like to continue this life
With a determination
Ever, ever . . .

My father was an ex-employee of the postal department. It had been fairly long since he had quit that job. Since I had been the daughter of an ex-employee, my first writing was published by the Postal Employees' Welfare Fund in Biratnagar. It was arranged by Bhim Koirala. He was also possibly an employee there. I do not know where he hailed from, nor am I aware as to where he is now or what he does. But in any case, he had extended a hand of cooperation toward me at the time.

It was in the year 2055 (1998) that I appeared before my readers with my first collection of poems, *Sankalpa*. The number of my readers had also increased, albeit in some measure. I had received one thousand rupees as my honorarium for that work and that was my very first earning. Although, prior to that, the then parliamentarian Rakam Chemjong had rewarded me with twelve hundred rupees by way of an encouragement for having exhibited some talent in literature. He had also rewarded four other women of the district besides me at the time. He had been associated with the United Marxist—Leninist Party (UML).

Some namesake big guns of the village remarked, saying, "A poor man's daughter was purchased by the UML for twelve hundred rupees, a deprived girl who had seen nothing was coaxed and cajoled with that amount."

I was furious at hearing such baseless comments. I felt hatred toward the intellectual level of those so-called educated people and said, "If the UML had purchased me for twelve hundred rupees, buy me for twenty-four hundred rupees yourself. If you can buy and sell human values, go ahead and do it." When I had said so, they were perhaps of the opinion that to taste me was not worth it. No more did I hear any such moments since then. I was conscious, albeit a little, in the matter of thoughts and ideologies, even when I had been an adolescent, it may be said, because I myself never thought of harming anybody nor did I wish for anyone's discomfiture. I also never liked any person who thought of harming others; possibly because of that attitude, I kept on walking along my own path and drove my life's chariot in my own manner and style.

Oh yes, never in the past I had seen so much money earned by dint of my own labor. As such, I considered myself quite fortunate. I had been elated because I had never hoped to see and enjoy such pleasant moments in life. Now I had started pouring out my miseries and pains by way of letters of the alphabet only. How could a person like me, who had always lived in miseries and troubles, ever hope to detach myself from them? Nevertheless, the pages of my life had started getting painted with the colors of delight and pleasure. Life, it appeared, is both a pleasure and a pain.

People who had read and liked my first book would write letters of appreciation to me. They would congratulate me for having come out with a creative writing even though I had been disabled and infirm. Some would also urge me to go for a second reprint. Here also I felt the pains of deprivation, because the inability to bring out publication in time in response to the demands of the readers was also an outcome of deprivation. The more prominent periodicals coming out of the capital would not spare space for my writings. I used to feel, *Why this discrimination between the high and the low?*

I had been setting forth along a separate journey while storing in my mind similar bitter experiences. Meanwhile, Baal Manch Nepal, an organization, reportedly selected me as the best child (juvenile) talent and awarded me the Kavitaram Children's Literary Talent Prize. My journey ahead became easier and smoother hitherto. Also, a year later, came the announcement of the Asweekrit Vichaar Saahitya Purashkaar, a literary award, having been awarded to me. It is said that it had been rather tough for the proponent of that award, because none of my publications had appeared in the market so far. I wonder how the matter was resolved, but the award was given to none other than me. Many people, including Dr. Kavitaram Shrestha, Lekhnath Bhandari, Bijayaraj Acharya, and Harigovinda Luintel had come forward to encourage a newcomer like me established at the time. It was by catching their helping hands that I had crossed the winding river of life. Life has brought me up to this juncture. *Oh life, what shall I call you—a curse and pain, or a beautiful boon of nature?* I had, at long last, started asking such questions to life itself.

So far I had not been capable of publishing any book. I didn't even have the means to sustain myself, then where could I have obtained the money needed to publish a book! My literary life had also been forging ahead amid such scarcity and pains. There would be hordes of people coming in and out of our house. There were times when we did not even have time to partake of our meals. I was also a human being and it was natural for me to feel lazy at times or to get fed up. How could I have satisfied the curiosity of everyone? I couldn't. They would only express their grudges and never appreciate my problems. I told them time and over again, "Do place yourself in my position and reflect for a while whether it is easy or difficult for me." In the course of a similar meeting with people visiting our house, I came across a publisher toward the middle of the year 1999. His name was Basudev Shakal. He said he hailed from Sankhuwasabha or Chainpur. He is presently said to have built a house for himself somewhere at Gaurighat in Kathmandu.

Those days he had set up a firm called Makalu Books and Stationery in Kathmandu and used to publish, sell, and distribute books and periodicals. He proposed to get my second collection of poems *Aafnai Chitaa Agnisikhaatira*, published (literally My Own Dead Body toward the Fire). As that would have given me an opportunity to reach my readers afresh, I readily accepted his proposal. Through him, I also got in touch with another person who wanted to publish my third book *Maanche Bhitrakaa Yoddhaharu* (The Warriors within Man). She was Sita Gurung, a resident of Sanepa, Kathmandu. Those days she had been an employee at Royal Nepal Airlines. They had my two books published and also made arrangements for my entry into Kathmandu. I had personally received the Ashweekrit Vichaar Sahitya Purashkaar literary award only on my arrival at Kathmandu. My fourth publication *Awashaanpacchiko Aagaman* (Arrival after Death), a collection of writings on various genres, was published by Ashmita Mahilaa Prakashan Griha, with financial assistance from such Kathmandu-based organizations as Sanchaar Tatha Srot Sanstha, Martin Chautari, Anaupachaarik Kshetra Sewaa Kendra (INSEC), and Baal Majdoor Sarokaar Kendra (CWIN). Many people, including Manju Thapa, Usha Titikshu, Lekhnath Bhandari, Lila Adhikari, Ganesh Bhandari, Raghunath Lamichaney, Akhanda Bhandari, and Dandapani Upadhyaya had come forward to give a concrete shape to the project. At last, I had been established as a new creative writer.

I had come directly to the dazzling capital city of Nepal directly from a dark and remote area. Everything there was new to me; every face was new like a stranger. The only known faces around me were those of my parents and my younger sister Anamika, aged only a month and half. My parents gave birth to her at a much later age. Had they given birth to her earlier, there would not have been such a long gap between her age and that of mine. Our parents thought it an easy task to beget four or five children! Such an attitude is the result of ignorance on the part of the Nepalese people, and one of the factors of ruining the health of the Nepalese women. What am I to say to my parents? But even if I say nothing, I am astonished at what they have done, despite their being fully aware of it. There was also another younger sister of mine, Mausami, older than Anamika. She was also as pretty as a flower; what a soft and lovable darling she was!

Pleasure in Correspondence

$\mathcal{I}$ may have crossed just between seventeen or eighteen springs at the time. At that age, I was also keen on pouring my heart out to someone. I was slowly being known among the general people as a girl who scribbled out pieces of literature with the help of her toes. I can never repay the debt of gratitude I owe to those friends of mine who helped me express my thoughts and feelings in a more colorful manner during those days. Yes, a person apparently needs someone who lends a company to him or her and shares sentiments—and I was also in need of someone. At that age, many friends used to write letters to me. They would not only write to me but would also enthuse me to do something in life.

At the time I had begun writing, an older brother from Udayapur used to write to me letters filled with pure love. He is a teacher by profession. He said he lived in the village of Chanaute under Lekhani Village Development Council (Committee) and was named Dilchandra Nandan, although his actual name is Bishnu Muri Magar. I have not seen him yet; but he not only showered his brotherly love and affection on me, but would also write all the time, when I was sentimentally lonely, that I was not alone. He would pacify me with love whenever I was in an angry mood. A person like you must not be angry—he would advise me in his letters.

He is one among those who have loved me affectionately, who always inspired to continue the struggle of life, who became happy wholeheartedly in my happiness, who shared with me in moments of grief. By standing close to my feelings, he showed all honor and constant hope. He would write in beautiful letters. Occasionally, I would get tired of life and write to him, "Dada, enough is enough. I don't want to struggle any longer."

In reply, he would from time to time keep expressing his soft feelings in simple words and in a beautiful hand, saying, "My sister Jhamak, you should not be weak." I still remember how pure had his feelings been toward me. Till this day, my relations with him are as pure and friendly.

Like him, there was another friend from Paanchthar, Lingden by clan name, who had entered into correspondence with me at the time. His pen name was Akinchan. I also treated him as my elder brother and would express my feelings accordingly. I also remember yet another person, Sagar Mani Gyawali from Gulmi district. He was also a man with kind and gentlemanly feelings toward me.

In this way, I had met my friends connected through feeling and thought. But we did not limit our discussion to feelings merely. We shared in discussions and debates too. But when we disagreed about each other's points of views leading to debates, we stopped for sometime; we did not end up the relationship. We continued writing after sometime. We would not mention the point of debate in the next letter, and peace would resume. Thus, we continued enduring relationship of feeling and thought with many friends.

In that journey, we expressed clear variegated colors of thoughts and feelings. It was natural at that age; we would express anger and emotion, and sometimes restlessness and frustrations. Gradually, friends of feeling increased more; I don't remember their names however, but then, I will never forget their compassion, love, and affection.

Not that I did not have women friends who would also correspond with me, but also somehow my feelings and thoughts did not correspond with theirs. Like them, I did not know how to talk about subjects such as what to eat and what not to, how to dress, what makeup to use and the like. I was not physically good-looking as they were. I believed in beauty of the mind, and, despite their outward good looks, I did not find them internally beautiful. In my view, it's women like Mother Teresa, Madam Curie, and Florence Nightingale, who worked for the betterment of the world at large, who are truly beautiful.

Even while I was seventeen or eighteen years of age, not for a moment would naughty thoughts cross my mind. How would they? My limits were quite different from those of the others. For one thing, I had not been born with a physical shape like the other girls in general. Even a little restless feeling would not be treated as simple and looked at kindly. As a result, my exchange of letters with girls did not develop good relations. Whatever good relations I could establish through letters were with boys alone.

I looked at this peculiarity from a pure and untainted point of view. If you look at the world with loving and beautiful eyes, everything around you looks beautiful.

Those friends with whom I shared my pure and unstained feelings, oneness, and closeness, have left a deep impression on my mind's pages and they deserve to be truly respected. I shared not only closeness with them, but also the moments of my troubles and happiness. I do not know how they looked at me, but I never looked at them with a bad or selfish motive. All of them were older than me—as such they are my elder brothers, whom I will keep worshiping with flower garlands. As I turn the pages of my memory, I find their pure minds reflected all over their letters, which time can also browse through. How sweet were those moments! I feel happy the moment I recall them. Oh dear, what close and chummy moments they were!

Toward a Wider World

For the first time in life, I stepped into Kathmandu, the bright city of my dreams, in the month of Baisakh, 2057, that is, the Spring of 1998. I felt it myself. My goodness, what a huge city! So many people! Where are these people headed to? Where do they go, what do they eat? How tall and large buildings! I was awestruck and enthusiastic. The first time I had landed in Kathmandu, I was wondering where I was; I also wondered whether I was dreaming or was awake.

At the time, three of my books had been launched inside the vast and expansive auditorium of Nepal Pragya Pratisthan. Dr. Keshar Jung Rayamajhi, the then Chair of the State Council Standing Committee had done the launching honors for my two poetical anthologies, *Aafnai Chitaa Agnishikhaatira* (My Own Dead Body toward Fire (pyre)) and *Maanchhebhitrakaa Yoddhaaharu* (Warriors Within Men). At the time, he had been introduced to me as a high-profile personality. I used to feel, *No human being in this world is of either a high profile or a low profile. All are equal.*

I scribbled a blunt question on a small piece of paper in front of everyone, "Who is a great man and who is not?" He fixed his power specs, bent slowly, and read my words on the piece of paper. He must have thought that this girl is blunt and quite uncivilized. Drawing lines of wrinkles on his forehead, he resumed his seat of the Chief Guest. He sat silently except for a few words after the launching of the books. I thought, *It is the way big shots behave.* It appeared that I had not been able to show adequate respect toward Dr. Rayamajhi as expected by the others present. My publishers expressed dissatisfaction with me. The media persons close to the Royal Palace were said to have expressed much greater disappointment with me. One of them even came to my room and asked me, "Don't you like the king?"

No, I utterly dislike both king and kingship—said my mind. But instead of replying openly to him thus, I kept mum and merely smiled. For I didn't want to be known as an antimonarchist so early in my life.

Those who met me tried to throw one bait or the other at me. But I did not speak out my mind before anyone, nor did I mortgage self-respect and conscience before anyone. A kind of ideological war kept on raging that day too. They perhaps wanted me to petition and request the high people. But I rejected all such proposals. I thought, *How abominable they are!* But I could not express openly. It was my compulsion. But I didn't request any appeal begging some support. My parents, on the other hand, used to scold me, accusing me of being involved in politics. How could my poor parents know whether I was doing it or it was being done upon? I, a girl of a poor farmer, how could I be dishonest to the same class? No, I could not pawn my self-respect, could not do so even in my thought. That day, such thoughts kept waging war. I was not declined to lose that war either, because I was a girl who had been in search of an ideological freedom. In such a broad world, I could never agree that everybody should like my thoughts or ideologies nor they should accept mine.

Another of my books, a collection of miscellaneous writings entitled *Awasaan Pachhiko Aagaman* (Return after Death), was launched the next day in that very auditorium at the hands of *literati Shyam Prasad Sharma*. As it is, I had indirectly been exchanging my thoughts and ideas with Mr. Sharma, and the two of us would be discussing many literary, social, and other issues of contemporary interest through the medium of correspondence since much earlier. A kind of closeness and rapport had also been growing between the two of us for long. He is truly a simple man who loved me dearly. I would address him as *Thulobaba*, father's elder brother, and he also used to call me a daughter—and still does. But we had not met formally earlier. I was thus extremely delighted to have met such a respectable personality like him formally for the first time that day and also to have my book launched at his hands.

I have (had) not seen such a large gathering of people in my lifetime. It was a matter of another pleasure for me to see so many people at a time. I had been slightly awed in the course of the first day's function; but on the second day, I was not scared at all, and even put forward some of my views to the audience. I had requested my friends, writers, and artists to go to the people, share with them, and write a question of their freedom.

When I said that, a loud applaud could be heard. History will tell how far those clappers have become responsible toward people. But that day we could hear long and loud clapping. I thought they had welcomed the young writer there with a red flower in hand. Thus, the brilliant dream city of Kathmandu welcomed the newcomer with clapping.

I may say that I had, by then, got an entry into the world of Nepali letters as a newly established writer. I realized I had lots of responsibilities and challenges ahead. Those moments of happiness spread endlessly. As I reached that turning point in life, I had, at long last, started feeling that life was beautiful. After all, I was also a human being who could laugh at the time of happiness and weep at the time of sorrow.

Till that time, I had been watching a sky only from my kitchen—a sky that covered narrow corridor; the sun I used to see was also small. Now I had started feeling that my house as well as my world was very small; the world of others was seen, in comparison, as a vast and expansive one—a world which I had never seen hitherto. As a person who had arrived at this world walking along a bridge built by the pen, I had been quite allured by this dazzling town. Everything in the town was new to me. I would feel like constantly gazing at—and touching—the running cars. After all, a town is a town. That may be the reason why the village folk, once they come to the town, do not feel like returning to their old places. For their lifeless villages lack the dazzling lights of the town. On my part also, it is not that I did not shed tears when I had to return to my village after visiting Kathmandu. But I could also observe from a close range the bitter reality of this otherwise bright world, because the faces of small pavement traders were lined with dread and anxiety. They were worried about police.

What did this bright town give to many street girls and boys that thronged the garbage dumps searching for something or the other? What did it give to the *Naamley* load-bearing coolies? It does not even provide them with a good night's rest. Howsoever beautiful this town might be, it seemingly swallows whole the have-nots living here. Why does everyone like this cruel, dirty town? We can see the total picture of Nepal in the dirty cruelty of this town. It is seen in the torn tattered dresses of those who struggle for survival. From these torn clothes can be seen the nakedness of Nepal. Those who took me round Kathmandu town would often ask, "How did you like Kathmandu?"

I would be at a loss to what to tell them—should I tell them I like it or that I did not like it? I would prefer to keep mum. Likewise, when they saw some dhoti-wearing persons, they would comment, "These *dhotiwaalas* snatch away the share of this country's laborers and fill their coffers at home with the money earned here." I wondered why these so-called intellectuals felt that way. A laborer may hail from anywhere; if he is sweating himself out for us, I felt that our mentality was rather shallow and abhorrent. I did not find any human sentiments affinity or kinmanship anywhere around. I found a kind of emptiness on the faces of the people.

I found people's faces were deserted. Having collected such impressions, bitter and sweet, I returned to my own village from Kathmandu. I held totally different experience, even during a short trip to it. I regarded my native desolate. But I never got scared of reality nor was disheartened; I rather accepted reality.

In that dense forest of population, I frequented my visits—coming and going. This game is quite strange. I had to commute to and from Kathmandu many times. There were occasions where honors and awards would follow.

On one of such occasions, some people mooted the proposal that I should write a petition to the then king Birendra and queen Aishwarya seeking an audience with them. They may have felt that if I once meet the king and the queen, they might show pity toward me and give me something that could establish in life. There were people related to the royal court; they insisted much. They put pressures on me, saying, "You have to submit petition before the queen for an audience to be granted." Now I was in a great fix. I wanted to come out of that place. I kept mum, and on the plea that I was hungry, returned to my room, because I was the least inclined to write a petition to the king and queen in order to meet them. That attitude of mine enraged some people, but what difference did it make to me? Nothing.

Every person had their freedom of thought. Why should have some people been unhappy when I made use of that very freedom of thought was something beyond my comprehension. Or time will tell. Some people even said that I had been instigated by antimonarchy elements to take the stand I did, but it was not true—no one had tutored me. Whatever the people may have been thinking of me, life went ahead without stopping. That same year, a collection of my write-ups, *Samjhanakaa Baachhitaaharu*, was brought out by Sahitya Sadan, Kathmandu, as my fifth book. Thus, five offspring had come out of the womb of my mind by then.

It's not all a big deal to give birth to a child. A happy aspect in a mother's life is her capacity to bear healthy and strong offspring. While I leave it to history to judge whether I could deliver healthy and strong offspring from my mental womb, I can say this much, "I have also become a mother. How a happy thing it is for one to be a mother!" A girl considered as useless and relegated to the backstage has emerged into the field of creativity in order to sow and grow plants. How far people would have helped me in those flowers, time alone will say. Many people have helped me in planting and growing these saplings. It is perhaps impossible for anyone to please all people around the world—this is a hard reality of the human behavior. That's why I also may not have pleased all people, nor did I live up to their expectations, because I also had some features of a living being filled with a little conscience and bearing some thoughts. Some people might like them while other might not—that's but natural.

Hunger for Knowledge
and Proposal for Kathmandu

Yes, man's hunger for knowledge is apparently limitless. I also had so much hunger for knowledge that it had touched an utmost pinnacle. Wherever I would reach, I wanted to learn or pick up something new. This characteristic of mine had helped me quite a bit in the task of learning and getting to know many things. The knowledge and skills I had earned were not enough. As it is, a man's process of learning never stops from the time of birth to the time of death. When it stops, the life itself gets extinct.

I had just started experiencing life. In my case, it was not simple and easy to obtain even the rudiments of knowledge in a formal manner. In fact, there is not completeness of knowledge. Comparatively some are more knowledgeable than others. Moreover, it was impossible for me even to earn any formal education. Whatever little I had learned and known was by virtue of self-confidence and self-study. But those who would look for a balance in knowledge saw many weaknesses and shortcomings in me. Of course, all people have some kind of weaknesses and shortcomings or the other. I also had plenty of them. Some suggested that I should go through all the textbooks taught between Class II to Class X. Others might have felt ashamed to do; but I did not feel ashamed at all. I went through them all. But the way I went through them was virtually the opposite of what they had told me to do, because neither was I a child nor the kind of a person to obey everyone's bidding. I learned only to the extent that would be necessary and of use to me. Neither was it necessary for me to get my life stuck by mugging the theories of science, nor to dig out the secrets that the mathematical formulas would teach, nor even to draw the lines and angles of geometry.

Quite a few scientific truths, I had observed and experienced in the open earth itself. Even if I had not learned the arithmetical formulas, it was not possible for me to be either misguided or cheated by everyone, as I had picked up the necessary arithmetic that would come in handy in people's daily life—and that was sufficient as far as I was concerned. If there was the need for anything in my life, it was to go ahead of a narrow awareness so as to attain a broader one. Some people would ask me, "Do you also know English?"

I would say, "No, I don't." I couldn't catch what they would talk among themselves, as they looked at me, in English; I would imagine they were probably slighting me. Hadn't it been a case, they would have conversed among themselves either in Nepali or in some other mother tongues, I felt. I could not ascertain as to whether they had been showing off their knowledge and capabilities, or displaying their civilized one upmanship.

But I also had a keen yearning to learn the English language. Some people suggested that if I could have an access to a library, I would have more easily and quickly picked up the language; they even proposed to my parents that they would take me to Kathmandu. They also offered to arrange free board and lodging facilities for me. But my parents would hear of it on the plea that the household affairs would be jeopardized and the other children's future would be ruined. As for myself, I had a keen desire to read about and understand the world around me from a broader perspective, as also to learn about science and acquire knowledge to the utmost possible extent. In other words, I wanted to live in Kathmandu in order to acquire more knowledge. But

I was not physically capable of staying alone, as I could not do anything for myself, so much so that others have got to assist me even in going to the toilet, besides helping me put on or off my clothes as well!

Age and Studies

As my parents turned down such a nice proposal meant for my stay at Kathmandu, thereby nipping my desire in the bud to receive further enlightenment, I was furious with my parents. I thought, *What is the reason to prove that their family life will spoil if I went to Kathmandu?* Can't one of them look after the siblings? If both the parents won't separate, can't they send Mina to accompany me? What would have gone wrong if she were with me? My parents could not think that way. It seemed to me that, as far as they were concerned, it was enough if the future of their other children could be improved. It was not necessary for me to learn anything and to know anything for building up a base on which I could create an easier environment for living. Or, in other words, it was okay even if my future prospect weren't better. That kind of mind-set of theirs stood as an obstacle in the fulfillment of my desire to live in Kathmandu for learning something more, knowing something more. I returned to my village with a heavy heart. But even on my return to the village, I didn't cease writing, nor did I stop reading anything that would come my way.

Meanwhile, I had let it be indirectly known to my friends that I was in need of a teacher to coach me English language. On hearing rumors through them, a teacher came to my home itself. His name was Milan Dahal. We entered into an understanding that he will teach and I will learn. He had said that he hailed from somewhere in Jhapa district (now they say he has shifted to Kathmandu). Those days he was staying with his family in a house he got built slightly below that of ours. Now they say that having sold his house, he has shifted to Kathmandu. He was my first teacher in life. Occasionally he would display the bitter side of his nature, and at others more amiable—well, that is human nature. One should bear with everything. But even if he would make his teachings easily understandable to me, I would forget all about them the very next moment. He would get fed up at times and say, "No matter how much I teach you, you will not learn." It was natural for him to say so. My mind could not grasp as much as he taught because I was a human being, not a machine.

He could hardly teach me for two months, when he left the place on being transferred elsewhere. How much might I have learned within a matter of two months? He left, and I remained busy with my business. Time passed in this way.

After quite some time, I came across another teacher named Madhav Mishra. He has his house in Dhankuta, some distance below that of ours. He also could not teach me for more than three months—he didn't find time. That was the end of my learning of the English language. It stopped there.

As people saw that I had started learning to read and write A, B, C, D at a late age, they would say, "You have started studying now? Aren't you too old?" and the like. That was their way of mocking at me.

The notion that a person should stop learning to read and write at a certain age is totally wrong, however. As for me, age would hold a view directly opposite to that; for me, age would never stand as an obstacle to anyone's education and learning. A man can learn anything at any time that is favorable to him. That's why I would reply to those who taunted me and ridiculed me, saying, "This was the only moment that came with an auspicious omen for me to study. Though I am quite grown up in age, a child in learning." I smiled. That kind of reply plugged their mouths, as it were; for they didn't dare teasing me anymore. Though I was grown up in Nepali culture, there was no point in sustaining every practice, if they were evil. But the question arises: *If the people in a society mock at a person when he or she wants to learn anything, what kind of a society or culture is that?*

As for me, my enthusiasm was never dampened, no matter who said what, because, in my opinion, whatever I had done was 100 percent right; what did it matter if the others considered it wrong?

In any case, had I been to Kathmandu, I needn't perhaps have terminated my English language lessons after mere five months, even though there also every man has a price. Kathmandu is a place where you will get everything if you have money and won't get anything if you haven't. There was no chance I would have money with me. On top of it, I was economically poor and physically so infirm. It wouldn't have been nice to expect others to be of help. As it is, it was getting difficult even to sustain ourselves on the earnings of our parents. What's more, there I would have been compelled to depend on the mercy of others. That wasn't an acceptable proposition to me at all. Even as it is, I had a little self-respect in me too. That's why I traced my steps back from Kathmandu to my own village.

I always loved my village; it was ever beautiful; a place where my life was deeply rooted; the climate and weather, the water, soil and everything formed my life cycle.

However, after my return to the village, I didn't find any person to teach me English language. Not that there were no teachers around, only that they would hesitate to teach me as I was a public person, and they were afraid lest their weaknesses and shortcomings be exposed and they might earn a bad name. What was more, since our house was located a bit further from the town inside the village, they considered the distance involved in coming and going a bit daunting.

The biggest hurdle, however, was a meager remuneration; although the first teacher who taught me English had also demanded a remuneration of five thousand rupees a month. What was the motive behind his demanding that much money for two to three hours' class wasn't known to me. As it is, even the earnings of my entire family wasn't that much. How can we survive by paying him that much? I didn't say to him anything; I only thought why people do think that money can be earned so easily. They regard money as everything. What a selfish world! But when he had an inkling that his demands had no chance of getting met, *he had come to terms.* In that sense, *he must be said to have been liberal toward me.* I came to know later that he had demanded such a huge amount of remuneration only to view his pride शेखी भार्नं (p. 160).

I felt very bad. I had not challenged him in wealth nor was I proud of anything. *What kind of* शेखी *did he . . . I don't know. Please check page 161 once more.*

૪

Disability and Our Society

The society had still looking at me as a pitiable disabled girl. Every deed I performed is linked with my disability. No matter how educated and cultured people might have been, their mentality is still savage. There is a traditional belief in our society that any disability or infirmity is the consequence of his sins in the past life, that it is a matter of shame for disabled persons to be brought out in public, and that they should be kept indoors all the time and the like. The eye with which people looked at me wasn't different either. So much so that even my creativity would be linked with my disability. Like if I wrote about the pains and agonies of someone, the readers would pitifully comment that I had portrayed pain since my own life is filled with pain and agony. Also, if I didn't know something, people would think that my infirmity had stood in the way of my knowing it.

But my thinking and approach was totally reverse. My thoughts, conscience, and feelings weren't different because of my physical infirmity. I wasn't helpless as people would think I was. They thought themselves complete in all respects; they thought whole and all in all themselves. If I didn't know anything, it had nothing to do with my body but with my brain and intellect. That's why I wouldn't like people to look or treat me with pity. I was also a human being; I also had ideas, feelings, self-respect—everything. But people regarded it just reverse. Even when I received any prize, award, honor, or medal, people would think that they had been given to me as I was a disabled person to write essays, poems, epics and so on. Wouldn't any of them deserve to receive any prize? In the eyes of some people, I had nothing else besides disability and helplessness. But I wasn't what they would see me like.

I was a useless person in their eyes; in my eyes, they were educated, civilized, great fools. Because I had done no harm to them, why do they have negative attitude toward me? I was a human being too; why do they try to link pity in whatever I deserve and win—prize, award, honor, medal and so on? But not all people in the world are good, nor are all people bad. If there is an existence of evil in society, so is there the existence of good. Even the so-called high-level people in the village would look at me with a hateful eye, even if they couldn't express it publicly. At such times, I would feel that this world apparently belongs only to the strong and the well-endowed; weak or infirm people wouldn't even be regarded as humans. I was also a human being, but my happiness didn't bring smile on the lips of anyone, my enthusiasm didn't mean anything to them. People would fling the flames of fury and the dart of jealousy and envy on me. I don't know why they considered me unshapely and ugly. But there were also people who loved me and saw beauty in me. There were those too, who would feel happy at my smile, laughed when I laughed, and felt sorry at my pains. That's why life was beautiful even as it was.

Man is apparently jealous by nature. They feel—*Why can't I achieve but only he?* The reason why the world would become displeased at a little progress I made was not for nothing that Poet Laureate Lekhnath Poudyal had written:

"Let me be the only one to eat well and wear well,
All pleasures and enjoyments for me,
Let all weaker ones die . . ." and so on.

How nicely he had described conscienceless and selfish people—I enjoyed it. As for me also, there was no reason to be puffed up at a slight achievement, nor to be distressed when I had a little setback. I was the same person, the only difference being that more and more people had started knowing me; I *had started being appreciated*. Initially, I would feel that was also a great thing. And I might have a secret desire in me for that. And perhaps natural too, for there was nothing unusual for a girl despised by the society itself to expect some approbation from the others and to expect a life similar to that of others. To be frank, I must have expected such appreciation in a slightly greater measure than the others; that's why, even if people only slightly pointed at my deficiency, I would be deeply and disproportionately disturbed or deeply hurt. But how could I be a person without deficiencies? Merely that I may have looked at the other people with a greater anger than was fair or normal.

They thought one should always bow and bend; they thought the disabled and infirm are not humans, but I don't yield to anyone. I never bowed down before anyone. Because, even if the others didn't regard me as a complete human being, I would take myself to be as good a human being as anybody else; no matter how ungainly others found me, in my eyes I was never so, because if a man cannot do justice to himself, he can do no justice to the others either. Whatever a man does, he should first be satisfied in himself; only then can he satisfy the others. It is, therefore, that I did never take up a thing that didn't satisfy me. Time goes on teaching the human beings one lesson after another. In my own life, it had been putting me to test; destiny was also doing the same. Apparently, poet Madhav Ghimire has put it right thus:

> A bo-tree plant will germinate
> even though it were by breaking a rock
> The power of creation is so,
> it will never fail in the world
>
> —Madhav Ghimire

In my case, even if I hadn't been a peepal tree that had sprung up by breaking through the crevasse of a rock, I had been born on this very earth—a creation of her own. And how could her creation be unsuccessful? But as I say this, it would be unbefitting of me to claim that I was a successful creation of the earth; it will sound an आत्मरति (self-praise/self-satisfaction). But I can say this much, "After all, I was also a creation of the earth like the others."

Perhaps she had also expected something out of me, which was never understood by a particular group of people. That group kept on insulting and casting aspersions on her womb and a creation thereof; the earth, on her part, kept on tolerating silently, without uttering a word of protest. She had also probably desired that I should myself prove it to the world that her womb and creation can never be that useless. And she kept on waiting till that time when it was proved that her creation hadn't indeed been a total waste. I stand on the present and ask those who claim themselves to be complete human beings: "Is it you that is incomplete, or is it me? And is the society's eyesight disabled and infirm, or is it mine?"

Self-respect and Labour

My sense of self-respect had seemingly been aroused since those very days when I had started recognizing the colors of life a little bit. During my childhood days, if something was given to the others and not to me, I would be furious and feel, "Why was it that it was given only to them and not to me? If they are entitled to it, why not me?" That could have been a mere childish envy or jealousy, but it also had, apparently, a tingle of self-respect mixed with it.

While we used to play, we would win some of the games and lose some others. When we would win, we looked as if we were the masters of this tiny world. When we lost, we would get irritated. What a bad habit, isn't it?

But almost anything one does during childhood days appears becoming or agreeable. If the children played together the whole day but quarreled or fought with each other toward the evening and went separate ways, but met again the next day and patched up differences, nothing would be taken amiss. In the tiny world of kids, all such things are considered natural. But grown-up people cannot do the same—that's why there are wars and killings. The rage of children is like a water bubble that bursts in a moment. They can remain happy in their small world.

Yes, I am referring to self-respect. When I do something that hurts the feeling of my small younger sister Anna (Annamika), she protests, saying, "If *didi* is free to do it, why not I?"

It is an outpouring of a small mind's self-respect, but we are not taking it in a proper spirit and we found scolding her instead, "Keep quiet, you fiend, you talk too much, little one."

This kind of thinking is wrong on our part. We feel that the small ones mustn't speak. I had also been badly influenced by a similar kind of thinking. A child has to listen to the senior irrespective of what they say. Sometimes they too become very rude. Even those in right position have tolerated injustice. But as I grew up, my intellect and thinking also began to mature. Up to the age of eleven or twelve, I had neither learned pondering over life, nor did I have any worries and anxieties, because I was content with mundane passions like eating, playing, sleeping and so on. However, as I grew up further, the process of thinking about the various aspects of life also started increasing.

Only after wings of awareness sprout in a man, does he ultimately begin to ponder over the various aspects of life. I used to be scolded even when my clothes go tattered earlier than usual. What was my fault in that? It was sure to be torn, why you scold me? I had begun to feel that even my own people would not understand my problems born out my disability. If I had something of my own, I wouldn't have been the target of such abusive language, I would think. I have begun to doubt whenever I am unable or ill as to why my family members don't look after. But there was nothing I could call my own. Everything belonged to the others. I had to depend on others for my life, for food, for clothing—for everything. Had I been able-bodied, I would even have eked out my living by slogging like a coolie laborer.

The more I advanced up in age, the larger became the size of my stomach and the back of the body. The burden on my parents had increased accordingly, because the amount of cooked rice that would meet the requirements of two or three persons earlier would be gulped up by me alone. The cloth that was sufficient for all in the earlier days would be used up merely in getting my dress made. That would make them all the more aggressive against me. "No matter how much clothes we buy for her, it doesn't suffice.

Let her wear the skin of a dog"—they would say. It's also true that my dress will wear and tear so quickly.

As I grew up further, my internal self would keep on saying, "Fie upon me that I cannot help depending on others even for the sake of living!" Since my very childhood days, I would dislike living as a burden on the others; but what difference did it make whether I would like it or not? Truly, how helpless and impotent had I been at the time? I was a mere parasite that lived off the sweat of others. Yes, I also had a keen desire to survive on my own labor and sweat; but alas, I wasn't bodily capable of doing anything.

Once I entered the literary world, people from various walks of life began tempting me with attractions of money and wealth. They wanted me to do tricks on the roadside and beg money. No, I won't, because I didn't have money or wealth, nor did I have a body complete in itself, but I did have other attributes of my own.

Of what use was money or wealth to me anyway? I merely had to live, that's all. I couldn't earn money by mimicry as suggested by many, which is why they were fire and fury with me. On my part, I kept on stepping on the same fire. My parents would admonish me, saying, "It wasn't good not to listen to them. One should obey one's seniors." But I would keep mum at such a chance. And they would quietly trace back their steps. Thus, no matter how hard they would try, my self-respect didn't bow down before them. Even after I had established myself in the field of literature, many people tried to undermine me in various manners. But all their efforts bore no desired fruit.

I am not beyond myself with pride, however, because a person doesn't come out successful in every examination. I have also been probably successful in some, while unsuccessful in the others. But I can assert this much: that I have never learned to run away, nor have I learned to request anybody even when I was in a trouble; that's why I became what I am. I became capable of surviving on the strength of my own labor; but as far as mental labor goes, I have fallen behind no one. People who have seen me say this:

"You make comfortably and, that too, while staying put at your own house." How easy they think it is!

Occasionally, when some people come to our house, my father says, "She has no work. She just sits and eats." As per his understanding, I don't have any work at all. I sit idle and eat at home. But I have not a moment's respite the whole day and I get dead tired by the evening; is that no labor? Do you count only hammering a piece of iron, carrying a heavy load, or digging a ground as work or labor? I have labored every single moment; I have sweated hard. It is not as easy as the onlookers think it is. A man has to survive, and that what makes him strive. I am also one of the many people who have been slogging for the sake of life. I have started enjoying the fruits of my labor. Yes, the enthusiasm of living on the strength of one's own labor is quite different, as I have found out. The pleasure is apparently different too. The colour of self-esteem, I also find, is also truly and singularly beautiful. Although this had been spilled over me long back, I have started recognizing this just now. Oh, what a beautiful color!

Men and Gods in Religious Faith

How beautiful the rainbow looks as seen sometimes while it is drizzling and when a blanket of cloud has partially covered the sun—the rainbow that spreads across the sky! What a lovely sight! Despite the fact that I never worshipped any God nor believed in divinity, I never slighted the believers when I met them. A man has his own kind of religious faith or belief; every person in the world is free to follow his faith in accordance with his tradition and culture. One is free not to observe the traditions either. Besides, one is also entitled to express his belief or the lack of it, and also to protest against the God one holds in reverence. Meanwhile, some may consider this as nonsense. But if we talk about all kinds of freedom, this also finds a place as one.

The colors of a man's faith and belief are as beautiful as those of the rainbow. All variety of gods also appear beautiful. Be it a Muhammad deeply engrossed in prayers, a Christ hanging from the crucifix, a Buddha imparting lessons to his disciples, or a Krishna dancing in the company of Gopinis, are the gods of any community less beautiful than others? At times I wonder as to why no god looks ugly or unsightly. As it is, man could never conceive of a bad shape or color in portraying his God. And how could he? He has been taught from his early childhood that he has been created by God himself. But why does a man laying his faith in one God quarrel with another who believes in different gods? Why do men give birth to a communal (religious) riot? Have the gods asked them to quarrel? I ask such questions to religious minds. They keep silent. It cannot be fathomed from their silence as to whether they are under confusion or are suffering from self-deprecation.

In my life, I also touched and groped around people who had a religious faith or a religious mind-set. But I never consciously protested against such a faith or such a mind-set. They would want me to be on their side, to speak well about them and to adopt their religion. But there was a difference between their faith and the faith I subscribed to. Their gods were different than those of mine. I subscribe to a man's faith—not to that of a class, group, or community. I would see gods in people's fine behavior and mind; I didn't put any faith in a god that was unearthly or belonged to a different world. The Christians would tell me, "Your disability will go once you lay your faith in our God." The Buddhists and Muslims would say the same thing, and so did the Hindus. I was in a quandary as to whose god I should revere and whose not to. The gods of all people looked alike before my eyes. As I looked at their shapely bodies, all were attractive and good-looking. It didn't behoove me to say that someone's (your) god was good and not that of others. That's why I kept mum. Just because I had remained noncommittal, I wasn't disliked by any of them. They would go on narrating about their gods for hours on end. I would at times even be irritated at their unending narratives; listening itself would become an ordeal. It was at such times that the fountains of my disbelief would burst against them and I would voice a disbelief in their gods as well.

If they had a nature of being quickly provoked and were in fact provoked, they would be fire and fury and left abruptly; if they were of a quiet nature, no matter how deep a dissatisfaction I would display, they would merely keep smiling and say, "Looks as if Jhamak is in a bad temper today." I may have hurt some people's sentiments in the process, or I may also have filled some hearts with some drops of delight. It seems life's like that and it's not possible to satisfy every pedestrian you come across in the course of life's journey. I gave the religious people a freedom to express their views; I could as well have refused to listen to them. Likewise, if they would get irritated on hearing my views, that would make no difference to me either, because I was the type of a person to be amused with myself and wanted to live life in my own style; I also had my own religion and my own gods—an originality in all things.

Some people would even treat me as an incarnation of goddess Saraswati, would place coins and touch my feet with their heads, or would make offerings of flowers and fruits; there were other who considered me a living replica of God. I would tell them in all humanity, "I don't represent any god. I would like to live as a simple human being." I analyzed that the thing called god is a creation of man's own imagination. What people may worship as gods were the good deeds of a man. If I had dishonestly and treacherously told people that I was an exact incarnation of god, it was possible for one more god to be born. I would perhaps have been installed in a grand and gorgeous temple built at a cost of multimillion rupees; countless people might perhaps have slogged in serving me and attending on me in order to attain salvation. But I placed before the veil of an untruth; I was a human being and wanted to live as such.

Some people would tell me, "Change your religion." But I neither needed to change any religion nor change my god, because my religion wasn't associated with any caste, class, gender, or community, nor was my god associated with any of those things. Most people may have thought that since I had been born in the Hindu community, I would also be bearing its banner. As I have said, whatever I may have been as a child, as I grew up I couldn't subscribe to any religious faith nor to any god of different denomination; that's why I was in a position to relish the taste and enjoy the freedom of being free.

Some people would also come to me and tell me about their having been made to change their religious faith. Likewise, an elderly dai (brother) came to me and narrated to me how his family had been forcing him to change his religion. The reason was that the family had been converted into Christianity. He hadn't liked that and had expressed his dissent. It appeared that he preferred to retain the Buddhist faith, culture, tradition, and customs that he had been following since his birth. But his family members had been subjecting him to various kinds of physical and mental tortures. Oh, what a cruelty! Some people subscribe to the Christian faith, while others subscribe either to the Islamic, the Buddhist, the Jain, or the Hindu faith. That is a matter of an individual's choice in religion. But what kind of an injustice is it to try to impose the same faith on everyone? It's surprising. Why is a man forgetting to respect the rights of others while using his own rights?

It was difficult to understand what that dai was saying. He had no voice or the power of speech. He could also write but a little. All he could do was to use gestures, and I could hardly understand that. What to do?—I was at a loss; but I thought I must somehow grasp his thoughts. It wasn't hard for me to perceive his disturbed state of mind, and I asked him to take a pen and a paper to write what he could and tell the rest with the help of hints and gestures. He wrote a few words with great difficulty and told me the rest in gestures. Somehow I could grasp what he had to say; he was very happy.

I realized at the time how happy a man became when he could bring out and make public the uneasiness, agitation, and suffocation that had been perturbing his mind. I was also pleased to be able to read a little of his mind. Others were saying, "We wish we could understand what this dumb and mute fellow wants to say." But so far they had remained unable to dig into the details of what he had in his mind. When they saw that I could comprehend what he had to say, they were flabbergasted and said, "He may look dumb, but it seems he is internally clever" and bit the tongues.

I retorted, "Is he dumb, or are you yourselves?"

There is a limit to toleration too. I listened to them without any reaction. They went on laughing at him; I witnessed that too. When things crossed the limits, I spoke, then they *yol* (puzzled); they must have thought, this girl is ठु'च्ची disguised as religious आतङ्क claiming—"If you don't do this, you may have to bear such consequences." But I was never scared by such आतङ्क. Because I had never done any injustice to anyone—not a slightest crime. I would just read them and throw in the dustbin. While reading such pamphlets or brochures, I thought, *How can people spare their time for such wasteful things, if they had utilized this for some beneficial work?* How foolish they are! I was not scared by anything when the journey of life was terrifying, but they might have intended to terrorize me so as to make me appreciate them, and show devotion toward their god forcefully. No one should think of overpowering me. I should like and love it before I should share a few words in favor. I did not like their proposal; I could not appreciate them. I did not waste a single word, nor could I sympathize with them. How could I? They were brute and जवर्जस्ती. Nobody was at our home that day. He returned to his place beaming with happiness. I pondered over him—how clean-hearted and honest he is, but why is such injustice meted out to him? Does any religious faith ordain that our behaviors should be unjust and cruel? I would keep on asking such questions with the religious people I came across. I would keep on telling them, "No one has a right to trample upon the freedom and independence of others."

I treated them most cordially; I think so; it is their time, how will they tell! I did not want to hurt anyone's belief and faith because I believe that every man is free to live the way he wants to. If someone believes in God, I see no reason to object to it; likewise, if one doesn't believe, we have no right to object. To conclude, I must tell this much with honesty—I didn't subscribe to or follow any religion as expected by the others. I always pursued the path of, and stood by, the religion of humanity widely known as *manab dharma*.

The Urge for Freedom

Since my childhood days, I was also desirous of enjoying all kinds of freedom enjoyed by human beings. To play mischief at times and to be subjected to rebukes at the hand of seniors, and at others to plunge oneself into, and come out of, the muddy ponds of life had continued unabated and on a regular basis. But perhaps the urge for enjoying freedom was infinitely ingrained in my psyche. The urge went on increasing as I slightly grew up. I would wish that I could also claim my share in matters of sex and intimacy. Not only that, I started seeking a place for myself in everything else. But no, I didn't find my share or a place anywhere. In everything, I saw the shadow of the men folk and also saw my own reflection crushed and trampled under it. I always craved for emancipation from this state. I don't know why, but since my adolescent days, I didn't feel like becoming a burden on anyone. I always dreamed of surviving on the labor, skill, and capacity of my own—a beautiful dream that was!

Fortunately, I was seemingly destined to live on my own talents. Yes, it is necessary that a woman becomes free in all senses and self-dependent economically. This is a lesson life has taught me.

Life, it appears, is made up of many layers. Once a layer is peeled off, another one appears. Apparently, it was not for nothing that Shankar Lamichhaney wrote his *Abstract Chintan Pyaaj*. He has written beautifully about life in that essay. He also enjoyed a kind of freedom in life and also enjoyed life's romances through his writing. I also had the intention of enjoying all kinds of freedom in my writings; I had a life liberated by youthfulness—a restless and fickle life. I wanted to enjoy all kinds of freedom in life. Those youthful desires, those youthful ardors, fervors, and passions—I wanted to enjoy them all to the utmost extent. As I would hold my pen, they would say, "Hold from this side." Others would say, "No, from that side." This pull and push continued; I stood for sometime and watched this game of rigging and pushing. That game was nice too. People may have imagined that they could understand everything and could discriminate between what was wrong and what was right. I could trace out the path on my own writing; I didn't need anyone to trace out the path on my behalf. Some people would advise me that I should write certain things and shouldn't write certain others. I disliked people standing on my way thus, because I was completely independent insofar as my writings were concerned—much more independent than in my day-to-day life.

In my practical life, however, various impediments of inequality would keep on standing in my way. Despite all my efforts, I was unable to untie those knots of impediments. Alas! It was seemingly impossible to easily wipe out the grime of irrelevant thoughts that lay settled in the minds of men for ages and ages. But one couldn't help making an effort either. It was impossible for me to remain uninfluenced by the inequalities in Nepalese society.

There are several disparities here—born out of gender, class, community and the like. I experienced them and I could not have expressed them if I had just heard about or just seen. Although I would look for an equality and assimilation in all matters, I had myself been at the receiving end of inequal behavior on grounds of cultural, economic, or gender differences. I had to bring the same voices of inequality and disorganization to the fore and had them mingled into the sea of literature. I used to enjoy doing this, because it wasn't a matter that concerned an individual alone. I never brazenly put forward my personal problems in my writings, as I reflected somewhere. It is said that sharing your troubles cuts them into half and sharing your happiness doubles it. Perhaps that's why Jagdish Ghimire wrote in his *Antarmanko Yaatraa* ("Do share your internal pains with all." He has mentally traveled much in his *Antarmanko Yaatraa*. Yes, I am also traveling mentally, and am talking the thoughts and contemplations as my mind desires. What I talk isn't the same as that of the others. I can't say there is a difference because the pain is the same and so are the problems. The only difference is that of style and language.

As I observed various pits of inequality, I struck against it with my pen. When they could not bear those blows, some people asked me not to go to the extremes and others advised me not to write much on political issues. I used to laugh within myself on seeing the imprudence of those people. At the very moment, I started erasing the line of demarcation drawn by them. I couldn't stay within those lines, nor could I become the camp-follower of any ism. They are free to draw any line of demarcation in my words and sentences or thoughts I have expressed, any principle or theoretical outline—they are free to do.

As I said, I cannot be restrained by the barriers placed by anyone, cannot keep myself within the lines of limitations drawn by anyone. They are to order me to write in this way or that. I don't follow any. A pen is free in itself, a writer is free in himself. What should be written and what should not lies within the discretion of the writer himself or herself. If he confines himself within the dogma of 'write this' or 'don't write this,' the pen cannot write free voices; the author cannot produce free thoughts. That's the reason why I kept on wielding my pen by breaking the barriers raised by the society and by going beyond the social, cultural, economical, gender-based, class-based, casteist, and communal barriers and restraints. I would do and write the same things that I had been asked not to. While doing so, I would feel the sweet sensation of becoming free and independent. I enjoyed in full the freedom of the pen and aspired to enjoy even more; that's why my pen kept on belching out all kinds of voices. In any case, my pen continued to run along its own independent periphery, that's all.

The Pen and the Dread of Death

I had been of a slightly pigheaded and stubborn nature since childhood days. That very temperament reflected itself in my writings. The colors of resentment and rage also got spilled over it. Voices of rebellion against disorder, defects, and disharmony came to the fore. My pen bore on its shoulders the voices of equality and emancipation against all kinds of discrimination.

At the time, a kind of storm was brewing from the jungles and it was pulling toward itself a fair number of men. The wind of rebellion was reverberating with voices of justice, liberation, and struggle. Village after village, settlement after settlement were getting enmeshed into that storm. It was natural to be so. There were many inequalities, injustices, and oppressions here. With a dream of eradicating them, many young men and women took to the jungles. The young sons and daughters would enter the jungle and raise guns, dreaming for a change; but their families at home would face the torture and punishment. The elderly parents of such young people would be made to answer to the armed forces and policemen as to where their children had gone. Quite a few of them would be beaten and thrashed; some innocent people would even be killed. Even the right to live was snatched away. Many children were orphaned, the laps of many parents got emptied; in fact, the country was passing through severely tragic times.

Yes, people were frightened even to speak out openly and frankly. Even if some guests turned up toward the evening, one would be scared to ask them to have the evening meal or to stay for the night. On the other hand, those who had gone into the jungles would also terrorize the people in a like manner. Incidents of killing innocent persons to torturing them, forcibly extorting money in the name of donations were going on unabated. As the evening approached, people would start talking in whispers. Nobody knew what would happen to whom, or who would be killed the next moment. It wasn't sure as to whether a person, who had gone out of the house in the morning, would return home safe and sound by the evening or would be killed. What an injustice? People couldn't even live in peace.

Those were also tough times for those who wielded the pen. It was all the more difficult for writers, poets, and artists who were just and freedom-loving. I was also somewhere around and I was being mentally suffocated on seeing the oppression, tyranny, and injustice cross their limits. I had been fire and fury on seeing innocent people being subjected to torture and cruelty. The wheel of time was also turning backwards as far as the suffering people were concerned. How devoid of breath and vital airs had human life been!

Even amid such scare and fright, time kept on moving along in its own speed. Or in other words, the life-wheel kept on whirling round constantly. Personally speaking, however, the calendar of the year 2057 (2000) got torn after handing over to me some packets of rejoicing and delight. With the advent of the new year, it was natural that a kind of new enthusiasm, a new exultation was sprouting, and plants of a new awareness were flourishing.

When no one cared to listen to my calm and peaceful creative voice, I was compelled to scream out loud. When the voice of humanity was suppressed with terror, my creative activity refused to remain silent. It started to toss up and surge up carrying with it the voice of rebellion. Once it ultimately started shouting in a surged-up and high-pitched voice, everyone heard it. As I spoke in such a voice, I was dubbed as belonging to this party, as that would have been a narrow and limited periphery for me. I couldn't have been tied to anyone, nor could I have remained halted within any kind of demarcation line.

As a person who by nature cherished freedom and an unrestrained life, as one who sought to live according to one's values and beliefs, as one who liked to mingle in the company of one and all, and as one who desired to live by pursuing a lifestyle of one's own under an open sky, I didn't feel like living under any kind of restriction. I couldn't tolerate the penetration of claws on humanity. *That's why I kept on shouting and screaming with blocked ears, by those who had pretended to be sleeping and, above all, by the closed time.* They were startled and alerted; alarmed, they became eager and active to break that pen. They might perhaps have thought they could get a good night's sleep if only they could twist and squeeze the pen which kept on belching out the voice of justice and humanity. That was why they tried variously to suppress my creations that they just started to bloom. *To nip them in the bud,* impotents that they were, they were so much frightened with the pen that they threatened to wipe me out.

Yes, during the very first phase of my literary career, I received a threat on my life. I didn't have any indication as to who was the person to threat me thus. Whoever he may have been, he was a coward, an impotent, and an inspirited fellow. Had this happened to a weak fellow, he would never have carried a pen anymore, would have killed himself, or would have cast his pen away. But I couldn't do that, because even if I had to die for writing or speaking the truth, I was prepared. Who doesn't love his or her life? I was also in love with my life. But if one has to live a terrorized and frustrated life, that was why I enjoyed all the freedom in life. Likewise, in my writings, I enjoyed a liberated and full-fledged freedom. I didn't have to undergo any bindings and frustrations. How was the one who had threatened me to know that I would be least scared or frightened with his cowardly and impotent threats?

I never wielded my pen behind the back of the people at large, nor did I ever indulge in stirring up false dreams and hopes. While living all the time in the people's common ground, I kept on speaking only on their behalf and lived a life of gay abandon. Yet I have never been able to forget that year, 2058, which has been inscribed in the pages of my life as a dark and black year. To speak the truth, I had to undergo a lot of mental sufferings and pressures. That was also a significant achievement of mine, attained by virtue of the truth that I always spoke or wrote about. That was the fallout of a rebellious voice and threatening utterances of an unsuccessful, cruel time to shout down the voice of a rebellious pen.

A Benumbed Mind in
Blood-Soaked Times

It wasn't only in my life that the year 2001 passed off a Black Year. That year was also full of unforgettable incidents and occurrences in the country's history itself. The process of painting the pages of history with sprays of human blood was continuing. Or, in other words, the earth continued being soaked in blood. A look at the earth soaked in human blood would appear extremely horrifying. Such a large-scale blood-letting was perhaps rare in our history.

That same year saw the Palace Massacre. King Birendra's dynasty was wiped out. As it is, the plays of numerous assassinations, rapes, political conspiracies, deceit, and fraud were being enacted in the royal palace since times unknown. Yet that day's collective assassination was truly heartrending. That also in a place where even the wind had to obtain permission to enter, where security personnel remained on duty twenty-four hours of the day and where not even birds and mice, no question of human beings, could penetrate the security ring of the armed forces. However, as it turned out, that was the most insecure and unsafe of places.

As the massacre took place, people were kind of benumbed, deadened. Doubts and suspicions had started raising among people about the efficacy of the country's security machinery from that very time. But it was difficult for anyone to speak—anything could have happened. That's why people kept quiet. The eyes of those with slightly soft and humane minds didn't dry up for days on end, as tears kept flowing. Elderly people used to say—"Our (nations') parents have been killed, what will happen of us?"

More knowledgeable people would say—"The queen bee has died, the other bees will perish themselves." We would frequently hear hearsay, comments, and doubts.

At the time, quite a few poets and writers came out with creations filled with lamentation and moaning. But I would be disgusted to read them, because I feel that our creations ought to teach people to smile at the time they are crying, ought to teach people to live with hope at a time when they are disappointed and frustrated. But why can't our writers appreciate this thing? To the contrary, they keep on making people weep by coming out with nothing but anguish and distress-filled creations. But I did not read such creations.

Personally, I would feel nothing but pain while going through those writings and I didn't want to be distressed in life by reading them. Life wasn't pain alone; it was *joys* too; also romance and radiance. And I wanted to enjoy to them all.

A kind or curiosity would also keep on rising in my mind. The people in that place who considered themselves the saviors of all others couldn't even save themselves; why? When false reports on the massacre were made public, the people totally refused to believe them. How easily had they tried to mislead the people! How gullible and dumb did the palace regard them! Even a child of seven or eight years derided and ridiculed the palace report. But when they would ask their parents about that falsehood, the latter preferred to keep silent. It was not out of choice they had kept quiet, however; it was rather a compulsion. Anything could have happened if they had opened their mouths.

But how long can such a silence, such a muteness, last? A man can keep quiet for sometime out of his love for life, but he could not maintain that silence for long. Initially, he began whispering, then began talking in a muffled voice—but that didn't please him. When he began speaking loudly, he forgot all about his love for life, about fear or dread, about everything. After that, he felt highly relieved and lived a full life.

All said and done, people had come to know and understand full well about the farce enacted by the royal palace. The terrifying and horrible face of monarchy was also exposed, and people slowly and gradually started to voice their muffled discontent. I used to think, *Why are people so much deep in grief?* I heard them silently. They used to whisper and keep quiet. Gradually, their discontent began being expressed. Their voice was suppressed. Yes, people would not like to retain monarchy any longer. But they were dismayed and annoyed at seeing all people place coins at Gyanendra Shah's feet and touching them with their heads. But was merely touching his feet enough? There were women who would have his feet washed. He could have stopped the religious women from washing his feet (while performing a rite), but he did not (it is a common belief that no woman should touch the feet of a male other than her husband). Obviously, he must have enjoyed the touch of the moment's tender hands on his feet. He regarded himself a master and them as slaves. He must have felt at the time that he was a true and heavenly personification of God. But he did not personify God at all and was merely the son of a human being.

What a practice even in the twenty-first century! Had he been unable to, it would have been acceptable, but his feet were healthy. People were demanding jail to the criminal. But who will listen to them? I could understand the meaning of being a ruled citizen. Why are people deprived of truth? My mind would be deadened by the scene of the country being washed in blood. My heart would be severely pained at the sight of human corpses lying about here, there, and everywhere. How inhumane was a human doing? The murders were also utterly cruel and animal-like. At such times, a journey of creativity would be difficult as it is; those who had chosen the path of freedom, democracy, human rights, and change would find the task of wielding their pens all the more daunting. I was also a writer filled with similar values and beliefs; my creations would therefore reflect the people's voices of change because I was myself a daughter of the common people. How could I be dishonest with them? That's why my pen carried along with it the voices of justice and kept on following the brighter aspects of the revolution.

The roots of despotism were spreading and further in the country. They were driving the nation toward a deeper darkness. Justice-loving poets, writers, and artists were raising the voice of democracy; I also kept on raising the voice of justice in my writings. It was impossible for the poison-tree of despotism to find such views easily digestible; what they rather wanted was to spread the poison through the world and make it to take the entire world in their grip and make the latter rotate in the reverse direction.

But those who dreamt of a new age would find the views on equality easily digestible. Those who wanted to curse me kept on cursing. But at the very place stood innumerable suppressed minds who continued to applaud me. Those who cursed me were getting lost in the crowd of those who would clap their hands in my praise. Those who wanted to give birth to a new age didn't try to erase my marks. Directly or indirectly, they built a path for me to walk along. Time passed amid such sweet and bitter experiences, the calendar got torn, and a whole life also kept on getting torn on installment basis.

Emergency and Terror-Filled Times

Life was terrible; it was full of fear. Hardly had the first one or two months of the year 2001 passed, when an emergency was imposed throughout the country. Incidents such as murders, terrors, and rapes were growing apace. Conflict, it appeared, was truly terrible. It could drag anyone to the death-pit anytime. It wasn't even possible to talk in raised voice. The armed soldiers were let loose. They enjoyed the freedom: they got busy in harassing people. They not only badgered those involved in the war, but also the common people. They weren't the only ones to terrorize the people, however; those that had taken to the jungle at the time weren't also far behind. If anyone joined the ranks of the army or the police for fear of the latter, they would intimidate his parents, wives, brothers, and sisters. Many would be inhumanely killed while others would be made traceless. When one becomes heartless, he apparently can do anything. The victims said, "Feed us and give donations, if not a son or a daughter we claim for war." They come to us. Out of fear some joined the government army or police force. As a result their parents, wife, and siblings were terrorized. Others were killed brutally or disappeared them. Oh, what a cruelty! Once man's heart is removed, he remains capable of doing anything.

People were panic-stricken on the face of terror. In the pretext of searching for the terrorists, the armed forces would frighten the common people. They would beat and *belabor* innocent people or otherwise unnecessarily harass them. Not only that, the army men were also reported to have been involved in rapes, murders, and other inhumane acts in one village after another. In some rural areas, the army men were said to greet people with words like, "Hello Comrade, Red Salute" and, should someone respond in the same vein, they would pounce upon him, ask him questions like "Where is your leader?" and thrash him, kill him, or do whatever they liked. Stories of their molesting and gang-raping girls on the threshold of their youth were quite commonly heard. The element known as humanity had drained out of them all. The terror-stricken eyes of everyone looked like they were begging time for the safety in their lives. Truly enough, nothing is apparently dearer to man than his life. Once the series of sensational atrocities multiplied in the villages, people migrated from the villages to the district headquarters, from there to the larger towns and cities, and from there to the country's capital, and those widowed with some wealth didn't even feel secure there either and left the country altogether to move to some other lands abroad. Grown-up young men and women were not to be found in the village—some had joined the ranks of those jungles, some had joined the police or the army, while the rest had either migrated to the cities or left for foreign countries. The rural areas were desolate, inhabited only by the elderly, the small children, and their mothers. And the cadres of both sides would torment and torture them. What a bastardly behavior!

The army conducted search operations in our village as well. They flung open every single house of the villagers. But somehow, they spared our house—God knows why. The armed forces, however, would consistently come to our place and cast a hawk-like eye here and there. More people used to visit our house than those elsewhere in the village; for me, everyone was alike—none more, nor less. I would behave alike with everyone, laugh and chat with them. The armed personnel would come to our place in the pretext of meeting me and stay for hours at a stretch, would look at each and every item in my room to their heart's content so as to find every article bearing the Marxist touch in them, so much so that even the posters depicting the portraits of movie stars appeared to bear a Marxist tingle in their eyes!

Marxism is a scientific philosophy which is not bad in itself. All people have a philosophy of their own, because every person has his or her points, overview, conscience, and outlooks (consistent garne) that all add to form a philosophy. But I don't know who taught them that everything of Marxist is offensive. That made them cruel against it. Poor dears, their consciences did not enable them to differentiate between what is good and what is bad. Could it be that their higher-ups had instructed them in a similar manner?

As I said, they would see a Marxist tingle in every single article of mine and say, "Everything around here is Marxist. Do you read a lot of Marxist literature?"

I would feel like asking, "Did you see Marxism even in these walls?" But it wouldn't befit me to behave as they did. Had I done that, what would have been the difference between them and me? On top of that, they had law in their hands along with guns, and most significantly, they had orders from their higher-ups to shoot at anyone who talked in favor of life. One had to weigh every single word before uttering it before them. A mere word would be enough to wipe out a person's life. Occasionally, however, it would be too much for me to bear and I would say, "I am an independent writer and there is no rule that dictates what I ought to read and what not to. It's not that I read only Marxist books—I read as many different books as I can lay my hands on." That would shut their mouths and they would go their own ways.

The period of emergency happened to be so terrifying, in fact, that people dreaded speaking even what they couldn't do without. They would remain panic-stricken that anything could happen to them anytime. How would such a panic spare my house? It didn't. The armed force, I repeat, had been let loose to such an extent that they were free to enter anybody's house in the village and do whatever they chose to. So much so that they could even take the life of anyone they liked. Some soldiers, dead drunk on alcohol, would come to me and tease me with questions such as "Jethisaasu" (one's wife's elder sister), wouldn't you ever like to get married?"

"Fie on you! Don't you feel ashamed, you impotent bastards, to cast your evil eyes on my flower-like younger sister? And as for me, I have not gone as much crazy as yourself with an overdose of sex-lust and I am not in a mood to marry"—I felt like retorting and driving them away. But I was a mere commoner and I had my limits that I couldn't cross (पंक्ति confusing छ, text हेनैं). Instead, I would grind my teeth and say, "I heard what you said and understood what you meant. Go away, get out!"

At the time, they are said to have come across my younger sister Mina while she was walking along the road and to have said nasty things to her. *Oagh*! What makes these wild animals called "men" to stab their penetratingly evil eyes on the girls in general?

Occasionally, army officers would also visit me and urge me to cooperate with them. I would tell them to respect and uphold human rights by not letting their soldiers loose.

My writing career kept on proceeding ahead even in the midst of such ups and downs. Till that time I had also suffered many setbacks and passed through many mishaps. I had also seen life in a slightly different light and understood it—that life is also a struggle and strife. One has to face some tough turns as also some smooth ones. Life, in any case, is life. I had been through a lively moment even at that critical juncture.

☒

Voice of Emancipation from Darkness

It seems life often passes through difficult circumstances as it goes along. *Was my life any different? Others had to help me through my toilet, or washing was unable to move about without the help of others, couldn't look at or* see things properly without the help of thick and high-powered glasses. What a miserably bonded life! Couldn't even wash the mouth after partaking of food without the help of others! Others had everything—I had nothing! Alas! But coming to think of it, I had something that the others lacked.

Even though I lacked everything, I had a strong will to live. If I meant anything, they were my thoughts, sentiments, and desires—in other words, the great truth of assuming a human form. The world is ever changing, and it moves along—this is also a truth. Those who ruled the nation did not know this. Man possesses feelings, desires, and ambitions. They are free to express their points of view related to them. They did not understand this great truth. Another is that this life is ever changing progressively. But those on upper hierarchy never realised this. A human being is a form of life that inhabits this very world. His wishes and desires are free and keep on changing—are in a state of flux—that *I was also another truth.* As a person who wields the pen in pursuing this great truth, I cannot leave my pen even under the most difficult circumstances of any kind whatsoever. How can I? My pen is the only bridge that links me with the world. Even if it was possible to live without it, life wouldn't have been either easy or smooth. I had been known to the world also as a wielder of the pen. I

would break their pens to fulfill their
ı sold their souls. I wasn't prepared to
th my own existence, conscience, and

not out of my selfishness; *weightier*
by selling my soul. I use the pen for
ntry's internal conflicts greatly harass,
ı burnt of the conflicts that tolerated
a great tragedy did the country have
ally those who became the victims of
tolerate? It seems people were in utter
ıment they underwent! My hairs stand
he mere memory of those days makes
'hen Gyanendra Shah was placed on
I snatching away even the minimum
itical parties put *some kind* of ban. He
declared his son as the crown prince just on the eve of the Dashain
festival. No one could extend support to these steps of his. People
had started burning internally with rage. But what was one to do?
The people of the lower echelons had to tolerate whatever the
higher-ups would do. They felt suffocated; God knows when this
would explode. That may explode any moment. How could that
palace know all this, the palace that was serving various blood
baths and forgeries? How could it understand popular desires?

The king had only known to exploit the blood and sweat of
the poor people. We, on our part, placed that very person on a
god's pedestal and kept on making offerings of an incarnation
of Lord Vishnu. But after all, he was also merely a human being
like any of us, born of the wombs of a woman. Why then were
we expected to regard him as Lord Vishnu's incarnation? What
kind of a tradition was it that made a man king as soon as he
was born? Such questions would arise in my heart since the very
adolescent days. But even if I asked someone, no answer would be
forthcoming from him or her.

But after the palace massacre, people came out openly against
the king. The nib of my pen was also raising, directly or indirectly,

its voice in the favor of republican setup. Instead of directly supporting or opposing anyone, I advocated in favor of peace, democracy, and independence in my poems. As I never penned cheap political slogans, there were people who thought that I had not raised any voice in favor of democracy and republicanism. That was also natural in a way, because I wouldn't send most of my writings for publication in the media and periodicals. That was a very bad habit of mine. A few of my writings would appear in the media only if my friends took the initiative of taking them or getting them published.

I could express my feelings in writing under any adverse conditions. I wasn't afraid of life. But I would see quite a few people who lived under constant fear. That's why, perhaps, they would be scared to see me expressing my feelings. But I kept on writing. An expression of those difficult times as a collection of poems, *Naulo Pratibimba* (*New Reflections*), was published in the year *2003*. That book was published with the assistance of Madan Prasad Shrestha, who ran Marygold School in Dharan and whom I had met just once in Dhankuta. Thus, my sixth book was published with the help of people from Dharan and launched there. On that occasion, I met many literary figures from the eastern part of Nepal. In any case, even during those dark days, my pen kept on raising a voice of emancipation.

In the World of the Kantipur

Although I had visited Dharan a couple of times earlier as well, this time my stay in this place was of slightly different nature—as I had been the guest of someone who used to love me and respect me. Yes, I was staying in the house of the same Madan Prasad Shrestha where I used to receive a treatment similar to a daughter.

Truly, Dharan is a town of Laahu*rays*—those who go to distant lands, labor hard (mostly as military men) there, earn money, build fabulous houses on their return, and keep their families rolling in wealth and prosperity. As you look into the faces of people here, it gives the impression that not a line of distress or penury runs across them. But the crowds of *dokay-naamley* load carriers thronging places like the Chaataa Chowk, Bhanu Chowk, Puraanu Bazaar, and the like, with downcast looks make one feel that this place isn't much different after all—the life of the poor and the downtrodden is the same here too.

In any case, I enjoy staying in Dharan because, despite its plus and minus points, there are a few people here who appreciate the value of a human being. Even at the time of launching my sixth book—a collection of poems entitled *Naulo Pratibimba*—I got acquainted, albeit a little, with the creative writers of eastern Nepal. I know some of them with their faces, colors and others with their thoughts and behaviors.

That evening, Dharan was about to settle for the night. I could see that people there enjoyed the cool evening breeze of the otherwise hot summer evenings as they sat around their brightly lit balconies. I was also made to join them. At the time, a lady came near me, looked at me for a while, and, with smiling face, said, "How are you, Jhamak?" I vaguely remembered having seen her earlier while visiting the Ghopa Camp for a medical checkup. At that time also, she had behaved with me in an intimate manner and had given her name as something akin to "Jwala." As I didn't show any reaction to her query, she said again in a raised voice, "I am Benjwala Shrestha—Madan Sir's daughter." Only then did I smile.

We entered the room and started chatting. As we went on chatting, it appeared like we had known each another for long and been old-time friends. Our views about the women were similar. She turned the pages of my diary and went through them. I had jotted many things about women on those pages. They apparently touched her. After going through my diary, she said, "Oh, how interesting! It would have been nice if these ideas were made public!" Then she added after a while, "Are you interested in writing for the *Kantipur*? A friend of mine has her husband working there. It could be done."

I made no reply. My silence agitated her, as she said, "Don't say no, Jhamak. *A capable one-person* like you should appear in *Kantipur*."

I don't have the habit of giving my consent in haste; I did likewise that day. I only agreed after quite a lot persuasion on her part.

Then I started writing columns. At the time, Yuvraj Ghimire was the editor, and he was also pleased. I was then a lone female column-writer in that newspaper. Prior to that, I used to receive a monthly allowance of a thousand rupees from the Ministry of Women and Child Welfare. That would somehow meet my expenses for exercise books, pens, and so on, and some clothing. But that wasn't paid every month, only on an annual basis.

It seems human relations are based somewhat on sentiments but mostly on money. In order to keep on maintaining these human relations, I also needed money—money to turn this way, money to turn that way! So much so that every human breath also cost money, as it were! Occasionally, I was even constrained to cover out domestic expenses with the help of money I had received as prizes.

Joining the *Kantipur* as a columnist made life somewhat easier and more smooth. My economic condition improved more. But the political situation was highly unfavorable. To wield the pen under such circumstances wasn't a bed of roses. But a work is a work. Whether comfortable or otherwise, I felt that one's own earning provided a greater pleasure than those given by others. How joyful it is to live by the sweat of one's own brow! Many would be lured at seeing the money I had earned by dint of my labor, *would sort of cover it.* It was natural for those who always looked at me with jaundiced eyes not to appreciate anything done by me, because their attitude itself wasn't positive. However, I always looked at life from a positive viewpoint; that's why I also drove its chariot with a positive outlook in life. People would say that the editors and columnists wouldn't look *eye toward* one another, but my relations with the editor always resembles one between a brother and a sister, as Yuvraj Dai was always affectionate toward me. I would also respect him as an elder brother. Benjwala *Didi* had played the role of a bridge connecting the *Kantipur* and myself.

I started appearing every week in *Kantipur* with the column "Own Surroundings" *since . . .* That also led to widen my contacts with the readers. I started considering life as my own and pleasurable. Although it was a difficult task in itself to strike a balance between my literary and column writings, I had to make a success on both grounds, nevertheless.

The *Kantipur* didn't merely make me a columnist; it also helped establish my identity and provided a base on which I could sustain my life. I wielded my pen on various subjects. I used to raise the issues of women, children, and literature, besides the incongruities of the society, which my readers would read with relish. I would lose myself among the colors of letters and words. And I dedicated myself to the noble cause of letters and words.

Paints, Brushes, and Canvas

From my very childhood days, I used to draw outlines of objects such as flowers, men and women, dogs, cats, rabbits, and the like, with the help of a twig on the bare earth. They were taken little notice of by anyone. Later on, as I became familiar with letters of the alphabet, I would occasionally draw those very objects on the exercise books, and those would receive slight praise by the onlookers. I would be puffed up with pride and draw them again. My guardians, to the contrary, would scold me for having misused and wasted the exercise books in that manner and would warn me that they would no more purchase such papers for me. But I would nonetheless keep on drawing pictures.

After sometime, when I made my entry into literary creations, I began to color letters and words—I would be delighted to do so; sometimes when I liked to draw, I *used the same exercise* book. My passion for drawing pictures by using black, blue, red ink colors has slackened now. I very much liked the red vermillion powder that Mother would put on her forehead while going to the markets, and looking at the mirror, I would apply the same on my forehead with my foot. I would put on a *tikaa* paste on my forehead with the help of my toes. But it would start itching intolerably soon afterwards; small rashes would also erupt on my skin. It was because I was allergic to colors; but despite that, I would feel like playing with them and rubbing them on my person. बाँकी

When I had been to Dharan for the launching of my sixth publication and stayed there for about a week or so, I would occasionally feel bored in absence of anything to do. It was summer, and the sky above was open and clear with only minor patches of clouds at places. One day, as I sat on the balcony of Madan Sir's house, gazing at the vast blue sky, poet and painter Narendra Bahadur Shrestha showed himself up. He is also a businessman. It transpired that he had come from Kathmandu in order to participate in my book-launch. He had prepared the cover design of my book *Naulo Pratibimba* and had also penned its preface. We had also met another couple of times prior to that.

I have a habit of lightly bantering, playing potter (?), and joking with people slightly more than necessary. That day too, I badly teased him. "Not being a trader myself, I am never in a position to carry a bagful of money, although I have no complaints."

Had I made such comments on any other persons, he or she would certainly have been enraged but not Narendra Dai. On the contrary, he let out a loud guffaw and said, "What to do? I have to survive." I added, "Please don't cheat the world in the pretext of surviving." He became grave and replied, "I also possess the heart of a human being. That's why I write poems, paint pictures, and carve statues." I felt that I had offended him quite badly. And, while picking up a blank piece of paper lying nearby, I jocularly and playfully drew the sketch of a woman's face on it. He had been quietly eyeing at my work. Once I had finished the sketch, he spoke, "It seems Jhamak doesn't merely offend people. She also knows the art of pleasing them. I never knew you are endowed with the quality of an artist and painter." I thought, *I should not have drawn. I showed my poor knowledge, yet he appreciated.*

I kept on gazing idly at the sky, forgetting in the meanwhile what had been going on around me. Nor did I take notice of Narendra Dai or pay attention toward him. I hardly realized that, in the meantime, he had gone to a shop nearby and fetched along with him a brush, a canvas, and some paints. I only came to know about it when I had been abruptly awakened by the knockings on the door. The absentminded person that I am, I hardly notice the goings-on around me once I get lost in myself. Occasionally, I even forget having already partaken of my food. At times, when my mother or younger sisters ask me to do something, I either don't hear them or, even if I may have heard, forget it the next moment.

Similar was the case that day. I neither noticed when Narendra Dai had got up and left me, nor when he returned from the shop he had gone to. After he had returned with the stuff he had bought for me, he told me, "Start painting pictures." How could I refuse him? I said OK and took delivery of the brush, canvas, and paints from him.

I mentioned before, I love playing with colors. I was delighted to get colors today because words were becoming insufficient for me. Narendra Dai would also tell me, "Activities like writing poetry, painting (pictures), and carving are meant for one's own happiness. You are a creative artist who should not pen political write-ups." But I could never agree with him. Because activities like writing poetry, painting, and carving aren't meant merely for pleasing oneself, but we do so for the sake of life. While creating life, we express thoughts and ideas too. A creative artist must be allowed to use his or her conscience. Beliefs like what one should write and what not are wrong in themselves. Such concepts as one should write like this and one should not write like that are absolutely wrong founded. I am a human being too, not an animal. I had good reasons to have possessed my own ideas, opinions, and thoughts. I never meant literature as a medium of pleasure or recreation. Nor did I take it as a medium of exposing mere imagination. Because I wanted to connect life with literature and express thought in literature. I painted pictures with the color and brush Narendra Dai gave me. I tried to search for the color of life and of thoughts in those pictures too. *I cannot. Somehow many of them got torn. How spoilt! But I can say I was a learner only. Therefore why apply color? It was disorderly, lines became imbalanced—it was merely a practice. To continue doing was my fate. I always wanted to connect life with literature, present my thoughts and ideas in* the shape of literature. I would look for the colors of life in words, for the fragrance of thoughts, and for the paradigm or test of arts. I had a different of philosophy my own.

For the first time, I painted a cover sketch for my seventh book, *Pardaa, Samaya ra Maancheharu ( )*, a collection of short stories. Vivek Sirjansheel Prakaashan, a publishing house belonging to Vijayraj Acharya, had organized a function in the month of Ashaar *2062*, in order to simultaneously launch nine books penned by an equal number of authors, out of which one was my above-named book. But somehow, someone else had been credited for the painting of its cover sketch instead of me. I was deeply aggrieved. I told the publisher about it, and he begged forgiveness.

Our blunt and thoughtless utterances addressed at someone often create uneasy situations. At times, his or her sensitivities are badly hurt. On such occasions, it's nicer to express one's view through colors. Ultimately, life and even creation is only colors. I liked the colors of life best of all and our experience, suffering grief, and happiness that flow together. It's true that I liked tears and pain, sometimes ecstasy too. The colors of my thought didn't match those of Narendra Dai or of my sentiments, but just because of that, there was no question of the color of a tender human heart being defiled or soiled. That's why I looked at him with love.

I also drew the cover sketch for my eighth work *Bemausamka Aasthaaharu ( )*, a collection of essays myself. It had been published by Jaleshwari Shrestha, a Kathmandu resident. It was said that she was involved in business and trade; she is also a writer. When she asked me for the manuscript of my work, I handled over to her the draft of the collection of essays above-named. She had it published in the year *2006*.

I had already done the cover sketches for two of my own works. A bimonthly periodical, *Rachanaa*, which has glorious history of its own and which has been successful in leaving its own stamp of *originality sphere of culture* and literature over the last forty-six years, also used my cover sketch in its issue for the months of Phalgun and Chaitra issue in the same year. I have a long association with Rochak Ghimire Dai, its chief editor; he is a very lovable personality.

The first exhibition of my arts and poetry was organized under the auspices of Q Art Gallery in Kathmandu; the exhibition included some of my paintings along with nine poems. I had come from the world of words to the world of colors—in the long run, the world could look at me from different angles *(?)*. I have the agility of a child—I am always curious to learn anything, get an idea of anything new. It is said that creative persons are a serious lot. But I didn't acquire seriousness at any time. As already pointed out, I would like to crack jokes with anyone—talk frankly and openly with any person. Many people who have met me have liked such openness; others may have internally called me bad names as well. As it is, I easily mix and mingle with people anywhere—it doesn't take long for me to make myself at home at any new environment. That's why I am what I am—can't be like any other.

I would have perhaps never entered the world of arts and paintings hadn't Narendra dai handed over to me a set of brushes, colors, and canvas. Presently, I feel delighted in playing with colors and paints. I have now started looking at the world not only through words but also through colors.

Grime Formed in Their Mind

$\mathcal{I}$ have spoken against superstitions, tyranny, lapses, and perversions. My words weren't disabled or helpless. They were bombs and explosives in themselves. Naturally, the coward and impotent were frightened and fled away from them. Those who had pretended to side with me and hold my hands started shunning me and turning away from me. Even in my life as a writer, I was exploited and tormented in various ways—my life passed through those experiences as well. This life itself taught me that it was not enough to see fair and handsome faces, because an abhorrent nature and behavior could be lying concealed inside them. Some friends, who were closer to me earlier, had also gone their own ways. Many of them had already set up their homes, sired children, and become parents—others were also following their footsteps. As they were tied to their own domestic drudgeries and responsibilities, it wasn't easy for them to keep on befriending me as hitherto.

There were also others who had started shunning me and shying away from me. As it transpired, they had been afraid that their children could also be disabled like me if they continued meeting me. My god! Disability wasn't something contagious or infectious—so should they have been scared? Fie upon the degraded mentality even at those that were supposed to have been educated! I didn't need to meet such persons either, for my life wasn't something to be despised; it was priceless in itself.

A little sister who lives above our house has been kept confined in a dark room of her house, because she is disabled or infirm. They say it would invite shame on them if they let her come out.

Poor soul, she can neither enjoy the sun's warmth nor breathe in the cool air outside. She also has a life, but what a difference between the life of an able person and the disabled! Just because she is disabled, has she no right to bask in the warm sun or to breathe fresh air? Her elder brother holds a college degree and her sister-in-law is also well educated. If they can't treat a human being as human, of what worth is their education? The meaning of education is to learn how to behave like a human being. But there are such educated and civilized people in the world, whose certificates aren't worth more than a toilet paper—they can as well be torn and thrown away.

But as I say this, let me not be misunderstood; I am not casting aspersions on many other educated and civilized people who have led the world from darkness to light—the people who have emancipated many others by providing the latter with the light of knowledge and consciousness, thereby helping them cast aside the mist of ignorance. My mind bows down to their feet in respectful obeisance. Whatever educational attainment a man may have had, and howsoever civilized he may be, he will not be in a position to think or work in a proper manner as long as his brain is filled with the filth and slime of outdated, superstitious thoughts.

Some people who had been seen by the world as educated and civilized, I found to be totally uneducated and uncivilized. Others may dub me as an insane or an extremely vain girl as I say this; that's OK. But I still feel that education must be seen in actual life, in one's behavior and manners; besides, that life must come in handy to others in actual practice. Only the person who transforms his education in life is worth being called educated and civilized, as I see it.

One day my sister Mina told me, "Saru's marriage was cancelled on the reason that her elder sister is disabled." It was done in a moment when they had fixed everything, according to the Hindu system, calculated the auspicious day, and exchanged garlands between the boy and the girl. There are still such people *as have* rotten mind; they live in our society and call themselves civilized. But actually it seems they are still at the level of animals. They could not come out of that animal civilization. According to Hindu tradition, once a girl's garlanding or exchanging of flower rites has been over, she is considered his mate, and she cannot choose any other male, as she is regarded impure. *Moreover, what happens if her marriage contract is also broken?* Who else will be a greater fool than one that breaks marriage contract? Moreover, what will you call him who broke marriage other than a greatest fool? Is he at all any civilized and educated?

Once I met a teacher with a Ghimire family name. He told me he lived in the southern plain lands (Madhes). It came to be revealed then that he was worried about the break of his lineage. His only son was mentally retarded. He got him married to a girl, but she had deserted him soon. He told me, "I have sufficient wealth. You can squander as much as you wish for luxuries. *There is no scarcity to run life.*"

And I thought, *Fie on men! Are those material satisfactions enough for him? Is he worried about his son or his lineage—the family line?* I told him what I thought. He had no answer, was ashamed of but replied. At all *corte (cost),* one needs to continue their lineage too. *These who are worried about their continuity and at the cost of humanity, what kind of education will he impart to his students?* I thought.

Some of my disabled friends tell me of many an injustice heaped upon them; some say they had been turned out of their homes; others complain about having been deprived even of food, water, and shelter; yet others hold that their families had disowned them and deprived them of their share in family property. As I hear such stories, I get deeply pained and aggrieved. It's a matter of shame to say that we are living in the twenty-first century when a man being deprived of the life of a human being, when a man hasn't received the treatments as human being. Knowledgeable people tell us, "All human beings are equal." But do those people who are confined inside some dark dungeons and deprived even of sunlight and fresh air also come under this definition of equality? Not even fresh air can enter. In which century is this life still? When I think my heart is full of agony, and I feel too sensitive. When I compare their *lives, I feel* animals survive in a better way.

Irrespective of how much a person is educated or cultured, the cloud-like dark patches born out of superstitious beliefs and stored in his or her brain seldom vanish and go away. That was one of the reasons that led some of my close friends to shy away from me. They had so deeply sunk into the muddy swamp or quagmire of superstitions that they simply couldn't pull themselves out of it. Also, that was the reason why they could never appreciate the tenderness of a human heart; nor could they recognize the beauty that lay inside it. After all, it appears that the world keeps on moving amid these very sorrows and happiness. Life also follows suit. I never hated life and so could grasp the essence of being a human being.

I never complained against those people who distanced themselves away from me on the belief that I was a symbol of some kind of evil or misfortune *(?)* and who were alarmed at the prospect of their offspring sharing a similar fate like mine if they came near me. On the other hand, I sincerely wished them good luck. After all, whether or not anyone was close to me, I was bound to fight my life's battle on my own. I did fight my life's battle single-handedly. I also kept on discharging my duties and responsibilities, come what may. I never shirked away from my integrity *(?)*.

This wide world wasn't inhabited only by the kind of people who despised me and looked down upon me. There were also people who looked at me from a positive angle, were favorably disposed toward me, and loved me. Their eyes were like flowers, and they saw a flower in me too, didn't see the blemishes in me. Again, there were those who always kept on running away from me, shunned me. They had been running away from their own souls as well. A question arises: Should we call them educated and civilized or superstitious? When is the grime and filth of blind faith ingrained in their brains going to be wiped away? How nice it would have been if the black clouds of superstitions were blown away!

$$\text{☖}$$

Words Versus Guns

Those days, the country had been rendered *jarjar* (?) *(devastated or decayed)* by incidents of murder, rape, and terrorism all around us. The army would claim that having won the fight, the rebels would claim that they had been victorious. But who had lost and who had won was something that the people in the lower echelons of society had no way of finding out. When they came face-to-face with either of the two feuding groups, they would meekly tell them victory had been theirs. Because both the groups had guns. Their guns could be directed at the people and could crack against them at the slightest suspicion—killing the people on the spot. The killers would perhaps brag out, "This will be the plight of our enemies." What cruelty, barbarity, and heartlessness! This land had turned into a slaughterhouse—anyone could be killed anytime, anywhere.

King Gyanendra had taken the reins of power in his hands and had deprived the people of their basic human rights too. He had even imposed a censor on the newspaper, radio, and TVs. The people on their part kept on worshipping him as a god's incarnation, while the same divine incarnation would go on suppressing them. Elderly village people would tell us that it was a sin to speak against him.

But a human mind is a human mind; it cannot tolerate when it's too much. The village elders also started saying in a hush-hush voice, "This is beyond toleration. What a great bloodsucker is this incarnation? It would have been a great relief if we could do away with it." Yes, there were orders to shoot anyone who would speak or write against Gyanendra Shah. The army and police had been deputed to carry out his orders. They were so much unrestrained that they were free to do anything.

In those difficult times, it wasn't easy in itself to uphold the faith reposed on the pen. But I had been doing the same thing. It was a daunting task to wield your pen from inside the barriers of guns and gunpowder. With the onset of the king's direct rule, I discontinued contributing to my column in the *Kantipur* for about a month and switched over to literary writings. But whatever I wrote would be directed against barbarism, cruelty, and inhumanity. My collection of essays, *Bemausamka Aasthaharu*, was a product of that period. It contains a voice of rebellion against the cruelties, injustice, and tyranny of those days; it also raises a voice in favor of the womenfolk, who have been suppressed from age to age, in a frank and forthright manner.

It had also been necessary for me to withhold writing my newspaper columns for some time with a view to elicit people's reaction and to read out their minds. But a kind of frustration and anxiety pestered me all through. I experienced the pain of a writer *denied the* opportunity to express his or her views and opinions.

Those days, Narayan Wagley was the *Kantipur* editor. I had a fairly smooth relationship with him. I found him to be a good-natured person with a positive outlook—and it wasn't difficult for me to mix and mingle with him. I would occasionally also tease him, "What's this, Narayan Dada? Have you forgotten me?" He never got annoyed and would send me SMS, saying, "Jhamak has been in my mind." I would be delighted as there was a sense if intimacy and warmth in his words. I learned that those days they had to edit every word in the *Kantipur* under a close watch and supervision of the army. But Narayan Dai used to publish my writings without editing out a single word—Gyanendra Shah's men were getting more furious with me out, I know not why.

I used to hear somewhat about the stories of ancient Raama Rajya, King Rama reign, and Krishna Raajya, since my childhood days. It was said that Raama, as a king, had kept his people happy; so was the case with Krishna when he was the king. Even when

Raavana and Kansa were kings, their people weren't unhappy either. All the kings and emperors of history—whether they had been gods, demons, or humans—had thought about the happiness and welfare of their people. But the Nepalese monarchy, which considered itself to be an incarnation of god, never thought of its people's welfare. An inheritor of the same legacy, Gyanendra was all the worse in the sense that the process of killing and getting killed rose sharply during his reign. He was so drenched in it. I had been witnessing all that the incarnation did and was also a victim of it all.

Occasionally, a question would arise within myself quite involuntarily. Truly, the foundations of one's relations with others get shaken when either the others fail to understand you or vice versa. No matter what relations you have with your parents or your siblings, they mean nothing if they understand you. In my case also, my relatives neither understood me yesterday or today, nor will they understand tomorrow. *What little my relatives would feel at the time was that, because of me, all of them would be ruined and whatever little I am immovable property they had owned would be confiscated. I would try to impress upon them, time and again, that I hadn't done anything unconstitutional, that nothing would happen to their property and that, if anyone had to be ruined, it would be done but me.* But they never understood my point of view. I would always be all alone in the sphere of thoughts and sentiments. Man is born alone and dies alone. Naturally, I was also born alone, but in my case, I also had to wage a lonely battle for the sake of living. There were nothing but barriers and walls around me. Long time ago, I had read in Parijat's memoirs about Sukanya, her younger sister. It was Sukanya, I had learned, who had made Parijat what she had been. I had admired her. In my case, I wanted to extend whatever assistance I could in order to make the democratic movement a success, but my family never respected those thoughts and sentiments of mine.

I had been confused as to what to do. I had become some kind of a lunatic. At the time, it was my younger sister Mina who used to carry my writings and deliver them to the pro-democratic newspaper and periodicals behind the back of other people. That was how I could participate indirectly in the democratic movement. Mina not only helped carry and reach my writings up to the shores of the sea of democratic movement, but she also actively assisted me in every step that I would take. I salute that unseen and unknown fighter who lent her helping hand to me.

Dhankuta Got Burnt!

As one reads between the lines on the people's faces that hide within them the pains and agonies, it wasn't difficult to understand why Dhankuta all the time appeared so calm and quiet. Perhaps Dhankuta had been burning with the same pain that its people were burning.

Many must have denounced Dhankuta, others created नरसंहार *(massacre or bloodbath)*, and still others made it infamous. I find this name (Dhankuta) friendly and amiable. It was the place where *I had been born* and brought up. I found the same earth, where I had begun developing my wings, dear and amicable. But at the same time, my love can never be limited with a place that is a mere speck on the map, because I am a human being. Whichever piece of the earth I touch with my feet, I feel like it's my own, and whichever place I reach appears to be like my home—I take pleasure there. I have no home of my own in Dhankuta—I stay in a small cottage built with the blood and sweat of my parents.

My day's routine begins from a small room in that cottage. Since I wake up, my struggle starts and the days end in it. I occasionally imagine how nice it would have been if I could live in a house built with my own blood and sweat. Even if in an imaginary home I become happy for some time. I don't want to be a burden on anyone. Whichever place my life leads me to is my own land. There are so many people who spend their entire life under an open sky. I live a life of ease in comparison to theirs.

As I said, Dhankuta is my birthplace. But those didn't want its development ruined it. Perhaps it was the very pain that was behind the burning of Dhankuta. I learned that, long time ago, this was also the place where the Chhintaang incident had taken place and the voices for justice that were raised at the time had been suppressed.

Since the time I began understanding Dhankuta, it seemed that its hills and slopes, forests, rivers and rivulets, plants and the grasses all have been seemingly caressing me with their love. But among the people here, I could mix and mingle with only a limited few. I feel a little more at home in an informal surrounding, because I crave for a kind of fondness and amicability. So my familiarity is limited to a few. But the few that I have been able to acquaint myself with are sufficient for me.

Men are open to few. Sometimes when my friends meet me, they used to say, "How complacent you are! You have forgotten us. Who knows, you may once forget Dhankuta itself."

Then I would reply, "Wherever may I live, if it does not love whole heartedly, I cannot call the 'geography' my own. No geographical border becomes my place." Then they would keep quiet. Perhaps they thought, *What a foolish girl! In any case, Dhankuta was calm, quiet, and peaceful.* The process of people pouring into the district headquarters and its periphery from the surrounding villages was multiplying by leaps and bounds. It appears that a man is prepared to leave behind all the property he owns and go elsewhere for the sake of remaining alive. The plight of the people living in the throes of internal conflict was the same. The sounds of bombs and gunfire were being heard from places beyond. People had started feeling that Dhankuta itself will also be engulfed in the fire of conflict in the none-too-distant future. The armed forces, equipped with arms and weapons, hadn't ceased patrolling the nearby villages. They would also harass innocent people without any rhyme and reason. When we saw that, we would feel like cursing all army men and policemen. But at the same time, we would see sweat and perspiration with them—poor people, how helpless they were! They were bound to obey what the higher-ups ordered them. A wave of democratic movement was raging the nation. But they were following orders only. Their life is not under their control. Man is writing the boundary of gun. His desires and ambitions are also confined within this. And he has become like an aggressive animal. Oomph, what irony!

Eventually, Dhankuta was also getting involved in the movement for democracy, because the conscious minds among its population weren't prepared to compromise with the tyrannical times and regime. Yes, among those minds mine was also one. For I could never, for a moment, support the royal regime; my wielding of a pen was never meant to strengthen anyone's brutality and dictatorship. My pen continued to lend support to the voices of change, equality, and freedom. It kept on writing about the new age and the new consciousness, and the dreamers of beautiful dreams carried its message across to the common people elsewhere. As I had been staying all the time in remote Dhankuta, it wasn't an easy task in itself to remain in a close and constant touch with the capital. To raise a voice of justice from a corner of the country, where even books and newspapers aren't readily available at all times and in sufficient numbers, was a challenging job in itself. What's more, those were difficult times; the police people kept a hawkish eye on all, and if anyone was seen returning home with a book, newspaper, or periodical purchased in the town, he or she would have to face police-checks all along the route and answer countless questions and enquiries of the policemen. But after all, it was a part and parcel of their daily routine.

The media, however, extended their full support and cooperation to me. *Kantipur Publications* not only assigned to me, for the first time, the task of a column-writer, but they also provided me with a convenient tool to reach its readers and establish contacts with them; although I lived in a darker corner of Dhankuta, that helped me spread my democratic thoughts through my writings to various sections of the people. The press played a significant role in the course of a democratic movement. Many creative writers and pen-people associated themselves with the press and fought their war in favor of freedom and democracy. I was also one among them who participated in the movement through writings. Had I not been disabled and infirm, in all probability I would have been behind the bars and would have been subjected to various mental and physical tortures. Even as it is, people who had been deputed by higher authorities kept on tormenting me mentally in various ways. At times, there would be subject to cross-examinations in the room itself. But nothing incriminating or unconstitutional was found; if there was anything unconstitutional, they were my sentiments, thoughts, and words. As my writings were rebellious, they may have suspected me of having links with faces involved in unlawful activities. That was why, too, the armed forces may have kept me under a close surveillance.

In meanwhile, King Gyanendra shamelessly staged a farce of an election; the entire country was his stage, and the participants in the farce repeated their play in Dhankuta as well. A few days prior to the staging of that farce, our father had gone to the town and returned with a rumor they had heard there—that those who didn't go to participate in the elections would have their hands and legs chopped out. My father had returned home hurriedly. I thought, *He is somehow an educated person. Why is he not understanding?* It was the terror created by actors of King Gyanendra. A sort of people wanted not to witness the farce—they had come out in the protest against the vulgar and shameless scenes that would be staged.

The clever agent enticed by the juice that would come of election entered our village. The so-called big shots in our village started to participate in the festive mood of election—performing a farce that is. In our village, simple (ignorant) village women were given roles out of which the big shots would exploit selfishly.

Even the simple woman rejected to participate in that farce. When nobody was prepared to watch the performance, their feast was spoiled. However, the characters led entered our villages with their followers; their courage proves they must have been lured by a large share.

The previous night sounds of bombs and gunfires were heard along with sounds of people screaming. Most people were deeply asleep, but those sounds not only disturbed their sleep but also scared them to the hilt, almost making them lose their senses. In the silence of the dark night, frightened people huddled themselves inside their houses.

I have never been able to forget that night. The sounds of the gun used to reverberate so close to the house that gave us the impression they were hitting at the walls of our house or the nearby trees. We were scared with fright that the bullets would penetrate our walls and enter inside. Those who set the fire of war must have delighted. What a dread to those who work under them! Had they wanted to put out the fire, they could have protected people instead of preparing for the drama.

The phone rang early the next morning. A voice from the other end said, "Are you all still alive? Dhankuta is said to have turned into ruins yesternight." Dhankuta in ruins? I fell as if *I was tumbling down a waterfall.* A commotion gripped the people. "The electricity office building isn't there, the bank building isn't there, the prison house isn't there," it was said. Everything was in a shambles. Dhankuta was also gutted in the conflagration of the conflict.

At that time, some friends were in prison. They were very frightened. They had lost hopes for life. They told me, "Thanks God, *he survived!*"

Truly, the next day, some simple village folks were made, by way of coaxing and cajoling, to proceed to the polling booth and to cast their votes in the town elections. The media kept on blaring, "The elections were held successfully." What was the sense in spreading the news of the farce having been successful when there weren't any spectators to see it?—I thought within myself. Outside the auditorium and the stage, those people that had been raising their voices against the despotic regime and in favor of justice, kept on being martyred. To say the truth, human blood was flowing continuously all around that stage; the despotic walls were getting soaked and dissolved by that blood. It's truly said, "Too much of everything is bad."

Once Dhankuta had been bombed and gunned out of existence, a kind of numbness gripped the people. They used to be apprehensive even if they came across an unfamiliar face. When everything had been turned into ruins, people were constrained to pass their nights in total darkness—as if it was still a sixteenth-century life. People were compelled to live in a complete blackout for about a month and a half. In the absence of electricity, all the communication equipments were also out of commission. I had a ten-band Chinese radio in the name of a medium of information. But that wasn't mine own; it belonged to a friend, Devi Bahadur Shrestha. He hailed from Tangechha in Bhojpur district. He used to stay in our house in pursuance of his studies as well as in order to eke out his living. He used to visit me earlier too. He was a very nice man; a kind of intimacy had developed between the two of us. He would address me as *didi*, elder sister, and I affectionately called him Devi.

Human beings become closer through feeling they are closer by way of thoughts. He is one among the few people that are close to me. I am happy to be with him. I have exchanged joy and pain because I have loved him like my own brother. We come from distances—both geographically and relation-wise. Only our relation is based on feeling or unselfish love, which is beautiful in itself—is sweet in itself. I had to sustain life by penning down stuff with the help of the flickering light of a kerosene lantern. I would then bundle the writings inside an envelope and send them. When that would reach its destination and when would it appear in print was another anxiety in itself. Some of them would even get outdated, old, and *tattered* by the time they reached; thereby my love's labor would be lost! That was pain resulting out of the conflict, which I had to bear; not only me but all people had to bear. But those who had blown out Dhankuta with bombs and gunpowder may have been basking in the glory of their job and feeling self-satisfied.

In any case, Dhankuta had burnt with its own internal pain, with the fire of the conflict. It kept on burning and my mind also kept on burning along with it. It continued paining me somewhere inside my mind for long.

Belief Flowed Down With Tears!

That I had been born at a time when the skies were in tears may have been a coincidence—at a time when people had to live by the sweat of their brows. I must have given troubles to my mother in such a time. How was it possible for the mothers-in-law to accept with grace the fact that a daughter-in-law, who would have been expected to toil hard at home during such a season, had been confined indoors with a childbirth? On top of that, my grandma belonged to a so-called upper-echelon Thakuri clan. That day also, hardly had her son arrived at the threshold of the house after a whole day's work in his office, she is said to have said, "You may be elated at the thought that your wife had begotten a nice offspring. She has given birth to a mere skeleton." In fact, my grandmother is only a representative character of those days—an average picture of the plight of women. By the way, I am talking about the *rejuing* of the rainy summer.

Yes, I had seemingly opened my eyes for the first time as I had been dropped down to the ground. I really enjoy this season endowed with greenery everywhere. What's more, how delightful in itself is the moment when the sun just brightens the skies after the latter have ceased shedding tears!

It was perhaps because my life had started in the rainy season, I also had to keep shedding tears at the various twists and turns of my life. But when the sky used to weep, its teardrops would soak the earth. The cool rain would reach the roots of plants and trees and give the life, and they would grow green. The earth would look *vebant*. On the other hand, I used to weep when pierced by excessive pain, and the teardrops would wash my grief and sorrow. Then I felt a great relief—my pains and agonies would also flow out along with the tears, making me feel unburdened and relieved. In fact, it appears that I had been born to undergo pains and to struggle with them. My life also saw nothing but pains, experience nothing but the marsh and swamp of tears. That's why I am very much fond of pains. I also love tears, perhaps because I had to go on weeping many times in the course of my life. Science confirms, weeping is wholesome.

However, I wasn't born a weeping Tom. As a child, people regarded me as one pleased and contented with myself. Only when I was under a terrible pain, I would scream out aloud. It's true that, shedding tears would bring you relief. I could feel coolness. Once you weep, you should do so to your heart's content. Then one steely fresh like flower—*should life like* one. The laughter that has disappeared in your lips should revive. I wept many times, and while I laughed, I did so wholeheartedly, and enjoyed a lot. All my evil thoughts also washed away with it. Even if have wept quite often in life, once I laughed, it was a full-throated laughter. During those difficult times, when walls had surrounded us from all sides, I had stood up against them. Even if no relatives of mine—or no one for that matter—would back me and support me, it was my soul, my thoughts, belief, and my conscience that kept my morale high. The tormentors of those days, it transpired, had intended to entangle me that way Hensovia granulate, a parasitical plant, does and to eliminate me without my becoming aware of it. Their pain appeared to decorate me with a medal described as Gorkha Dakshin Baahu, class four, that had been awarded to me even during King Birendra's lifetime in the year *2000* but which hadn't been handed over to me yet on the occasions of a Constitution Day many years later when democratic struggle was at its height and thereby to disgrace me. But I had not enquired about it; I didn't care about it. Because I never expected prize, award, medal, honour, I worked hard for myself. I earned a little out of it and saved some. I was content and happy with whatever I got. But if someone offered me honour, award, or prize, I never said no.

I didn't want to be uncivilized. I *juked* with all sorts of people talked, chatted, enjoyed. But I was determined in my opinions. Nobody complained against it. While honoring me with that medal when during King Birendra's regime, nobody asked me a single word. Perhaps they used to ask nobody. *In those only those* close to the court were offered the medal Gorkha Dakhseen Bahu first, second, and third class. We citizens were entitled to have only fourth and fifth.

I was merely nineteen. Naturally, I was glad to be honored for my work at this age. Many of my friends congratulated more on that occasion, because I had neither used any effort in obtaining the medal nor tried to please the courtiers. How I was given I feel surprised. But there was no question of my obliging those parasites by wearing *doen* my head, a symbol of calumny by accepting the medal on a Black Day in the midst of a black congregation during those dark days. My soul, beliefs and faith, and conscience, nothing would allow me to accept it. As a person who had stood in favor of freedom and democracy, I couldn't have gone there to wear the medal by trampling over my self-confidence and self-respect; as such, I didn't go.

But that incident had sent an earthquake-like shudder in the mind of my parents—they had been extremely terror stricken—that the step I had taken was sure to ruin them and invite all kind of misfortune. "This unrighteous and evil one wouldn't even let us live here by having our property confiscated too." That day they had cursed me and scolded me with all bitterness at their command—so much so that I even had to skip my dinners, as I was bellyful with their bitter and endless rebukes.

I was also furious with my parents that day, and I felt like quarrelling with them and screaming against them, as the scolding had crossed their limits and I wasn't in a position to tolerate anymore. But alas, I had no words! How accursed was my life! That day I found my life itself as a great burden and didn't even feel like staying in their house anymore.

As I had been telling, that award had been announced in the year *2057* but hadn't been handed over to me at the time.

I had also, on my part, never bothered to make enquiries about it, as I didn't care. As it is, I have never craved for any prizes, honors, awards, and medals. I would toil hard on my own, and whatever little I would earn out of it and save was enough for my subsistence, and I was contented with it. But I was also quite firm and stubborn when it came to my thoughts and allegiances.

I was never asked a single word when the award had been announced during the lifetime of King Birendra. Probably those days, it wasn't the practice to ask anyone. I was just entering into my nineteenth year of age at the time. As a young and immature girl, I was naturally pleased with the news of the award. The announcement of the award had also pleased my friends, and all of them had congratulated me and extended their best wishes. But since I had done nothing to make the people in the palace happy, I had been amazed as to what made them offer me that award. I had also been called to receive the award. But because of my personal reasons *(reservations)*, I hadn't been able to attend the award function, and the issue had remained pending.

Sometime later than King Birendra's family massacre, when a despotic regime took the nation in its firm grip and I started expressing my views against it, concerned people started making enquiries. Possibly, people associated with the dictatorship had reckoned that I was hungry of recognition and honour. "As she would learn that she was going to be honored with the award, she might definitely turn up." But a person dedicated toward freedom and democracy would not accept a proposal of receiving such an honor during those difficult times; it wasn't acceptable to me either.

At the time, my younger sister Mina's intermediate examinations results had been announced, and she had come out successful. She was beyond herself with joy. And it was natural, because if one's years of labor bring out the desired fruit, it is indeed a matter of delight. She beamingly approached the parents and conveyed the good news to them. Father appeared to be slightly pleased and said, "You have improved your life." But Mother was very much angry; she didn't speak to her for three days. On seeing Mother's anger, she came to me with a downcast face and asked, "Why was it that they weren't happy at my success?" She was disheartened and disappointed with herself. But even then, she was saying, "It's immaterial whether anyone is happy or not. I have studied for my own advancement." I didn't make any reply to her but said to myself, *Bravo, you have recognized at least yourself. Even if the others aren't happy, I am.*

Yes, neither the skies nor the earth treats *us women*folk as equals, even the wombs that give birth to us despise us as women. The courtyard and the piece of the earth where we are born and grow up do not belong to us. We even do not belong to the family or the clan we are born to. We aren't regarded even as human beings. I am a person who clamors for an equal and parallel sky, a parallel earth—one who looks for a parallel point of view. But I never got to see that.

I had my own faith and belief, my own views and opinions, outlook, understanding, and pattern of thinking; I also wanted to live a life of my own choice. I didn't want to borrow anyone else's pattern in living; I wanted my own style of living—that's why I had to shed a lot of tears as I lived. But I didn't compromise with anyone. I lost many things in life too; perhaps what I lost was not meant for me either. In the process, I also lost my tenderness and gentleness and became a rock myself. When a person has to undergo pains and sufferings at every step, such pains and sufferings also start tasting good, as it were. Occasionally, a person has to be pinched and pricked by something; once those pains and sufferings are over and recovery takes place, a person starts experiencing coolness and composure. A person experiences pleasure only after a hardship is over.

A human being is a bundle of pains in itself, because he or she causes the pain on his or her own. That is the pain of living, or survival. Because it is much more difficult to live than die. Death in itself is a beautiful art, and death is also a great delight—as some people in the world would say. But I say the exact opposite—"Living is a beautiful art and *death?*—an eternal truth of life. Not a death that results while running away, but the one we opt on our own in the course of a struggle. It is in defending the same faith and belief of mine that I had to shed copious tears, but even then, the walls of discrimination kept standing erect. How would they melt just on the strength of tears? Only when they were struck with the hammer of thoughts with full force, they started crumbling. *I did the sufficiently moistened the faith in life.* Let me put it this way: the faith in life rained down with tears. Although I myself was thoroughly drenched in that rain, my faith in life and survival neither ever melted not crumbled.

Life in Cliff and the Smile of Orchid

No matter how difficult times I went through, I kept on searching for life, because if there is no life on earth, it will be of no significance. Yes, life has a special role in making the earth and the world a beautiful place. I continued writing all the time about human lives and urged all to stop human massacre, urged all also to stop the blood-river from flowing. In return, those who had been digging human graves threatened to bury me in the same grave, to have me blown away by the same blood-river. But I loved life. I loved to write songs of life and read them, even if there was life in my letters and words and *understand voice connected* with it. The rulers and administrators of the time were startled to hear those very songs of life I sang. They wanted to choke my voice, break my pen, and put me in a situation where I could neither live nor die. But their intentions were never fulfilled. If they had their way, the voice of my life would have stopped for ever, my pen would have been broken, and life? It would have been a living corpse.

I am a person who would like to flower, blossom, and spread on my own. As I saw the flower blooming along the edges of the courtyard, I also felt like enjoying the same freedom. On seeing them smile and laugh, I felt doing likewise too. And I tried to enjoy the same freedom and to laugh the same laughter. But nobody liked that and so dubbed my voice anarchist, letters anarchist, and words anarchist. I enjoyed the same anarchy.

Those who believed and thought they were living under the rules and regulations were themselves the greatest anarchist who wanted to turn the hands of the clock backwards. I kept on speaking against bondage and restraints. All efforts were made to put me silent. Those efforts didn't bear any fruit, although it's true that many human beings have sacrificed their lives on the altar of this earth. Those that dreamt of a new creation also kept on sacrificing for the sake of their country, Mother Nepal continued suffering its punishments, continued getting drenched in the blood of her children, and continued to suffer the pangs of her laps being emptied. Her eyes hadn't dried for a long time, and she had been stunned in herself. On seeing Mother Nepal getting stunned, I said, "No more should we let her remain stunned, and her eyes must be made to dry up." But that stunning replied, "No, Mother Nepal must continue weeping, and her chest must continue to be thoroughly drenched in blood."

Of course! Mother Nepal, your children had sacrificed themselves in the Great War of the movement with the hope of seeing the ripples of happiness spread on your face. People had stood themselves up in order to attain justice, freedom, and emancipation by jumping across the tall walls of a closed time and oppression. We may add that people had surged up to the brave struggle against injustice and suppression with the objective of seeing that Mother Nepal's blood, flowing for years, would stop. In this crowd of people I had also mixed and mingled through my writings. I have already mentioned that I didn't have to bear the burnt of the army and police batons or wasn't sent to jail; yet I couldn't remain untouched by mental torment. Had I been a whole person, anything could have happened; I may have been spared only because of my physical disability.

When those that looked at me with crooked eyes rose to power, even the monthly allowance of a thousand rupees that I had been receiving since the days of the Sher Bahadur Deuba government was discontinued. Because I hadn't been able to assist those who wanted to turn this earth into a human slaughterhouse. I had rather kept on saying, "This human slaughterhouse must be closed down." The leader of this slaughterhouse wanted to swallow up *while*—*if not* I had to cover his cruelty and praise his deeds.

To do so meant to sacrifice myself. It could be equated with the task of sacrificing in that slaughterhouse. I could not follow such a wretched path because I wanted to live human life and wanted to see the world with beautiful eyes. How could they like me? I had upheld the torch of humanity against all forms of barbarism, a torch of justice against injustice and oppression. And would they have liked me? *Even otherwise, on what basis could I have that despotic regime that had sucked the blood and sweat of thousands of people and inhumanely murdered many justice-loving people?*

There was no way I could do it.

I could not support the slaughterer, the person whose heart had been removed, support at any cost. I stood, propped up by letters, and spoke thus:

Even the हिरिचमिरा *(white ants)*
When their wings grow
Enjoy freedom of flying in the sky
By forgetting the dread of death
How could the meaning of
Being human being be
Equated with to be put in cage
Living a life of horrible fear!

I have said above that the royal regime never liked me because I had been carrying with me bombs of words, gunpowder of thoughts and ideas against it. I had become an eyesore to *that* regime; it wanted to suppress me but couldn't. The only thing it could do was to snatch away the monthly allowance I had been receiving, and it did that. It would even have liked to snatch away my *grub away* from me but couldn't. What else the villainous characters of barbarism could do other than harassing the helpless common folk? As for me, I had warned them that I would rather prepare to die than utter an untruth. Those that had been fire and fury with me were burning themselves in the fire of their rage.

About a thousand females from around the world had been nominated for the Nobel Peace Prize of the year *2005* possibly on the grounds that they had raised the voice of justice, freedom, and democracy. Nine women from Nepal had been included in that list of nominations *(nominees)*, of whom I was one. Merely receiving a prize was not a big deal for me; what was more significant was to take part in that movement. It was, of course, a matter of regret in itself that the women's movement was deprived of the Nobel Peace Prize. But what I would say in the capacity of a member of the movement is this: "Our struggle is continuing. While we will keep on fighting till the end of our lives in order to attain that beautiful world of justice, equality, and peace, we will also make our future generations stand up in this struggle."

When a cactus is in bloom, it celebrates the festival of flowering on its own, writes literati Sulochana Manandhar. She loves this festival. The flowering celebration of cactus and my own celebration of freedom that I did in harsh time are comparable. At this moment, I feel like conveying this to Sulochana Sister. My life is also taking part in the celebration of cactus. I liked the celebration of life above all, that's why I denounce cowardice and have confined writing.

I have a dear younger brother, Bishwas Namsong. His house is in Khandbari of the Sankhuwasabha district. He has been affectionately addressing me as an orchid, Sungava, as he likes that flower very much, he says. Why he likes Sungava is because it blossoms in any kind of difficult terrain, according to him. I also feel like telling him, "Your Sungava has been laughing uninhibitedly as she searches for life even in difficult. Didn't you like that smile?" Truly, I had been likened to a cactus in the eyes of Sulochana *Didi*, an orchid in the eyes of Bishwas and a Bhirphool, a flower in the *redge*, in the eyes of my dear elder brother, Dahal Yagyanidhi. All the three designations point toward the same thing—a symbol of toughness and *valiance*, be it a cactus, an orchid, or a *bhirphool*.

Hadn't I toughness in me, those parasites born in difficult times would have tied me round and wiped me out of existence. But despite all obstacles, I had those parasites sliced and nicked. I didn't merely seek to survive under any circumstances, not did

I consider it signification merely to live. Because even an animal has a life of its own, so does a bird in the forest. What I am is a human being. A human being must live in the interest of human beings. That's why there was a difference of *the sky land the earth* between me and animal. I lived life in a human sense and enjoyed in full the freedom associated with itself. Even despite craving for a mere life, I never lived under frustrations even in the midst of the most adverse circumstances. I always lived with a gay abandon; that's why I blossomed like cactus in the words of Sulochana *Didi*, smiled in the mind of Bishwas Bhai like an orchid, and flowered like a *bhirphool* in the words of Daaju Yagyanidhi.

As the Dark Fog Dispersed

As the dark fog disperses and the day becomes fair, people start boldly coming out into the open. The spotlessly clear and bright sky after the rains and the flowers in full bloom with the rain-water just evaporated from them are the things I really find beautiful to look at. But the sky above our country had not been cleared of the smoke of the gun and the gunpowder for a long time. The earth had not stopped getting drenched in (human) blood either. The people who had stood up against the tyranny and barbarism were either being mowed down with the bullet or were getting their throats squeezed and strangled. Oh, you villains of an unbridled regime, people are braving your gunfire and lining up in their struggle for democracy! The people would never accept an arbitrary rule that had kept the country locked-up in a dark dungeon. Those that headed the dictatorial regime were at their wit's end in face of the people's sacrifice and even imposed a heavy censorship and communication—so much so that they even had the telephone lines disconnected. We had felt like a real prisoner at the time as we had been no less a victim of mental torture than those behind the bars.

Mother Nepal was finding it quite hard to carry the embryo of a democratic republic inside her womb. Justice-loving Nepalese wanted to save and protect that embryo—that's why we had been waging a war against those who wanted to terminate our Mother's pregnancy by way of an abortion. Mother Nepal was also extremely scared at the prospect of an abortion that would kill the baby she had willingly conceived during that dark period.

Numerous offspring of youth sacrificed their lives just in order to keep the embryo in your womb out of any harmful way. Only when her chest had been thoroughly drenched with that blood, could she finally relieve herself from the pangs of childbirth. We were also in extreme delight to see the smile all over her face. Our mental skies, so far darkened by the fog, were cleared up, our lips which had lost their smile for long, got it back once again. To observe the faces of people beam with happiness, I found, as a matter of greater pleasure. The country found itself reborn into a republication atmosphere once it had done away with the season of Gyanendra Shah (April 2007). Mother Nepal, how happy you had become on that day! We creative people were also equally happy because our pens had been freed from the bondage, letters and words had felt emancipated, and choked voices were getting themselves released. The weather was golden-hued and radiant, as it were.

The Nepalese people *over happy*. It had been very difficult for them to break long tradition in which they were used to and grown up. No matter whatever the culture, it is subject to change. All objects in this world are liable to change and the human civilization is all the more progressive and prone to change. The Nepali society cannot remain untouched by this phenomenon. My grandmother, who had lived during the old Rana regime, would say, "The old autocratic regime was much nicer. People would at least live in peace." She did not live to see and experience the post-1991 democratic period. Moreover, had she lived to experience the decade-long period of conflict, how much more pained she would have perhaps been.

My aunt, who had lived during a part of the conflict period, would also say, "What has the world come to? Man has started sacrificing man in the way he would kill an animal." Those were the views reflecting the times they each had experienced. But human civilization was in a state of perennial flux.

The Nepali society, which had been ruled by one dynasty for long, never had the opportunity to live and move with freedom.

Pluralism for *him* was limited to the words, it was never put into practice. It was as if only his dynasty was born to rule. Was it that *his* dynasty alone was pure and that of the others impure? As it is, the Hindu tradition regards the king as an incarnation of god Vishnu; but how can a dynasty, which for ages has slaughtered human beings, be regarded as divine incarnation?

History had been looking for a change. It is said that once the ant starts growing wings on its body, it indicates a fast approaching death. Truly, Gyanendra's season also came to an end in like manner. The sky overcast and darkened with the smoke of gun and gunpowder gradually started getting opened-up. The end of a season of tragedy had given rise to an enthusiasm and ecstasy. The people who had thronged into the towns and cities started returning to their village homes, and those who had left for foreign lands started returning to their own country. Mothers had started expecting their children's safe return home toward the end of the day. A newly married Hindu woman had ceased fearing that her vermillion would be wiped out untimely. Our souls seemingly start rejoicing once the process of human blood-letting slows down. I was among those who rejoiced at the time. Perhaps those that had a desire to stop even the blowing wind were not rejoicing, however; they would have liked the wheel of time to rotate backward. But the time-wheel did not oblige them. How then would their minds be happy?

The people, on the other hand, desired that no human being met an untimely death and Mother Nepal desired that not a single drop of her offspring's blood be spilled on any limb of her person. These desires had been fulfilled at least to a limited extent.

That day the heads of those who had regarded themselves as powerful and who had dreamt to prolong their rule on the strength of the gun had truly bent down. The assassins of human beings must bow down their heads in front of history in a like manner. I am a person to pen down the history of life with those times. There are many gardeners to water and help the plants of democracy grow; I am one of those gardeners.

I kept on delightfully gazing at the radiant sky that had been cleared of dark clouds. What a brilliantly golden-hued sky! How enticing and charming! There is no barrier to limit its expansiveness—it can expand itself to its heart's content.

Touching the Wounds of Conflict

In fact, the country is still suffering from the pain and agony, time is still suffering, and the entire age is suffering. Although loss itself results in agony, but seen from another angle, it also provides the base for new creations. For example, a diseased tree withers and dies, which is also a kind of loss. Another seedling grows there and replaces it, which is also a creation. Had those who had gone into the jungles not blown the horn of republic, had rivers of blood not flown, the country would not have transformed itself into a republic so soon. This is an established truth. The monarchy wouldn't have to come to an end—that's another bitter truth. But the country had to pass through the throes of an unprecedented tragedy and experience an unprecedented and terrible fight, which is an equally undeniable truth. A full generation of the country did not merely go into a conflict; the productivity associated with it was also lost in the course of that conflict. The nation's future associated with it was burnt down in that conflagration.

Another thing, most of those who had taken to the jungles were kids aged sixteen or seventeen years. To make them play with guns, gunpowder and bombs was in itself detrimental; those above us the leaders played the same detrimental game.

After all, their war was directed against the government; had they involved slightly mature people in it, the country would have suffered less. It's because the young ones start recognizing the colors of life at that stage and because their awareness isn't fully developed at such an age. Their education also remains incomplete. Yes, if those that ignited the fire of conflict from the jungles had given a timely thought to this aspect of the problem, the country would not have suffered such a misery. I get extremely pained when I see the faces of the girls who have just attained youthfulness and those who have lost their lifemates, as also the kids who have been orphaned even before they could fully recognize their parents. I have seen those young ones, whose parents had ruthlessly been murdered right in front of their eyes, with their faces filled with resentment and rage. His or her tiny mind has strongly determined to take revenge. My mind gets stunned when I see the *undried* eyes of the parents. Yes, this is the wound of conflict and *terribly painful,* which a person apparently finds difficult to bear.

I wiped out with the words the pus and blood oozing out of the same wounds of the people—what else could a person who played with words does? I wiped the flood of their tears with the cloak or mantle of sentiments. A man who hailed from somewhere in the West, and who had earlier been a Nepali Congress worker, had both his legs and one hand chopped off on the plea that he was a spy. I had come across him in the course of a seminar in Kathmandu. Not only one but both of the conflicting sides have played upon the bodies of men in such a cruel and inhumane manner as to deprive them of their bodily tools of earning. Killing insects and human beings was regarded as the same thing. Those that kill celebrate like it was a victory—what kind of anarchy is this? Is this, then, the meaning of a republic? Questions kept on arising in the mind—time couldn't elicit an answer; probably it had no answer with it. In fact, an orphaned child is questioning those who had massacred his parents in cold blood—what had been the fault of my parents that they deserved to be killed thus? Those young women whose vermillion had been wiped out ask: "Why was my vermillion prematurely wiped out?" The wounds of conflict are still causing pain. And why should not they pain? The bloody sacrifice of tens of thousands of people has left behind it a terrible agony. Those that were sacrificed had been dreaming of a bright future ahead. It was natural for them to dream thus; but all dreams cannot come true—this is an eternal truth.

It is difficult to completely eliminate the ill-feelings born out of a conflict. The sound of bombs and gunpowder is still being heard; we are still hearing the news of men getting killed. The sounds are getting mixed with the voices of regionalism, communalism and with the reverberation of the nation being torn apart. I feel like telling them here, "Stop all this. The country is yours as well. The nation also goes through the same pain and agony that you have to bear when a limb of yours is torn apart." Let's voice this slogan: "Violence-free society and a beautiful world in mind." Will you join me? Will you add your voice? If so, please have a look on the faces of those helpless orphans; it is our duty to raise hopes in them. Look at these young widows who were just in their youthful age; don't they have right to enjoy the pleasures of life? Look at those parents who have lost their issues. What agony and grief they are undergoing? Let's not live for us alone; let's live for them too. Let's think for them. *How beautiful and people might this world have been* if we were to live for other's joy and happiness, all sorts of violence would have disappeared.

In order to eradicate the ill-feeling and wounds caused by the conflict, let all of us speak out in one voice, "Human beings are imagining a beautiful world devoid of any violence." Would not you like to lend your voice to join that of mine? If you are prepared to lend your voice, do look at these tender faces of the orphaned children—it is our duty and responsibility to give rise to fresh hopes in them. Look at the faces of the young widows—do not they have the right to live a life of happiness? Look at those rendered infirm and disabled as a result of a conflict—what pain and agony they are suffering? Look at those parents that have lost their children—how much pain they are going through? How long are we to live for ourselves alone? Let us also live a little for them as well. If all people were to sacrifice a little bit of their self-interest, all forms of violence would cease to exist in the world. The world would have been beautiful and peaceful.

We still hear the news of people being killed by explosives left or buried during the conflict period. Many are being wounded and maimed. What a tragedy! The nation is still undergoing the agony of conflict. Pens are still recounting, narrating the story. What a pain to the writers as well. When I put into paper, I also feel grieved. When the wound itches, my heart weeps. I have seen the policemen's or army men's wives widowed; some are quite young, others middle aged. Some have remarried. However, the Nepali society does not show much respect to them. They are confined to the demarcations drawn by culture and tradition. How strange it is! If you try to allow your life freely to look for happiness, you will be a sinner and if you spend life (being restless) you will attain *heavenly* bliss—in the next life. Many of them constrained by different problems fail to marry. Their youth withers away; their desire for sexual contacts and pleasures get frustrated. Moreover, they will have to bear the burden of the male partners all alone. The burden of children and other immense losses of material and physical are uncountable. I wish we would *(could)* be spared the trouble of writing about this pain any longer.

The Rays of Life

The process of tides rising from the river and falling back on the river itself continued. Torrents enter the river, so does flood; the river becomes muddy, but ultimately is transparent once again. My life resembled a river—at times muddy, at other times flooded and in spate, and then like transparent water. My creations appeared like ripples when life was in a surge, like a flood when life was in spate and like clear water when life was transparent. Creative persons get impregnated when they become happy, as also when unhappy. My womb was not also barren, and I wept along with my creations when my heart was in pain and laughed with them when I was happy. If truth is to be told, creations are like my life's inseparable friends, with whom I can share everything. Creations are also my life's identity, without which I do not feel convenient.

My creations are the outcomes of an intercourse with life's moments, consequences of having loved life. They are also the results of my affection for society, country, and the world at large or the entire humanity. As a creative writer, I could *never ever* take sides with cruel and inhuman activities. I can neither call a white thing black, nor can I pretend to have seen a black thing as something white. The principal love or cherish of my writings comprised of humanity, peace, freedom, and democracy. How nice it would have been if we could establish an all-inclusive, harmonious society based on equality! A piece of the heaven imagined by man would have been here. I kept on wielding my pen with that dream, I scanned and scrutinized the feelings and desires of the common people with the help of my words, and I kept on squeezing the pus and blood out of their natural wounds. It's okay whether I am praised or blamed. The weather has changed for the better even if in a small way.

Even in the midst of various ups and downs in life, the journey toward freedom continued. Even if the moments of my personal life were accursed, I have distanced myself from them and kept them out. The upcoming moments of my life will hopefully be alluring. The world belongs to me as well and I am alive. So many persons have been allured as they see this life. They tell me, "How fortunate you are?" They are tempted by my luck. The primary thing is that I have already struck down yesterday's unfortunate lines of fate; I have already broken them into a thousand splinters. Yes, I have myself drawn a new fate line after having erased out the old one. Possibly, no more will people call me an unlucky girl. Life's battles were lost at times, were won at other times. There were moments of pleasure and pain, easy and uneasy experiences, along the course of the journey. My legs may have got tired and weary on occasions, slow down at others. But the life's battle did not culminate anyway; that's why, life's nameless stream flowed on in a lively manner. People say that the lines of our destiny are drawn by fate; but in my case, no fate had his hand in drawing my fate line, and even if a line had thus been drawn, it gave me nothing. That's the reason why I rebelled against the fate that was in store for me.

Some people might comment, "This girl declared a war against fate and the destiny." But is it wrong for unfortunate persons such as myself to attempt drawing golden fate line on their own?

The Hindu culture has a tradition of worshipping power. The underlying significance of power is to activate a living being like the water, land, wind, sun, and other factors providing the human beings with the capacity to move or walk about. Our culture has the tradition of worshipping honour of the Sun god. We also worship water in the form of rivers like Narayani, Kausiki, and Mahakali as we consider them to be symbols of divinity. What I have now started realizing is that these elements of nature are regarded as the supernatural power. There is also a power inside humans—the urge for living and the power of self-confidence. The Newari culture has a tradition of worshipping one's own soul, known as *Mha Pujaa*. That's seemingly the worship of a man's power that is lying within human beings themselves. Creativity is also a form of the same power—ray of my life. I have been all the time following those bright and golden rays—all the time . . .

Hands of Cooperation

He is a politician by profession and has established his identity as one. But he was very affectionate toward me. Yes, I am talking about Gopal Guragain, whom I had first met toward the close of the year 1999. In our very first meeting, I had responded to him rather curtly and in a pinching manner. Initially, he kept mum and merely assumed a grave countenance; he only spoke slightly later. He may have thought, *What a rude girl!*

Since that day, he would occasionally keep coming to my place. Had he been of a different nature, he would perhaps have never visited me again out of spite; but he didn't do that. On the other hand, the more I pinched him with my words, the closer he would get. Unlike many creative writers, I wouldn't, however, spit venom against politics and politicians. I would chat with political activists freely and without bias, but would tell them that their politics must be people-oriented.

With the advent of democracy, all people breathed a sigh of relief. Gopal Sir started getting all the more close to me but he never tried to impose his political views on me. Rather, he would say, "You must remain independent and must widen the sphere of your thoughts and visions." People like Gopal Sir have extended their hands of cooperation toward me, have endeavored to make my journey toward a flowering easier and smoother. A body named Jhamak Ghimire Saahitya Kalaa Pratisthan, set up in the year 2006 in his own initiative, has been functioning until the present time. Following the advent of democracy, I have also started receiving a monthly pension. My life's journey is becoming smoother. Truly, the moments of my life yesterday had been tough and difficult. Of the many hands that have helped make my life's journey easier, one is that of Gokarna Bista. He hailed from Gulmi, and was a youth leader of the CPN (United Marxist Leninist) party. It seems he was greatly impressed with the talk I had with him when he had visited me once. On his part, Gopal Sir has bestowed a fatherly love and affection on me. On an institutional level as well, he is the one to labor hard for my cause. Devi Bahadur Shrestha is another. I saw no trace of self-interest in his toils and exertions on my behalf.

People thought they were doing politics on me; they thought they had put special influence on me. How prejudiced were their mind and eyes! I kept on pushing ahead with my writings in a free and independent manner. I didn't find any topic or subject not worth writing about. Some writers who are my friends twitched their noses as they commented on my writings, "Seems you are also involved in politics. Your writings these days are mostly on political topics."

Oh my god, what a narrow outlook they have! I keep on telling such brainless stupid, "I am not into politics, nor do I have any political party to extend support to. But I do write political articles because I am also a representative of the common people. I give a voice to their sentiments and aspirations through my pen. But if such an exercise is interpreted as being into politics, it only shows your brain is deficient in thinking and understanding."

Some of my friends have joined politics, others have joined politics, some are media persons, others are teachers, and still others are advocates, doctors, and engineers. With each, I have a friendly behavior. We discuss and share and differ, again we leave each other as intimate friends.

Gopal Sir is also a very simple-minded and straightforward person. He seems to have chosen politics simply with a view to serving people. He has not apparently done anything immoral under the garb of a politician, which is why he became dear to me and also honorable. I am prone to be easily *provocated,* and he isn't unaware of my nature. Occasionally, he lovingly advises me, "You should learn to restrain yourself as you have to discharge many a responsibility given by the age." In course of my association with him, I have come to know that he is a creative talent in himself, but his time and attention have been divided into various fields.

Occasionally I tease him, saying, "You have tasted various things in life; it *is time* you also taste literature."

He replies, "Let me not do that. Our duty is rather to extend our assistance to creative persons like you."

Truly, how nice it would have been if the administrators of our state also possessed a purity of feelings and thought like those that Gopal Sir has; Nepal's creative personalities wouldn't have been dying a dog's death in that case. I wonder if these people will ever understand that the country's arts, literature, and culture go to form our identity.

Yes, I did not give up writing. My new publication, *Jhamak Ghimirekaa Kavitaharu* (Poems of Jhamak Ghimire) was brought out by Pasina Prakashan in the year 2008, with an active support from Modnath Prashrit who had come to me once. Such an assistance and cooperation received from a creative writer, whose works I had read since my adolescent days and had admired, made me consider myself fortunate, because I have still to flower-up and still to proliferate. People like Gopal Sir came into my life and have been playing a significant role. It will be an injustice if I fail to remember such persons. I am quite fortunate, as there are many people who love me, who nod their heads in support of my pro-life thinking, and who raise their hands to cooperate with me.

Life: Whether a Thorn or a Flower

Similar to the way a flower blooms amid thorns and blossoms delightfully, life, likewise, seems to flower amid toils and tribulations. But man intends to live without having to face wounds and injuries, without undergoing pains and afflictions. His desire is to spend life in a smooth manner. But life does not always travel in a plane surface as desired. Would it always pass as smoothly, we would not have been able to savor life's delights. It is just because man has to undergo the throngs of pains and agonies, he keeps on fighting to attain happiness and bliss. Likewise, a flower would not perhaps have been so beautiful had it not been for its thorns. On my part, I also sought through pangs and pains. No one can expect to live his life smoothly and evenly. Every life has its share of pains and pleasures, of injuries and wounds, of twist and turns, and of lanes and narrow alleys—that what precisely go to make life as charming as a flower in bloom.

It is just because I had to move ahead braving difficult twists and turns, alleys and gullies that I'm presently passing through a phase of life that is simpler and more convenient. Not that my personal life is not still filled with entanglements and bewilderments; it is life's eternal destiny and all people have to accept it. I also accepted this destiny and therefore, survived. But a stage has come when my survival is not for myself alone, and my struggle no longer need to strive toward that end. I should live a life that is meant for others as well. My struggle should also be geared toward that destination. Howsoever long or short my life will be, I should henceforth live a life that will be meaningful and purposeful for my society, for my country, and for my universe. Yes, there were contexts when I have had to brave accusations that I choose the pen merely in order to earn name and fame. But no, I didn't choose the writing profession just for the sake of name or fame; I was perhaps destined to earn my entire livelihood through writing. Did I or did I not make any sacrifices and consecrations? This is for time alone to judge. I leave the responsibility of such judgment to itself. I shall not shrink away from the responsibility of being answerable even if I am made to stand in time's judgment *(witness)* box. I surrender life to that time. I sacrifice life for that age. Life is no more my own. My only concern at the present time is whether I shall be able to be a flower of creativity blossomed in the manner desired by the present time and age. Let death not mock at me and laugh. Let it also not come untimely, because I still have to deliver much else for time's sake.

Even when death claims me, let no one cover a faith-ordained shroud over my dead body, let no *kriyaputri* conduct mourning rituals for me, and let no one set a fire in the funeral pyre. Nor am I willing to feed the crows and vultures. I feel like experiencing with ease the way the god of death lashes his cutting whips on me. And I offer my corpse to those scientists whose studies and experiments broaden the horizons of medical science. I must bow down in obeisance to my mother's womb that bore the pangs of childbirth while delivering me and the mother who has kept on giving me company through life's course. And Mina? That companion, without whom my life's journey would not have been possible; a person who never sought credit for herself, but, on the contrary, had to suffer many a reproach, and yet never showed any ill-disposition toward me—I have been internally expressing gratitude toward her and saluting her. Besides, I would also like to offer a bouquet of red roses each to all the other characters—male or female, known or unknown—who have ceaselessly helped make my life's journey smooth. Today, a simple girl whom the society had showered insults and pushed into the backwards, is standing in front of you in the shape of a young writer. To those who had treated this life as an accursed one yesterday, I throw this challenge—"Do tell me whether life is a flower or bed of thorns?"

In conclusion, as I pursue life's grandeur and effulgence, I speak through these lines:

May you be living under darkness,
But I shall live such a life, such a life,
That keeps on pursuing the brightness of moonlight
And cast aside past accursed times as rags.
Let life be effulgent, bright as a light aglow,
Like a leaf made multi-hued by a dazzling moon,
Like bright colors spread thereon.

Jhamak Ghimire in a Glimpse

Name   : Ms. Jhamak Kumari Ghimire
Literary nickname : Jhamak Ghimire
Date of birth :   July 6, 1980 (Friday)
Father :   Mr. Krishna Bahadur Ghimire
Mother :   Mrs. Aasha Devi Ghimire
Child/Issue : Eldest one
Birth Place : Kachide, Dhankuta Municipality-3,
Dhankuta
Education : Self-Study
Interest/Hobby : Literature, Painting/Art
Contact (phone) : 00977-1-4330334; 00977-26-520302
E-mail :   tu.govinda@gmail.com

Works (Published all in the Nepali language):

- *Sankalpa* (Resolution—An anthology of poems) 1998
- *Aaphnai Chita Agnishikhatira* (My Burning Pyre—An anthology of poems) 2000
- *Manchhebhitraka Yoddhaharu* (Hidden Fighters Within Man—An anthology of poems) 2000
- *Awasaanpachhiko Aagaman* (Arrival after Death—Miscellaneous collection) 2000
- *Samjhanaka Bachhitaharu* (Sprinklings of My Reminiscence—Collection of articles) 2000
- *Naulo Pratibimba* (Nobel Images—An anthology of poems)
- *Parda Samaya Ra Manchheharu* (Curtain, Time and Man—An anthology of short Stories) 2005
- *Bemausamka Aasthaharu* (Untimely Beliefs—An anthology of essays) 2007
- *Jhamak Ghimireka Kavitaharu* (*Jhamak Ghimire's Poems*—An anthology of poems)

- *Jiwan Kanda Ki Phool (Life: A Flower amidst Thorns—An autobiography in prose)* 2010
- *Raat Ra Bhootpretaharuko Santras (Ghosts and Nightly Terror—An anthology of articles)* 2010

Prizes, Honors, and Medals:

- Kavita Ram Children's Literature Talent Prize, 1998
- Rejected Thought Literary Prize, 1999
- Captain Late Gopal Prasad Welfare Prize, 2000
- Prabal Gorkha Dakshinbahu-IV, 2000
- National Youth Service Fund Felicitation, 2000
- Gunjan Family Felicitation, 2000
- Parijat Memorial Centre Appreciation Letter, 2000
- Progressive Writer's Association (PWA) and People's Cultural Association Nepal *Felicitation*, 2000
- Impair Talent Prize, 2000
- Narottam Das Indira Devi Shrestha Trust Felicitation, 2000
- Melody Group Honour Letter, 2002
- TEWA Appreciation Letter, 2005
- Nepal National Democratic Youth Forum Felicitation, 2006
- Banita Publication Biratnagar—Honor, 2006
- Nabarang Literary Academy Jhapa—Honor, 2007
- Monthly Allowance and Honour from the Government of Nepal
- Regional Talent Prize, 2008
- Dr. Bimal Bani Prize, 2005
- Dhankuta Talent Prize, 2009
- Uttam Peace Prize, 2007
- Shankar Lamichhane Talent Prize for Essays, 2010
- Bhadra Kumari Personality Prize, 2010
- Gunjan Talent Prize, 2010
- Dilliraj Upreti Memorial Prize, 2010
- Padma Shree Literary Honor and Prize, 2010
  - Madan Prize, 2010

Printed in Great Britain
by Amazon